PRAISE FOR *THE CONFIDANTE*
BY CHRISTOPHER C. GORHAM

"*The Confidante* covers four decades and some of the most future-shaping legislation ever passed by the U.S. government. Through it all, we can see Rosenberg's fingerprints across the nation's major events. As a result, Mr. Gorham's biography is also a mystery. How could we have forgotten such a woman?...What *The Confidante* provides, with cinematic color and encyclopedic clarity, is a resurrection of that history."

—THE WALL STREET JOURNAL

"This is a must-read for everyone. Christopher Gorham has written a book that is a fascinating look at the years between The Great Depression and The Cold War, and one woman who had a huge impact on all of it. A woman whose name we should all know."

—THE GLOSS

"(Anna Rosenberg's) immense influence on American politics, multiple wars, and America's public affairs, long overlooked, is once again brought to the forefront in this wonderfully told book, perfect for readers of history, biography, politics, and feminism."

—BOOKLIST

"An adviser to presidents from Franklin Roosevelt to Lyndon Johnson, Anna Rosenberg (1899–1983) was a prominent national figure whose present obscurity is perplexing. Gorham, a lawyer and American history teacher...delivers a vivid account of her eventful life.... Even history buffs may be surprised...A well-deserved first biography."

—KIRKUS REVIEWS

"An eye-opening biography of presidential advisor Anna Rosenberg...
This is a fitting tribute to a trailblazer."

"Christopher Gorham's authoritative new biography will put Anna Rosenberg where she belongs: among the most outstanding yet unsung women of the 20th century."

—NIGEL HAMILTON, AUTHOR OF THE *FDR at War* TRILOGY AND *JFK: Reckless Youth*

"Anna Rosenberg was a dynamo of a woman. Christopher C. Gorham's engaging and deeply researched biography *The Confidante* will leave you with two thoughts: 'Why did I never hear of this woman before?' and 'Thank goodness she's been rescued from obscurity!'"

—KATHRYN SMITH, AUTHOR OF *The Gatekeeper: Missy LeHand, FDR, and the Untold Story of the Partnership that Defined a Presidency*

"An outstanding narrative-driven debut that exemplifies why we read history in the first place. Anna Rosenberg's gripping saga should be read by anyone who enjoys a story of achieving success by overcoming long odds."

—STEPHEN PULEO, AUTHOR OF *Dark Tide*, *The Caning*, *American Treasures*, AND *Voyage of Mercy*

"Rosenberg was a woman who rose to postings that were supposed to be the preserve of men, and she was a patriot who helped us win World War II and protect the home front. Heroine, indeed."

—LARRY TYE, AUTHOR OF *Demagogue: The Life and Long Shadow of Senator Joe McCarthy*

"Gorham's biography is a must read for anyone interested in the FDR years and anyone concerned about current crises. *The Confidante* deserves a wide audience."

—ANDREW KERSTEN, AUTHOR OF *Labor's Home Front*

Matisse at War

ALSO BY CHRISTOPHER C. GORHAM

The Confidante: The Untold Story of the Woman
Who Helped Win WWII and Shape Modern America

Matisse at War

CHRISTOPHER C. GORHAM

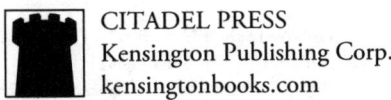

CITADEL PRESS
Kensington Publishing Corp.
kensingtonbooks.com

CITADEL PRESS BOOKS are published by

Kensington Publishing Corp.
900 Third Avenue
New York, NY 10022

All Kensington titles, imprints, and distributed lines are available at special quantity discounts for bulk purchases for sales promotions, premiums, fund-raising, educational, or institutional use. Special book excerpts or customized printings can also be created to fit specific needs. For details, write or phone the office of the Kensington sales manager: Kensington Publishing Corp., 900 Third Avenue, New York, NY 10022, attn: Sales Department; phone 1-800-221-2647.

Library of Congress Control Number: 2025936284

First hardcover printing: October 2025
ISBN: 978-0-8065-4416-8

ISBN: 978-0-8065-4418-2 (e-book)

10 9 8 7 6 5 4 3 2 1

Printed in the United States of America

The authorized representative in the EU for product safety and compliance is eucomply OU, Parnu mnt 139b-14, Apt 123
Tallinn, Berlin 11317, hello@eucompliancepartner.com

For Elizabeth

"The pain passes, Matisse, but the beauty remains."
　　　　　　　　　　　　　—AUGUSTE RENOIR

"Art is a form of courage."
　　　　　　　　　　　　—VICTOR HUGO

Contents

Man Out of Time

> "Shadows are rare here. There's sunshine everywhere except on you."
>
> —F. W. MURNAU TO HENRI MATISSE

> "Today you're a great genius—tomorrow they'll despise you—it's only natural."
>
> —HENRI MATISSE

NICE, FRANCE
1938

The Mediterranean sun was already fiery by the time the flower sellers opened their stalls at the Cours Saleya marketplace in Old Nice. To the dismay of the small-time merchants and café owners, tables remained empty, and the open-air square did not see its usual throng of perspiring tourists and Frenchwomen toting woven baskets. The cacophony of languages—French, English, Italian, and Russian—used in bargaining for antiques, leather goods, or watercolors was only a murmur. The crowds had been thinning through the spring out of fear of invasion from Benito Mussolini's fascist

Italy—just 30 kilometers away. Thousands of Niçois and visitors alike took refuge inland, away from the southeastern tip of France and the frontier with Italy. The few café habitués in Cours Saleya that day could hear chirping birds, church bells echoing from other quarters in the city, and the fluttering of the French tricolor angled from a balcony.

At the eastern end of the market at 1 Place Charles-Félix sat a seventeenth-century baroque palace bathed in sunlight. Since the 1920s, it, too, had been of keen interest to tourists. Behind the patinaed façade of mustardy gold lived the internationally famous artist Henri Matisse. Inside Palais Caïs de Pierlas, the high-ceilinged nine-room flat on the fourth floor with its views of the market and the sea, was Matisse, alone. A sight that would have been a rarity in the decades before, when the sole purpose of his wife, Amélie, daughter, Marguerite, and sons Jean and Pierre—the familial raison d'être—was the creation, evaluation, and successful marketing of the father's art. "We are one of those rare families whose members live in unity."[1] Now, his children were scattered, and his forty-year marriage to Amélie was coming to an end. His sparkling Nice, once a refuge, was being hollowed out by the threat of war. And his immense reputation was waning.

Long-term locals no longer saw the well-built man who sailed, sculled, and took dancing lessons at the Casino. At sixty-eight, Henri Matisse's strong build and square shoulders were less so; his broad, high forehead showed wrinkles; and his reddish hair and beard had turned white. "Matisse had the look of a man who had never been young and would very soon be old."[2] Another commented, "Matisse's face does not suggest his talent—he looks a healthy, well-to-do bourgeois."[3]

As always, when outside of his studio, he was conventionally dressed in woolen trousers, buttoned shirt, jacket, and hat. After meeting the artist, the young Englishman Quentin Bell described him as "comfortably plump . . . assisted by an excellent tailor." Matisse, he concluded, "might well be eminent in the world of insurance or real estate."[4]

Despite his sedate appearance, at the core of Henri Matisse was a seething desire to paint, which had not slackened with the passage of time. He "could think and talk of nothing else" but his art, said the daughter of Simon Bussy, an old art school friend of Matisse.[5] His art "devoured" his life; it was a "vortex sucking everything in."[6]

Matisse's revolutionary exhibit at the Salon d'Automne of 1905 had made him a star. Critics howled at the "barbaric and naïve" forms and the "color madness," but collectors took note.[7] "It took a lot of gall—guts—to paint it," Matisse said of the Fauve style, "but much more to buy it."[8] The Steins and the Cone sisters took the risk, and Matisse became "King of the Fauves." In the years that followed, Henri Matisse found his critical reception and respect dimmed. Older than many of his fellow modern artists, Matisse was no longer seen as a leading figure of the vanguard. The Cubists attacked him; the Surrealists ignored him. "All these fellows who normally said hello turned their backs."[9] His paintings in the 1920s were derided as facile and self-indulgent. Where once he had been recognized from New York to Moscow as one of the two giants of modernism, now Matisse was a decorative painter while Pablo Picasso was "the great renovator."[10]

Exiled from the avant-garde, Matisse found no home with the traditionalists; he was too far out in front to comprehend. His important works just before and during World War I, like *Bathers by a River* and *The Moroccans*, which he considered "pivotal," left collectors and critics lost at the crossroads. To one critic, they were "pathological," another saw them as a "decomposing corpse of Intelligence." "If one isn't hurt by their malice," Matisse wrote home, "one is by their stupidity."[11] Quoting Eugène Delacroix, Matisse said, "We are not understood, we are acknowledged."[12] To Marguerite, he complained, "It's not the good life with no cares. It's still a harsh life . . . surrounded by almost total incomprehension." The odds of his ultimate recognition as an important modern artist stood no better than the toss of a coin, he said sourly. "That shows how little confidence I have in public reaction."[13]

Unlike the "wild beasts" whom he'd once painted with, the husband and father of three children came across as conventional and bourgeois. "The real Matisse," reported one magazine, "hurries to open the door in his gardening clothes when you ring the bell." He went to bed early, maintained a rigorous work routine, hummed dance-hall tunes, and made sure his son Pierre put in hours practicing the piano. When his fellow Fauves were just scraping by, Matisse owned a home with a telephone, bathroom, and central heating. In an era when private automobiles were a rare commodity, Matisse drove a second-hand Renault. "Of greatness I could see no trace," judged the merciless Bell.[14] It seemed impossible that this grand bourgeois was the deity who created *La Dance*.

Matisse's wounded feelings were not imagined. Matisse's celebrated Fauve works had become stale, his paintings of the postwar years were dismissed as mere still lifes, pretty pictures of seaside hotel rooms, and voyeuristic studies of lounging women. His wartime masterpieces existed in a world that had yet to understand them. Many of his greatest paintings were hidden away in Russia after its revolution, others hung mute and unseen in the mansion of the wealthy American Dr. Albert Barnes, and still others languished in storage after being torn from the walls of German galleries, as the Nazi regime considered Matisse a "degenerate artist." "People know nothing of your previous output," Marguerite's husband, Georges Duthuit, told his father-in-law.[15] Françoise Gilot, Picasso's companion, gives a first-hand account of an ugly scene in Picasso's atelier where *la Bande à Picasso*—Georges Braque, Max Jacob, Marie Laurencin, and André Salmon—mocked Matisse as "finished," a "non-entity," while throwing cigarettes, matchbooks, and matches at *Portrait of Marguerite* (1906), a gift from Matisse that Picasso displayed in his studio.[16]

In the summer of 1937, France hosted the *Exposition Internationale* attended by forty-four nations and dedicated to art, technology, and modern life. The Parisian planning committee decided it would be deliciously provocative to situate the massive pavilion built by Nazi Germany directly opposite that of the Soviet Union. In photographs from the official exhibit pamphlet, the two enemy buildings face each other across the Trocadéro fountains like gargantuan chess pieces as the Eiffel Tower rises in the background like a queen. The architectural confrontation gave the Expo's latent sense of looming war the ballast of brick and stone. On other buildings and walls throughout the capital were 718 murals painted by an army of artists commissioned by the French government and the City of Paris to beautify the world's art capital for its worldwide guests.[17]

Neither his government nor his city bothered to invite Henri Matisse.

THE ENDURING FAME of the great artist Henri Matisse is such that his surname alone is sufficient to conjure the man and his art. *Matisse*: holding palette and brush and wearing a wide-brimmed hat. *Matisse*: the blue nudes and effortless arabesques, the gleaming green of a palm frond, orange-red, or the blue-green spiral of dancing figures. "I had never seen a thing so simple and so calculated," wrote the American journalist Dorothy Dudley in May 1934 upon Matisse showing her his work-in-progress mural, *The Dance II*. "Colors enter the world through Matisse like harmonies through Mozart," in the words of the late art critic Peter Schjeldahl.[18] The current of Henri Matisse's modernism was carried by several charged lines: groundbreaking Fauvism, experiments in chilly Cubism, exotic models in couture backdropped by patterns horizontal and vertical, and late in his life, paper cutouts "brimming with clanging colors."[19]

What more can be said of this "secular saint" of modern art, whose life, straddling two centuries, took him from "lamplit parochialism" to "international media blaze"?[20] Prior to his death and for seven decades after, waves of scholarship have added layers of understanding to Matisse's career. Among the first studies were Alfred Barr's *Matisse: His Art and His Public*, in 1951, and Raymond Escholier's *Matisse: Ce Vivant*, published five years later.

It took thirty-two years after his death for the world to gain a greater understanding of Henri Matisse. A large exhibition at the National Gallery in Washington, DC, in 1986 coincided with the publication of the memoirs of Lydia Delectorskaya, Matisse's companion from the outbreak of World War II until his death. That same year saw the publication of a forty-year-old memoir by Jane Bussy, the daughter of Simon Bussy.[21] Massive studies by experts in Leningrad, Moscow, New York, Paris, and Washington, DC, were published, including Jack D. Flam's *Matisse: The Man and His Art, 1869-1918*, and the Musée Matisse in Nice was renovated and enlarged.

A cultural exchange with the Soviet Union meant some of the most important Matisse works could be seen in Los Angeles, New York, and Washington.

In the decades that followed, the publication of Matisse's letters to his son Pierre, an art dealer and gallery owner in New York, and Hilary Spurling's definitive two-volume biography, *The Unknown Matisse* and *Matisse the Master*, allowed for a deepened understanding of his personal life.

It was there where the idea for this book was formed.

When I read Spurling's biography several years ago, I was particularly intrigued by the contents of a footnote—a 238-word footnote—which addressed the question: What did Henri Matisse do during the Occupation of France? Between 1986 and Spurling's biography, two books were published examining the acts and omissions of painters like André Derain, Picasso, and Matisse, as they navigated their artistic lives in a France divided into an occupied north and collaborationist south. One was Michèle Cone's 1992 study *Artists Under Vichy*, and from a French publishing house that same year came *L'Art de la Défaite* (*The Art of Defeat*), by French scholar Laurence Bertrand Dorléac. Matisse, according to Cone, was "supremely indifferent," essentially sitting out the Second World War, living in relative comfort in the unoccupied Mediterranean city of Nice as beautiful models and sumptuous things provided grist for his ever-deeper journey into modernism. Hilary Spurling, in her footnote, questions the basis for Cone's assertions. In this teapot-sized tempest, I found the potential for a story of art and war, creation and desecration, collaboration and inspiration.

What did Matisse do during the war years, 1939-1945? Did he simply paint his way through the war, ignoring the German occupiers and the Vichy government's compliance with their aims—including the expulsion and deportation of Jews—or did he seize a patch of the cultural battlefield, and if so, how exactly? Was he among the artists who were censored? Did he work around the restrictions? How did his efforts affect his fellow citizens? Did Matisse, as Cone asserts, take advantage of the Parisian art world from which other artists, so-called enemies of the Nazi regime, had been forced out?

And what of his family, friends, and fellow artists? We know his estranged wife, Amélie, and his daughter, Marguerite, participated in the Resistance. Matisse's letters to his son Pierre and friends Charles Camoin and Pierre Bonnard reveal his worry about their wartime ac-tivities and whereabouts, as well as those of his son Jean, who was engaged in sabotage against the enemy. Through his letters to family and friends, and using English, French, and Italian sources from the war years onward, this is a narration of Matisse's life and art in the context of the four-way war waged along the French Mediterranean coast among the Germans, Italians, Allies, and Resistance. To ex-amine the life of Henri Matisse and his family during the Occupation of France is to also explore the choices forced upon them and their fellow citizens: courage or survival, authoritarianism or democracy? In telling this story, I also aim to reveal the humanity of the man who could seem conventional in his habits but whose art broke so free of convention it "flickers halfway between the imagined and the seen."[22]

CHAPTER ONE

La Famille

"I had seen the true inspirers, the caryatids who, by supporting the weight of the temple, enabled the artist to become fully himself and to create."
—FRANÇOISE GILOT

AVENUE DES CHAMPS-ELYSÉES, PARIS, FRANCE
OCTOBER 15, 1905

The elegant Parisian crowd filed into the Grand Palais, the architectural masterpiece built at the turn of the century by the French Republic along the city's grandest avenue and dedicated "to the glory of French art." In the nave, under the largest glass-domed ceiling in Europe, the crowd took in the monumental space, large enough to host equestrian events, and girded by more steel than the Eiffel Tower. On this day, the Palais was host to the annual art exhibition, the Salon d'Automne. It was a new era, and the salon was a showcase of new artists and new styles. In its first two years, the event had featured lesser-known artists alongside some of the most respected names of French art: Paul Cézanne and Auguste Renoir. The well-heeled Parisians, men in dark coats, bowlers and homburgs, and

1

women in elaborate Victorian hats and long dresses ambled about, deciding which of the eighteen rooms to see first: landscapes, portraits, sculptures?

Those who chose Room VII were witness to an unfolding scandal. Patrons were shocked, not by what was in the center of the exhibition hall—stately, almost scientific marble busts, inspired by Renaissance sculptors like Donatello—but along its walls. The crowd murmured as it took in the raw, pure power of the collection. Viewers squinted to make out the names on the canvases awash in bold pinks and greens, turquoise and orange: *Who could be so audacious as to present this as art for respectable Parisians?* The rough and obvious brushstrokes, the lack of local grays, browns, and blues; garish hues unrelated to the objects they depicted, and so bright as to hurt the eyes—it was the work of Charles Camoin, André Derain, Albert Marquet, Maurice Vlaminck.

Even in a room full of color, one painting in Room VII stood out. A seated woman under an elaborate hat looks over her shoulder at the viewer, her long neck and high, sharp cheekbones giving her an almost birdlike appearance. In one of her gloved hands is a fan. She offers a hint of a frown. The work's fidelity to conventional portraiture ends there. The woman's almond eyes under dark circumflex brows punctuate a face deliberately flat and mask-like. A slash of pale green accentuates the woman's Gallic nose, her ear is a wafer of orange pink, and a horizontal brushstroke of pine green is the shadow along her brow. Her matte black eyes are not meant to convey the animating spirit of the sitter, but to communicate the interior aim of the artist. The elaborate hat she wears sits "like a galleon, loaded with wildly colored fruits."[1] Clouds of teal, rose, and lemon-yellow swirl among beams of rust, lavender, and indigo; its energies held together by a belt of tomato red. *Woman with a Hat* is a galaxy of color.

What was *the color of your wife's dress?* a critic asked the artist.

"Black, of course," replied Henri Matisse.

Two days later, on Tuesday, October 17, 1905, the Paris literary magazine *Gil Blas* published its review of the Salon d'Automne exhibition. The art critic, Louis Vauxcelles, corralled and dismissed in a few sentences most of the artists in Room VII, showing disdain for the "virulent imagery" of Derain's *Bateaux*, and Vlaminck's "terrible looking" entry. But for the creator of *Woman with a Hat*, he devoted a full paragraph: "M. Matisse is one of the most robust and gifted painters today. He has courage." Although he could have indulged in "easy bravos," Matisse "prefers to wander in a passionate search . . . for more vibration, luminosity." That Vauxcelles respected Matisse's courage more than *Woman with a Hat* or the paintings of his cohorts was made clear by his preference for the perfectly rendered statues in the center of the exhibition room, "It is surprising to see the honesty of these statues in the midst of this orgy of pure color: *Donatello chez les fauves.*"

Les Fauves. With that phrase Camoin, Derain, Marquet, Vlaminck, and Matisse became *Fauves*, the "wild beasts" of the Parisian art world. *Woman with a Hat* was derided by critics and conservative patrons. The exhibition jury members had even requested that Matisse withdraw the portrait; the chair of the hanging committee overruled them.[2] To the younger, more adventurous painters in his circle, including Pablo Picasso, Matisse's portrait was speaking a new language of color. Better yet for the thirty-five-year-old Matisse and his wife, Amélie, was the purchase of the painting by wealthy American collectors, the Stein family. To Gertrude Stein's brother Leo, Matisse's bold portrait was "a thing brilliant and powerful . . . it was what I was unknowingly waiting for."[3] Just a few years earlier, Matisse was struggling to provide for his wife, two young sons, and sickly daughter, complaining to a friend, "I'm not earning a penny. My little girl is ill. We're all freezing—I shall probably have to give up painting."[4] He sold sketches in a Montmartre tavern for a few francs and earned a few sous gilding leaves on the cornices in the very exhibition hall where his canvases were now mounted.[5] Now, in the autumn of 1905, Henri Matisse, the latecomer to art who looked and dressed like the lawyer he had once trained to be, was the face of the French avant-garde and becoming a leading figure in modern art.

His Fauvist period was successful but brief. *The Green Line* and *Bonheur de Vivre* were sold to the Steins, where they became subjects for the Saturday evening salons held in Gertrude and Leo's apartment at 27 rue de Fleurus, and Michael and Sarah Stein's apartment around the corner at 58 rue Madame. *The Young Sailor, Self-Portrait, Blue Still Life*, and *Woman with a Branch of Ivy* soon also appeared on the Steins' walls. The wealthy Russian Sergei Shchukin added Matisse to his collection, the dealer Berthe Weill lent his influential support, and *Blue Nude: Memory of Biskra* became the first of many Matisse paintings to become part of the modern art collection of the Cone sisters of Baltimore, Maryland.* In 1909, after years of painting in empty bedrooms and converted convents, Matisse built his first studio at the villa he had rented for his family in suburban Paris.

But as the art critic Louis Vauxcelles had noted, Matisse was a searcher, and his art career in the ensuing years took unanticipated turns. The younger artists he'd briefly outflanked—Picasso, Georges Braque, and others—turned to Cubism and Surrealism and became the darlings of French and international critics. The war of 1914–1918 warped French society, including its artists and writers, like a massive vacuum of intracontinental violence and illogic. "It should be the old and the infirm sent to die in holes," Auguste Renoir remarked bitterly to Matisse, "not the young with their lives before them."[6] Postwar Europe's foundations had been destabilized. The centuries-old rhythm of village life, where priests and prefects were the

---

* The Cones bought this painting from original purchasers Getrude and Leo Stein. When Picasso saw it, he said he didn't understand what Matisse was doing: "If he wants to make a woman, let him make a woman. If he wants to make a design, let him make a design. This is between the two." Walter Pach, *Queer Thing, Painting: Forty Years in the World of Art* (New York: Harper & Brothers, 1938) 125.

authority and women knew their place, was gone. The foundations of art, literature, and music were toppled, too. In the three turbulent decades after he gained fame, Henri Matisse continued to seek a painterly light. In his quest for "more vibration and luminosity," he sailed to North Africa, New York, and Tahiti and the South Seas. When in France, he worked in the southern city of Nice, where the Alps meet the turquoise water of the Mediterranean.

On marrying Amélie Parayre, a handsome dark-haired Toulousaine, in 1898, Matisse declared, "I love you dearly, mademoiselle; but I shall always love painting more."[7] Raised in an open-minded and well-connected family in Beauzelle, near Toulouse, it was a life Amélie accepted. Her family distrusted monarchists, Bonapartists, and the ties between church and state. Her father edited an activist Republican newspaper, her sister Berthe was a pioneering force in secular education in France, and Amélie, with looks "like a Spanish Queen," was ready to exert her energies toward a modernizing France.*

The gravitational force of the artist pulled in his family from the very beginning. The couple had a son, Jean, in 1899, and another, Pierre, in 1900. The two boys joined Henri's daughter, Marguerite, born in 1894 from an earlier relationship between Matisse and his mistress and model, Camille Joblaud. When she was six, Marguerite nearly died; saved by an emergency tracheotomy that required her to wear a metal cannula to widen her windpipe. Amélie loved the stoic and resilient young girl and treated her as her own daughter.

These early years were so lean for the Matisse family that Jean was sent to live with Matisse's parents in the north, and Pierre to Amélie's sister's home in the south. Marguerite stayed in Paris, while her adoptive mother, free of the little boys, opened a hat shop that

---

* One of the political connections of Matisse's in-laws proved disastrous for the Parayres when they were caught up in a nationwide scandal involving a young politician Fréderic Humbert. *L'affair Humbert* financially ruined Matisse's father-in-law, and when he was threatened with prosecution, Matisse relied on his training as a lawyer to clear his father-in-law's name.

provided the family with its main source of income. Despite the financial hardships, Amélie never wavered: she was "self-sacrificing" to her husband's artistic vision, while also being "effectively practical."[8] She was reserved, yet forceful; faithful, yet capable of wit. Posing uncomfortably for hours in a blue toreador costume for *The Guitarist* in 1903, Amélie began to pluck the strings. His concentration broken, Matisse tipped over the easel, paint splattered, and the guitar clanged to the floor. The couple howled with laughter.[9]

For many years Amélie posed and Matisse painted, and these twin obsessions were woven together. Home was the studio; the studio was home. It was an exhausting role, but one Amélie played without complaint. Upon seeing *Woman with a Hat*, a friend of Picasso's remarked, "Nothing about it was physically human. You had the impression that the artist had been much more preoccupied by his own personality than he was with his model's."[10] Matisse was self-absorbed, but the "chillingly inhuman" portrait of his wife said something about Amélie, too: she was strong-willed, courageous, and had a "passionate, exacting faith" in the direction of her husband's art.[11]

Over time the strain of being Matisse's wife, model, and personal manager, while his fame and demands for independence increased, took a toll. The paintings tell us that much. In *The Conversation*, which Matisse worked on from 1908 to 1912, the artist—a notorious insomniac—stands in profile in his striped pajamas opposite his wife, who is composed, seated, and dressed in black. Like the other paintings and drawings from this era where Matisse depicted himself, he is "oddly gawky . . . ungainly," a two-dimensional column, the crown of his head cropped by the edge of the canvas. In his sleeping clothes, the artist is in a state of temporal transience; Amélie, by contrast, is depicted with the elegant curves and sense of volume of her husband's later work. His hand is in his pocket, while her arms are comfortably rested on the arms of her chair—he's a petitioner before a judge. She is where she should be; he is not. The deep blue field that surrounds them and lies between them is less sea or sky and more midnight. "Violently original," the painting is a confrontation, a private late-night tête-à-tête that stirs a tinge of voyeurism in the viewer.[12] *The Conversation* is a brief filed from a troubled marriage.

"We were a family of artists," Marguerite explained. "The whole family revolved around the labors of the father."[13] Wherever the family lived, in their Paris flat, vacant convent, or a seaside cottage, the pattern of family life was based on when the patriarch was working and when he was taking a break. It was a house of rules: canvases had to be cleaned and stretched, rooms had to be tidy or vacated so they could serve as erstwhile studio space, paintings had to be framed and hung. Above all was the requirement of silence. Before dealers were invited to see the new works, Matisse, Amélie, and Marguerite conferenced for days evaluating the canvases before them. Painting was, in biographer Hilary Spurling's phrase, "the pivot on which the family turned."[14]

Matisse also collected artwork by Cézanne, Paul Gauguin, and others. These were cherished by the entire family, but none more so than their father's works. Where birthdays, weddings, and deaths marked the rhythm of time in other families, it was the completion of pieces that marked important divisions of time in the Matisse household. "I know the place your paintings occupy in our family," Pierre told his father. "Each one represents a period, a new enrichment of our common world."[15]

Yet the seemingly effortless serenity of so many of Matisse's paintings came at a cost. "A man who makes pictures like [these]," Matisse later told his son Pierre,

> is an unhappy creature, tormented day and night. He relieves himself of his passion in his pictures, but also in spite of himself on the people round him. That is what normal people never understand. They want to enjoy the artists'

products—as one might enjoy cows' milk—but they can't put up with the inconvenience, the mud and the flies.[16]

The "mud and the flies" started with self-doubt. Matisse had come to art later than most, and his virtuosity as a modernist was not earned through formal training but from some unknowable place. He entered "art history from essentially nowhere, as if by parachute. Never having had traditional lessons to unlearn ... Matisse innovated on something like whim—a privilege, without guidelines or guarantees, for which he paid a steep toll in anxiety."[17] Matisse likened himself to an acrobat, whose effortless airborne feats are in fact the product of countless hours of practice. Admirers at exhibitions saw the defiance of gravity; his family saw a man day after day struggling to reach new heights without a net. "Don't forget that my storms take place in my work," Matisse told Amélie, "which is the rudder that steers the whole house."[18]

In 1913, Amélie sat more than a hundred times for the *Portrait of Madame Matisse*. "A thunderous painting, in drenching blues and greens," the portrait depicts "a chic and stony woman leaning forward in a chair, with a black-featured gray mask of a face."[19] A friend of Matisse, Marcel Sembat, spent time with the couple that year and reported, "Saturday with Matisse. Crazy! Weeping! By night he recites the Lord's Prayer! By day he quarrels with his wife!"[20] Work on the portrait, according to Spurling, caused Matisse "palpitations, high blood pressure and a constant drumming in his ears." When Matisse had difficulty with a painting, he often worked himself into a heightened state, but this was "something like [an] exorcism. The portrait expresses no specific feeling but, rather, registers innumerable emotions, not excluding tenderness. The game tilt of Amélie's small head, sporting a dainty ostrich-feather toque, could break your heart."[21] Amélie had been "the happy counterweight to your fundamentally pessimistic nature," Marguerite told her father. And while Amélie would remain Matisse's wife, her time as model and manager,

champion and caretaker to her husband and his career was coming
to an end.

It was the last portrait Matisse ever painted of his wife.

Matisse first painted his precious daughter, Marguerite, when
she was six. More than a muse, she was Henri's favorite, and as a
sickly child, she was also a captive model. He always drew the ribbon
she wore around her neck to conceal a three-inch scar, a practice she
continued into adulthood.[22] Marguerite became a constant presence
in her father's studio, and with her father's encouragement, took up
violin and painting, eventually showing "considerable talent."[23] Matisse's moods were often reflected in his portraiture regardless of the
sitter, but when Marguerite was his model, he allowed her personality to reveal itself. In *Marguerite Reading*, she is a studious, serious
young girl, eyes cast down at her book. Dressed in a pinafore the
next year in *Marguerite*, a portrait of greater candor, her head is held
high with the "prim, shy pride" of a schoolgirl wearing her hair up
for the first time.[24] In *Girl with a Black Cat*, from 1910, she sits upright like a "Byzantine saint."[25]

Marguerite's centrality within the family is revealed in *The
Painter's Family*, a domestic scene from 1911. It is Marguerite who
anchors the canvas, queen-like, in a long black gown and a white
lace collar that would not look out of place in a European court. As
her brothers play checkers in plain matching short pants in front of
the hearth, the regal Marguerite, a look of concentration on her face,
clutches a book. Though Amélie sits to the right of her sons, you
would think it is Marguerite who is the matriarch . . .

That Marguerite is more articulated and actualized than Matisse's wife and sons may be because Matisse admired in his daughter
the traits he brought to bear himself: dedication—even devotion—
to art; abnegation of the appetites that would derail that devotion;
ardent, yet sober of mind; talented, yet disciplined. Her similar nature led Marguerite to possess an "exact and retentive eye" for her
father's works.[26] By the time Marguerite dangles a flirty high heel

in *Tea in the Garden*, an "extraordinary garden picture" from 1919, it was clear she had grown "from a child to a woman in [her father's] work," in the words of Kennedy Fraser.[27] "She's truly the life and soul of the house," said her brother Jean, speaking for the entire family.[28]

For over twenty years, Marguerite had joined her mother as the "piano and violin duet" maintaining the harmony of the family's life. They were the "two parallel columns at the entrance of Matisse's temple," so when her mother stepped away, Marguerite became the managing partner of the family firm.[29]

A painter in her own right, Marguerite was a critic of her father "trained by him to be as hard to please as he was himself."[30] "Your character, like mine," Matisse wrote his daughter, "tends to despair when things go badly, but forgets to take the credit for what goes well."[31]

She handled public relations and was the conduit to his most important patrons, corresponding for decades with the writer Gertrude Stein and Etta and Claribel Cone, the Baltimore-based sisters who were avid collectors of Matisse. She dealt with framers and gallery owners; she documented sales and filled out tax forms. Father and daughter "always collaborated," Marguerite's son, Claude Duthuit, later explained. "My mother was the only one known to [authorize] Matisse's signature for proofs."[32] Duthuit provides a candid glimpse into Matisse's world:

> When people came to choose things, my mother would put whatever drawings she intended to show out on the floor. Professionals and other artists thought it was normal, but for laymen [it was surprising] to see my grandfather's artworks on the floor. I remember my mother pushing the drawings with her toe.[33]

Marguerite Matisse was also the weathervane, attuned to the gathering storms in her parents' marriage, the lives of her siblings, and her father's art.

In time Marguerite, too, had to step away from her unofficial position as studio chief of staff. In December 1923, she married Georges Duthuit, a brilliant young scholar of Byzantine art. Perhaps reflecting Marguerite's social circle and disposition, their wedding was a small and sober affair, attended by the family, one witness (the painter Albert Marquet), and the art-collecting couple Michael and Sarah Stein.[34] Afterward, the couple commenced their life together with a trip to Vienna and plans for Duthuit to take an academic position in Cairo.

After marrying, Marguerite stopped posing for her father.

NEITHER OF MATISSE'S sons were equipped to act as Matisse's majordomo. Jean, the eldest, was far from the archetypical "good son." He was "famously difficult," according to one acquaintance of the family.[35] Jean was also rougher in looks and in temperament than his brother. Pierre had the Roman nose and erect bearing; his impassive face was almost birdlike, like his mother's, still and attentive at the same time; the kind of face always in perfect control, never to break into a toothy smile. In contrast, Jean had deep-set eyes and a walrus-like moustache. Compared with the well-coiffed Pierre, Jean could appear disheveled with his unruly hair and bushy eyebrows. In photos he allows himself to slump forward in an ungainly way. In his actions as in his dress, he lacked the discipline of his siblings. Jean's marriage to a struggling ceramicist, Louise Milhau, a divorcée with whom he'd had carried on an affair while she was still married, gave his parents a fresh reason to be disappointed.

When his younger son, Pierre, demobilized from the French Army in November 1920, Père Matisse arranged an apprenticeship for him with a Parisian art dealer. Pierre lacked the necessary talent to earn a living as a violinist or painter. But even the promise of a career in the Paris art world did not materialize when Pierre fell in love with Clorinde Peretti, a Corsican "hothouse flower," and hastily found himself in an ill-considered marriage. "I had a love story, the way young people do," Pierre said laconically.[36] The marriage lasted two months before Clorinde returned her ring and abruptly left the Matisse home. The episode left Pierre fearing he was a *triple raté*, a three-time loser. Their son, Henri Matisse wrote Amélie, "is a sick man in need of a cure…"[37]

Clorinde, too, was a loser. In deeply Catholic France, and especially in Corsica, divorce was hardly feasible. She was young, beautiful, and ruined.

To escape Monsieur Peretti, his murderously angry father-in-law, his own disappointed father, and the burden of failure, Pierre sailed for New York in 1924. Taking the cure of learning English with the hope of establishing an art dealership on a new continent perhaps seemed easier to swallow than sneaking around southern Europe always on the lookout for Clorinde's father, who sought to avenge his ruined daughter with the aid of a loaded revolver. Upon Pierre's departure, Matisse said ruefully, "I didn't give him all the advice I should have liked because things don't come to mind all at once, he left in such a rush."[38]

As the family drifted apart, they now sniped at and sometimes ignored one another across Europe and the Atlantic. Matisse remained "ominously silent for weeks [only to] volcanically erupt [and] hurl thunderbolts from Nice." In *la famille* Matisse, said Marguerite, fair moods and foul were as close together as the fingers on one hand.[39] The storms of her father's work had become a familial tempest. "We're not just living in a house that's cracking up," summed up Marguerite, "we're living through an earthquake…a raging storm and all we can do is try to keep our heads above water."[40] Just as ominously, Amélie wrote Marguerite to warn her, "Thunder was in the air."[41]

CHAPTER TWO

The Luminosity of Days

*"While he followed the progress of his hand on the
paper . . . the tension was so great that he remained
oblivious to everything else, in a trance like that which
enables an actor to perform his role in spite of a high
fever, or a partisan to march with a bullet in his body."*
—ELSA TRIOLET, "THE PRIVATE
LIFE OF ALEXIS SLAVSKY"[1]

IN A STATE OF SEMI-estrangement from his family and untethered
from their home at Issy-les-Moulineaux in suburban Paris, Henri
Matisse traveled. He spent time in Tangier, Morocco, New York,
and San Francisco, and voyaged to French Polynesia. In Tahiti, a
friend remarked to Matisse, "Shadows are rare here. There's sunshine
everywhere except on you."[2] When he *was* in France, after nearly a
half century of living in the north, Matisse sought a new milieu
under the sun.

The pocket paradise that is Nice sits at France's southeastern corner between the mountains and the Mediterranean Sea. Over the
centuries it had been home to Phoenicians, Greeks, Romans, Celts,

Franks, Alpine counts, British royals, Russian aristocrats, and Hollywood stars. Americans like composer Cole Porter, writer Edith Wharton, and dancer Isadora Duncan mixed with Europeans Pablo Picasso, Rudolph Valentino, and Coco Chanel. Oscar Wilde had lived at 9 rue de la Buffa, and Guy de Maupassant, near Musée des Beaux Arts Jules Chéret. Russian revolutionary Vladimir Ilyich Lenin lived at 23 rue Gounod, and his fellow leftist Leon Trotsky rather ironically resided on rue Droite.[3] The city had been home to German philosopher Friedrich Nietzsche and before that, future emperor Napoleon Bonaparte. The fashionable came for the nightlife, the wealthy came for the weather, and still others to escape the prying eyes of their enemies.

Henri Matisse came for the light.

"From my open window," he wrote on his first visit to the city, "you can see the top of a palm tree . . . sky and sea *blue—blue—blue*" (emphasis added).[4] When a winter storm lifted, Matisse took out his paints. "What made me stay was the great colored reflections of January, the luminosity of the days."[5] For the first several painting seasons Matisse made do with rented apartments and hotels, using canvases, paints, and brushes sent by his family from Paris.[6] His habit was to paint in the morning, usually in his bedroom. "From nine o'clock to noon, first sitting. I have lunch. Then I have a little nap and take out my brushes again at two o'clock in the afternoon until the evening."[7] His siesta was a necessary part of life in Nice. The window shutters are not just for the occasional *mistral*, the powerful northeasterly winds that clear the clouds and dust and leave crystalline skies in its wake. From the early morning until late evening, the sunlight can be relentless. "High noon is superb but frightening," he told Charles Camoin in a letter.[8] Color was everywhere: shiny cherries in the market, the cut-lime feathers of a parakeet, the basking façades of gold and rose. For a colorist like Matisse, "Nice provided the pictorial equivalent of laboratory conditions in which to reshape the future."[9]

Like a cyclist training for the Tour de France, Matisse ate spar-
ingly, drank modestly, and maintained a fitness level that his body
would allow, and otherwise conducted his life toward its singular
aim: to rise ready to pedal up the Alpine passes of modernism. "I
have asked myself every day if I were doing what was essential to
keep myself in condition to paint. All that is difficult. It means that
one must remain calm, balanced, clear of distractions. One must
make sacrifices."[10]

To break the monotony, Matisse played the violin or strolled the
city's gardens.* When Marguerite visited, he took her on painting pic-
nics during the day and to the Casino on the Jetée in the evening,
where they foxtrotted among the swells and swindlers. Matisse hiked
Mont Boron and rowed in the bay. He napped under olive trees and
walked the narrow alleyways under laundry that fluttered like the sails
in the sea. He ducked into shops selling wine, books, and spices . . .
then back to painting. The artist, he told the critic Léon Degand,
must "reduce his existence to the minimum . . . [s]implify life. Don't
admit anything useless."[11] And so Matisse missed important family
obligations, like his wife's father's funeral. Holidays and birthdays
came and went. "For me, [Christmas] was a day like any other."[12]
Alone and driven, the artist's only companions were caged birds and
a bowl of goldfish. The subjects of his paintings from these years act
as a kind of diary: his worn valise, a framed canvas, his violin and its
case. Through his interior scenes and still lifes of fruits and flowers,
Matisse transcribed the exotic color and clear light of the region.

He also painted women. Harem-garbed or half-clad, his models
"were drawn from the tide of human flotsam washed up in Nice between the wars."[13] Professor Catherine Bock, focusing on Matisse's

---

* Matisse had taken up the violin, in part, because of his obsession with his eyesight. In Matisse's first seasons in Nice, Amélie asked him why he was playing
the violin so much. He said it was his fear of going blind; if he did, at least he
could make a few francs busking in the street. See Escholier, *Matisse from the
Life*, 101-102.

Nice paintings held by the Art Institute of Chicago, notes the mute-
ness and melancholia. Matisse's models were:

> Gazing at the sea, pining at open windows, neither
> dressed nor nude, going nowhere, twisting in their chairs,
> inert on their couches with unread books and un-played
> instruments in their hands . . . absorbed in their own
> mute presence . . . available, bored [and] adrift.[14]

The ballerinas and ballroom dancers who posed for him might
have been a temptation for Henri Matisse, but his reports to his
family and friends were full of indulgences ignored. His "frugal and
monastic routine" was against the frothy tide of his adopted city. "In
Nice of all places," he joked to a friend.[15] In an understatement to
another friend, he described the "street life" as "interesting."[16] Matisse eschewed the rich local specialties of milk-fed lamb and stuffed
vegetables known as *petits farcis* for a simple supper of soup, hard-
boiled eggs, a salad, and a glass of wine. To Amélie, he wrote, "Nice
is utterly Niçois. I feel myself a complete foreigner here."[17] The self-
proclaimed "hermit of the Promenade des Anglais" signed his letters
home *le vieux solitaire*—the old recluse.[18]

Matisse's hotel rooms were as transitional and impermanent as
the city itself.[19] Nice in the years after World War I was a magnet
for asylum-seekers, rootless Europeans, immigrants, and penniless
musicians—making do and moving on when they could scrape up
train fare. The ancient port was at the edge of a Europe uneasily between a war that had settled nothing and another war that seemed
inevitable. Nice was also on the fault line of democracy and authoritarianism. Great Britain and France adhered to the rule of law, while
Italy and Germany had given themselves to dictators. "This is not a
defeated country," reported French General Émile Fayolle, after vis-
iting "defeated" Germany, only one month after the Armistice
ended World War I, "there will be another war in ten years, if not

sooner."[20] It wasn't just generals who sensed the danger. "Better not to think about it too much," Marguerite had predicted when Hitler set forth his twisted dream in *Mein Kampf*. "The future looks like the abyss."[21] There was a sense that the old world had self-immolated, and the new world order would arrive in a violent birth. The uneasiness of these "ravaged years," in Pierre Matisse's phrase, "seeped into the cracks and folds of the artist's consciousness."

After several provisional seasons in Nice, Matisse took a step toward becoming a resident when he rented a large flat at the eastern end of the flower market. 1 Place Charles-Félix is a four-story Italianate palais awash in sunlit ochre. "In order to paint my pictures," he explained, "I need to remain for several days in the same state of mind, and I do not find this in any atmosphere but that of the Côte d'Azur."[22] Converting a bedroom in his third-floor apartment allowed Matisse two adjoining sea-facing studios.[23] For the next few years, Matisse worked in these twin studios, spending the summers reconnecting with his family in Issy or treating them to summer holidays abroad. "I don't want any more struggles in my life," he told Marguerite, "I've got quite enough in my work."[24] As with his art, Matisse's relationship with his wife, Amélie, was marked by the push and pull of advance and retreat.

In 1926-1927, Matisse acquired a large double-sized apartment on the top floor of the palais so Amélie could spend the painting season under the same roof as her husband. At first, the breathtaking views from the top floor of 1 Place Charles-Félix contributed to a sense of serenity for Madame Matisse. "I get out a bit," she reported to Marguerite, "I sew, the time passes peacefully."[25] Amélie Matisse's presence high above the flower market was noted by the curious Niçois. Their building had once housed the *Sénat du Comte de Nice*, and its high ceilings, morning sun, and evening shade made it something of a stage on which the painter performed—his audience below the flower sellers, fishmongers, and flea-market *brocanteurs*.

The locals who admired the great artist proved a more agreeable audience than the art critics.

Matisse's Nice paintings were filled with lounging women and French doors and windows open to the sea. His use of color—rose, red, sky blue, mustardy yellow—remained without parallel, but his quotidian subject matter and his decision to experiment with perception (of color and light), rather than construction (Cubism), cost Matisse prestige from Paris and respect from his friends. Cubist Georges Braque "didn't condescend to look at what I've done," Matisse reported. André Breton refused to pay "any further attention to such a dead loss."[26] Unlike his large and complex earlier paintings, such as *Bathers by a River* or *The Piano Lesson*, they "gave no overt sign of disquiet."[27] The contemporary consensus from critics and collectors saw these as creations of a once-daring artist who had retreated to a seaside city to document its easy and prodigious pleasures. "The painting of Matisse is pure and simple delight" requiring no "intellectual effort," wrote art critic Clive Bell.[28] When he shipped paintings like *French Window at Nice* home, his normally supportive family gazed upon it in doubtful silence. By the 1930s, Matisse was "widely compared unfavorably to Picasso."[29, 30] Matisse was an "old lion," said André Breton, "who needed yet another Matisse *Window*?"[31]

This negative evaluation endured during Matisse's lifetime and for three decades afterward. "Once in Nice," wrote art critic Peter Schjeldahl,

> Matisse could go to work in his pajamas, with freshly picked lemons to paint, and newly waxed furniture, and the reflected glitter of a sunlit sea, and pretty women in never-before-worn summer dresses—and sometimes in no dresses at all. That is everyone's image of the early Nice paintings, and everyone is not entirely wrong.[32]

Yet Matisse labored on these works "like a carthorse." He pushed "further and deeper into true painting," he said, "searching for the density of things," and to "convey volume."[33] Perhaps time had to pass to see Matisse's early Nice works not as a surrender to frivolous decorations by a bored bourgeois, but as an artist making tactical withdrawals in preparation for an all-out offensive.*

Meanwhile, Amélie's melancholy persisted. Madame Matisse became so severely depressed she spent parts of each week in bed, only rarely venturing into town. "She's held up by the dressmaker," a deflated Matisse told Pierre on one occasion, "who is making dresses for her she'll never wear."[34] When he was home, Matisse tried to clear the clouds by taking Amélie on trips for mud baths and mountain air. The cures were temporary; it was "wretched to see her in such a state of misery and fatigue," Marguerite told her father.[35]

By 1932, neither the sea view nor the mountain air was enough. The family hired a full-time assistant to care for her: Lydia Omeltchenko. Madame Lydia, as the family called her, was twenty-two and a personality in process; a tall, blond Russian beauty, but lacking in

---

* Eventually, as the lens of time moved further and further away, Matisse's early Nice works came into clearer focus for art historians and experts. In November 1986, the National Gallery of Art in Washington, DC, exhibited 171 works Matisse had painted in rented hotel rooms, narrow apartments, and second-rate villas in Nice. To art critic Dominique Fourcade, these were works of "waiting and sadness," a "world behind glass . . . the world of the voyeur [where] communication seems impossible." *Anemones in a Terracotta Pot* wasn't just a pretty painting of flowers, it was a work of "amazing stridency . . . a kind of delirium withheld and released by the light in which the elements of this painting float." To another Matisse authority, Jack Flam, the images from Nice were replete with "boredom, claustrophobia, alienation, and sexual yearning." *French Window at Nice*, which had baffled the artist's own family, appeared to Flam decades later as a work of "almost gothic splendor." To Alfred Barr, in several works from the early Nice period Matisse had achieved "*tours-de-force* of virtuosity by bringing a great variety of colors and patterns into harmony." In Matisse's own words: "My destination is always the same, but I work out a different route to get there." See Museum of Modern Art catalog Henri-Matisse Retrospective Catalog, Nov. 3–Dec. 6, 1931.

confidence. Before her father died of typhus, he had been a respected pediatrician in Tomsk in Siberia. When her mother died of cholera in 1922, Lydia found herself an orphan at age 12. Raised by her aunt, the two left Russia and after a sojourn in China, they arrived in France. Lydia was accepted at the Sorbonne to study medicine, but she could not afford tuition. Instead of a blue-chip degree in Paris, she got a third-rate husband and was forced to trade on her looks in the playground of Nice, where she found odd jobs as a silent-film extra, dancer, and model. When her husband deserted her, she reverted to her maiden name. At this point in her short, operatic life, Lydia Delectorskaya had to rely solely on her intelligence and efficiency, traits that would make her indispensable to the family.

CHAPTER THREE

—

Lydia

"I do not create a woman, I make a picture."
——HENRI MATISSE

T HE MOMENT IN 1932 WHEN Lydia Delectorskaya knocked on his door was one of the pivot points of Henri Matisse's career. At the beginning of his fifth decade of painting, Matisse was struggling on a complicated installation for the wealthy American Albert Barnes, a self-made millionaire who was as prickly as he was rich, but who was possessed of "a remarkable talent for selecting masterpieces." When American journalist Dorothy Dudley visited Matisse for an interview, he told her, "You know he has 340 Renoirs, and 80 Cézannes... and some fine examples of Seurat... and a wonderful Greco." Now Dr. Barnes wanted a Matisse to decorate three lunettes in the loggia of the gallery of the château he'd built for himself in Merion, Pennsylvania, from shiploads of French stone. "He left me free to do what I wanted," Matisse said. "'Paint whatever you like just as if you were painting for yourself.'"[1]

Matisse saw the commission as a grand opportunity to conquer new artistic territory. Large-scale mural painting in France, as noted by John Russell, served an "important moral function."* Nearly every village, town, and city within France had a mural—not one of them painted by Matisse (nobody had asked him). These public works "set the tone for civic life . . . they came with an important lesson: painting mattered."[2] Given the chance, Matisse explained to Dorothy Dudley, "My aim has been to translate paint into architecture, to make of the fresco the equivalent of stone or cement. The mural painter today makes pictures, not murals."[3] To achieve this, Matisse abandoned his brush for a long bamboo pole with charcoal at its tip, and instead of a box of paints, he used large sheets of paper saturated in color. Standing on a scaffold, Matisse wielded the bamboo stick like a magician, constructing, erasing, reconfiguring, and repositioning. "He seemed to have no inkling that he was entering into a new manner, full of sap and vigor," remarked Matisse's friend André Masson, "a new phase marked by the miraculous alliance of grace with maturity."[4]

The Dance II turned out to be a years-long project.[5] The work was to be perfected offsite, then installed in Barnes's gallery, but it was so large Matisse was obligated to rent a garage at 8 rue Désiré Niel, a ten-minute walk from the Matisses' apartment in Cours Saleya. The ersatz studio had been used for the burgeoning motion picture industry in Nice. It was a vast space, "scrupulously swept, almost bare."[6] Worse, after toiling for months on the gigantic three-piece artwork, Barnes realized the measurements of the arched spaces provided to Matisse had been incorrect. The artist had to start all over.

For two years, Matisse labored to achieve his goal. "Groping my way forward," he groused to André Masson while walking home from the studio one day. "I've lost my touch. Everything I do has gone cold."[7] Balancing on his scaffold, with his meter-long stick held

---

* John Russell was the art critic for the London *Sunday Times* before joining *The New York Times*, where, in 1990, he became chief art critic. His wife, Rosamund Bernier, an art critic and friend of Pierre Matisse, met Henri Matisse in Vence in 1949. Pierre Matisse was Russell's best man when he married Bernier in 1975.

high above, Matisse obsessed over the mural and neglected easel painting. By using shaped sheets of painted paper to experiment with the design, Matisse was pioneering a style that would later come to define his mature work, but finishing the piece left the artist "tired and desperate" and "completely drained." He scrapped plans to exhibit *The Dance II* in Paris; instead, he and his dog held court at the garage where the visitors included the writer André Gide, the Bussys, the journalist Dorothy Dudley . . . and Lydia Delectorskaya.*

Dudley looked up at the large mural and was mesmerized:

> Eight giant figures against shafts of sky in a tremendous dance of goddesses . . . the sky vivid cobalt blue and brilliant rose . . . the [tone] of the flesh against the blue . . . the dancers appeared to move in and out, as well as existing on a single plane. We had come to see the fresco, but it was the fresco that dominated the moment and the place, so immediately engaging and powerful that it gave to this workroom the value of a [. . .] temple or palace.[8]

To some, it was the "synthesis of movement and stability," but to the acidic daughter of Matisse's friend Simon Bussy, *The Dance II* reflected an artist painting in circles. "The great dim monstrous de-individualized figures he had conceived began to wind themselves into impossible knots."[9]

The next day, both Matisse and *The Dance II* commenced the voyage to the wealthy Philadelphia suburb to install the massive modernist fresco. On the day of the event, in May 1932, Pierre arrived from New York City to join his father at the mansion of Dr. Barnes.

"Was the installation successful?" asked Dudley.

---

* Flam, *Matisse: The Dance*, Washington, DC: National Gallery of Art, 1993. The capricious Dr. Barnes refused to allow *The Dance II* to be seen by the public, so the impromptu exhibit at the garage was its only public showing. See Hilary Spurling, *The Conquest of Color*, 336-338.

"J'étais ravi," Matisse said. "I was thrilled. There in the Barnes Foundation [*The Dance II*] became a rigid thing, heavy as stone, and one that seemed to have been spontaneously created at the same time with the building."[10]

At the time, the patron, too, was happy with it. "One could call the place a cathedral now," he told the artist. "Your painting is like the rose window of a cathedral." Soon afterward, however, Dr. Barnes "turned the key on it and went off to Europe." *The Dance II* was not just a work of art, it was a "beguiling icon"—one that would not be seen for fifty years.[11]

The episode once again left Henri Matisse stranded on an artistic island. According to Pierre Schneider, Matisse found himself out in front but still out of step "not from his conservatism, but from [making] the transition to the characteristic work of the 1930s before any of his contemporaries.[12] What was the characteristic work of the 1930s? In that decade of economic collapse and political upheaval, artists from Russia, Mexico, and France sought to create works that bridged the gap between public and private art.[13] What Matisse hoped would be celebrated by the American public—a true mural, art as architecture—was instead hidden away as the private plaything of an eccentric millionaire. "Nobody has seen it," Matisse reported to Dorothy Dudley after the installation. "You're the only one!"[14] The journalist had hoped to place her piece with *Vanity Fair* or another well-respected national magazine; instead, the story of Matisse's long-overdue mural ran in the rather obscure periodical *Hound & Horn*.

Plans for his son-in-law to write a book on Matisse's art had long been discussed when Duthuit was back in France between research trips to museums in Egypt, Spain, and Germany. The handsome young scholar even held a membership at the Gargoyle Club in the Soho district of London. These plans met a dramatic end in 1933 when Marguerite discovered Georges had cheated on her with the beautiful wife of an English art critic. Matisse, of course, sided with his daughter and forbade Georges to continue work on the study. For Marguerite, who had been advised by Amélie to be devoted to her husband's career and who shared her father's uncompromising nature, the sin of infidelity was unforgivable.

Marguerite's separation from her husband was not the only change of circumstance in the Matisse family. When Madame Matisse abruptly dismissed her attendant, Lydia Delectorskaya's duties expanded. Between the family homes in Nice and Paris, Lydia oversaw the housekeeping staff, served as nanny for little Claude, Marguerite's two-year-old son, handled Matisse's correspondence, and waited on Madame.[15] When the family traveled to Paris for the summer, Lydia accompanied Madame Matisse in the sleeping compartment of the train and made sure stretcher bearers were in place to carry the ailing Amélie from the train to the waiting car. That she was employed by one of the most famous names in modern art meant nothing to her at the time. "I was an immigrant," she later said, "who didn't know a thing, who understood nothing."[16]

In the Nice studio one day in early 1935, Claude was napping, and Matisse was on his lunch break between sessions. The flaxen-haired Lydia, half listening for the next command, sat with her bare arms folded on the back of a chair and rested her chin.

"Don't move!"

By the time it registered, Monsieur Matisse had his sketchbook, and his eyes roved from her to the sketch paper, then back to her.*

The Blue Eyes became the first portrait Matisse painted of Lydia Delectorskaya, and it was a breakthrough. Tired, overworked, poorly treated by previous employers, Lydia, in a striped work shirt, was transformed into an icon of effortless beauty. Henri Matisse

---

* "Then, one day, he sat down with a sketchbook under his arm and, while I was scarcely paying attention to the conversation, suddenly spoke to me, 'Don't move!'...And soon, Matisse asked me to pose for him." Lydia Delectorskaya. *With Apparent Ease—Henri Matisse: Paintings from 1935-1939.* Paris: Adrien Maeght Editeur, 1988.

was at his easel once again. To Marguerite, it was "charged with everything that went before like a distant fire."[17] When Matisse's friend and rival Picasso saw the painting, he, too, tried to articulate its magic. "It is not like with any of his other models, there is a definite feeling, more than a casual aesthetic or sensuous interest."[18] The magic of *The Blue Eyes* might have been hard to describe, but it was clear there was an alchemy between sitter and artist. "[A]fter several months or perhaps a year, Matisse's grim and penetrating stare began focusing on me," recalled Lydia. With his intense gaze, perhaps Matisse was sizing up Lydia for the role he had always needed: manager, model, muse. "Drawing is possession," Matisse once explained. "Each line must correspond with another line that makes a counterweight; that is how one embraces, how one possesses—with both arms."[19] The impromptu sketch and the painting that derived from it were the embrace that formed one of the most fruitful partnerships in modern art.

As Amélie and Marguerite had done, so it was Lydia's turn to sit for Matisse. Besides his wife and daughter, there had always been models. Some of their names we know: Aicha, Annette, Antoinette, Dina, Elena, Henriette, Katia, Lili, Lorette, Monique, Nadia, Olga, Paule, Renée, Vilma, Zita. Others are forever committed to canvas, anonymous, nude, in a hat, or enrobed in a studio of props. They wear belts and bangles, combs and mantillas, Russian blouses, Japanese kimonos, Venetian robes, baggy pantaloons, Spanish shawls. A vase of anemones acts as a prop, or a bowl of lemons. Elegant or fetching, reclining on a Turkish divan, sleeping, sitting in an armchair, dancing, or standing, they are a parade of *jeunes filles* forever frozen in time as *The Italian Woman*, *The Girl with Green Eyes*, *Pink Nude*, *The Yellow Dress*, *Young Woman Sitting*, *The Breton Serving Girl*. Italian, Russian, Spanish, and French, metropolitan and colonial, they are, all of them *luxe, calme, et volupté.*[20]

If the parade of young women modeling for her husband bothered Madame Matisse, she labored not to show it. Amélie went so far as to treat these young women as "permanent members of the household."[21] The family invited them for meals, they helped them find jobs or openings at school, and some of them posed with Marguerite. The year Lydia moved into the Matisse home she proved to be honest, resourceful, proud, and loyal. Long of limb, athletic and lithe, she had the angular body type Matisse had, since his long working relationship with the ballerina Henriette Darricarère, desired. As Lydia herself remarked, Matisse did not prize the "great beauties" or the "beauty queens." What he wanted to see was an "inner life and an awakened spirit."[22] Matisse did not "idealize his models," said the artist Françoise Gilot, "he made them handsome, alive and solid; he made them real."[23] Lydia Delectorskaya possessed several traits that were common to his other favored subjects, but she also realized she was different. "Most of the models who had inspired him, were southern [Mediterranean] types. But I was a blonde, very blonde. It was probably for this reason . . . he had been studying me with a meditative, dour look."[24]

Lydia ably managed her dual roles as caretaker to Madame and studio manager and model for Matisse. "She could have run an army," said Hilary Spurling. "She had amazing capacities. She ran the studio, she organized the models, she dealt with the dealers, salespeople, the gallery . . . everything worked like clockwork."[25] A visitor to the studio described their relationship:

> The artist became tense and silent. His secretary appeared
> at his side holding drawing implements with the gravity
> of a nurse attending a surgeon about to perform a danger-
> ous operation. Almost holding his breath Matisse made
> a few decisive lines on a [piece of] fresh paper. . . .[26]

His studio humming, his interest in easel painting renewed, for four years Matisse painted nobody else but the blond, blue-eyed Siberian who lived under his roof. The attention was mutual. "Gradually, I began to adapt and feel less 'shackled'... I even began to take an interest in his work."[27] Lydia posed for several paintings that were later regarded as masterpieces in the second half of the '30s beginning with *The Blue Eyes* and including *Large Reclining Nude* and *The Dream*. Lydia seemed possessed of "some erotic-artistic combination, some alchemical formula... the catalyst to a heightened experience, she radiated a protective warmth that stimulated the creative process."[28] As Matisse's friend and fellow painter Pierre Bonnard put it, "A woman's charm can reveal a great many things to an artist about his art."[29] Of her patron, Lydia said, "He knew how to take possession of people and make them feel they were indispensable. That was how it was for me, and that was how it had been for Mme. Matisse."[30]

When Henri and Amélie declined to renew their lease in the palais at the end of the flower market, Matisse purchased at a steeply reduced price an apartment in the massive Hôtel Régina Palace in the Cimiez neighborhood above the port.[31] The quieter and cooler district had been favored by Romans of means who'd built the series of thermal baths on the plateau of the hill, next to *Les Arènes*, a medium-sized coliseum composed of an oval of sand and gravel surrounded by marble arches. Ancient senators and military commanders weren't the only visitors who relished the breezes overlooking the turquoise bay. The Hôtel Régina took its name from its most famous resident: Queen Victoria, who ruled the British Empire for sixty-three years and who escaped the London fog in a floor at the hotel for herself and her staff. The bas-relief, cupola domes, and bay windows were still there, but by the eve of the Second World War, the Régina was a "fantastic pile," chopped into private apartments, most of them sitting unsold.[32] Vacated in the general panic of invasion from Nazi Germany and fascist Italy, the grand hotel was literally a shell of itself, its vast empty spaces made it feel cold, especially in comparison with the sunbaked, bustling flower market. Like a bearded sea captain, Henri Matisse wandered the "vast, empty, echoing" hotel, with its pillars and "staircases like mighty shoulders."[33]

The apartment was a vast space with heigh-ceilinged studios and rooms on either side of the center hallway. Standing sentry was a six-foot-tall statue of an ancient Greek *kouros*.[34] On the stone and wood-inlay parquet floor was a small bench before the marble fireplace. There was a table and chairs, and everywhere fresh-cut flowers in decorative vases. In the conservatory were dozens of exotic birds. With panoramic views of the city and the bay, sunlight flowed into the space and filtered through the panes of the French doors.

At first, the Matisses' move worked well. Amélie was "enchanted" by the double-sized flat on the seventh floor. "It's like a renewal of her wretched life!" her sister Berthe reported. Matisse was "not so keen"; he always needed a studio full of props, and the new space was largely empty as movers and contractors had abandoned the city.

In the spring of 1938, while his wife settled in, Matisse took Lydia for a shopping trip to Paris. In the couture district near rue de la Boétie, he treated the young woman to half a dozen evening dresses. Once home, these dresses were hung in the studio prop closet alongside Amélie's diamond-patterned skirt and matching purple jacket that she had worn in *The Conversation*.

MATISSE RETURNED TO an unhappy kingdom and a royal edict. The queen on this day was Amélie Matisse, and she was less than enchanted.

"It's me or her."

The couple's friends tried to head off the brewing gladiatorial combat. Inside the half-installed residence, Berthe tried to calm her sister. After Madame Matisse shouted, "You may be a great artist, but you're a filthy bastard!" Simon Bussy took Matisse by the arm outside the hotel for some deep breaths to lower his skyrocketing pulse rate.[35] The family doctor weighed in saying the elderly artist was at risk for a stroke. When Marguerite arrived, Bussy gave her a "sermon" on the need to prevent her mother from "driving an eminent artist to his death." Bussy's wife, Dorothy, told André Gide in a letter that "after remaining bedridden for the last twenty years," Madame Matisse "suddenly rose up . . . and has shown the most terrifying energy" in her struggle with Monsieur Matisse.[36]

Madame Matisse would not be placated.

"It's me or her."

It wasn't Lydia's beauty that made her untenable, but her efficiency. Even Lydia's visits to Madame Matisse's bedroom to see to her well-being became "an insolent intrusion." Worse, the young woman had made herself indispensable to the artist, not only as his model but also his factotum, taking charge of his studio and his affairs while blossoming into something like an intellectual and creative partner to Matisse.[37] The artist had always "enjoyed the presence of women" and worked amidst "the cheerful loveliness of his young models," but Lydia Delectorskaya was no mere ornament; she was a women of substance, a "stronger personality," and as such she posed a threat to the order.[38] "Madame wanted me to leave," Delectorskaya later said, "not from female jealousy—there was no question of adultery—but because I was running the whole house."* To Matisse's children, seeing their father spend much of every day in the company of a "very beautiful young woman" was an "ominous development."[39]

On the very day he completed work on Le Chant, December 3, 1938, Matisse acted on the ultimatum. Lydia Delectorskaya could no longer live in the Matisse home, but in a compromise measure she was to return each day by bus to complete her household tasks. Often called an ice princess (even by Matisse), Lydia did not take

---

* This was an "ominous development" in the words of John Russell. On the issue of whether Matisse's relationship with Lydia was sexual, Hilary Spurling accepts Lydia Delectorskaya's account at face value, but others have their doubts. Art critic Peter Schjeldahl says, "Spurling loses me when she hesitates to concede a sexual relationship." Perhaps a clue is that upon arriving at Matisse's home one day, Picasso was surprised to find Matisse playing hide-and-seek with Lydia as he beckoned "coo-coo."

the demotion coolly. In a boarding house down the hill from the luxurious Matisse home, Lydia was overcome by self-pity. This expulsion was the latest tragedy in a life that was long on loss and exile. Perhaps from one of her unsavory neighbors, Lydia got hold of a pistol and, standing by the window, aimed it at her chest and pulled the trigger.[40]

When she opened her eyes, she realized she was unhurt—the gun had failed to fire. She tested the gun by firing it out the open window. But, as she told Matisse's biographer many years later, she did not have the nerve to turn the gun on herself a second time. When Lydia awoke the next morning, she boarded the tram at Galleries Lafayette, exited at *Les Arènes*, walked across the street to the Hôtel Régina, bearing the indignity of being demoted to daytime hired help for the Matisse family.

CHAPTER FOUR

The Piano Lesson

"We are, all of us, molded and re-molded by those who have loved us, and though that love may pass, we remain nonetheless their work—a work that very likely they do not recognize, and which is never exactly what they intended."

—FRANÇOIS MAURIAC, *The Desert of Love*

THE MATISSE FAMILY'S SOUR MOOD in 1938 reflected the national mood of much of France. Two years before, German dictator Adolf Hitler occupied the Rhineland, forged an Axis alliance with Benito Mussolini's fascist Italy, and civil war broke out in Spain between that country's fascists and loyalists. In France an ominous sign was the victory of the extreme right-wing Front Populaire. In 1938, Hitler was again on the move. In March, Nazi Germany annexed Austria and was threatening Czechoslovakia. From Paris to Nice, Lyon to Bordeaux, French citizens were ridden with anxiety. "Everyone is appalled by Hitler's latest encroachments," Matisse wrote Pierre, who had married an American, Alexina Satler, and opened his own gallery on Fifty-Seventh Street in New York. "On the whole, people don't say much, because they don't know what the future holds, but they fear it."[1]

For Henri Matisse the fear and uncertainty were compounded by the bitter memories of the Great War a generation earlier. In 1914, just three weeks after the outbreak of war, Matisse's hometown, Bohain-en-Vermandois, was occupied. The German Army, still in their spiked Pickelhaube helmets, defeated the British Expeditionary Force at Cateau. A French counterattack failed, and Bohain suffered abuse for the next four years. The town's roads were mined and its *mairie* set ablaze. Food was rationed, and residents were fined for noncompliance with the occupiers. Bronze statues and copper gutters were melted down for the Kaiser's artillery shells; automobiles were requisitioned, then bicycles, horses, and mules; telephones and radio telegraphs were confiscated; even pigeons had to be slaughtered for fear they'd be used for carrying messages.

Matisse was forty-four at the time and desperate to enlist. He bought himself soldier's boots and took a medical exam but was rejected from serving due to a weak heart. Crushed, Matisse appealed to his friend Marcel Sembat, a socialist politician, who advised, "What you can do is continue to paint well."[2]

For artists and writers who could not join their comrades, such advice was deeply frustrating. Though the President of France, Raymond Poincaré, exhorted French writers to use "their pens and their words" as part of a "mobilization of the intellect," to write or paint while others fought and died felt an unfulfilling task.[3] "All of this was very little," admitted Victor Giraud, literary editor of *Revue des Deux Mondes*, in his patriotic essay of 1917. "If you were to tell me these ink-stained pages were not worth a few good shots fired in the trenches—ah!—how right you would be!"[4] Hearing of a fellow painter's service, Matisse wrote, "I shall always regret that I could not be a part of these upheavals. How irrelevant the mentality of the rear must appear to those who return from the front."[5]

As Matisse wrestled with his sense of powerlessness in Paris, his family in Bohain was struggling under the Kaiser's yoke. Matisse's mother refused the local German commander's order to evacuate her home, so she was briefly taken into custody. Auguste Matisse, the artist's younger brother, was sent, along with four hundred able-bodied men, to a prison camp in Havelberg, in eastern Germany, part of the huge reservoir of involuntary labor from which the German Army drew without mercy.[6] During this time, Matisse had no news of his family for months, and his concern deepened with reports of the poor condition of civilians transported to the prison camp in Havelberg. "I'm not in the trenches, but I'm in a bad way all the same," Matisse wrote to his friend Charles Camoin. "The lack of news from my family and the anguish that comes from the continual suspense we live in—the little we know, everything they hide from us—all this will give you an idea of how it feels to be a civilian in wartime."[7]

In time Matisse followed Marcel Sembat's advice to "paint well." In the short term, he sold off prints and used the proceeds to send weekly shipments of bread and biscuits to the German prison camp, inscribing each, "For the civil prisoners of Bohain-en-Vermandois."[8] His long-term studio works during the Great War took on a new gravity.[9] The two paintings that best reveal this "grave and tranquil elegance" are the austere and inscrutable masterpieces *Bathers by a River* and *The Moroccans*.[10] In *Bathers by a River*, Matisse transformed his four semiabstract bathing figures by "cutting off the head of one, severing another's legs at the ankles," and leaving "mutilated, stone-grey caryatids."[11] The four panels of the massive painting begin on the left with a fetching green; but to reach the last two panels the viewer's eye has to traverse a "black maw," an "impassable trench."[12]

As Europeans realized the horror of their own technology—what explosive, high-velocity artillery and the machine gun could do to faces and bones—there was a sense that the past, the generations of priests, vicars, and village life, was gone forever. On the other side of that trench was the modern world. "This work could only have been painted in 1916," says art historian Catherine Bock about *Bathers*, "at the moment when the enormity of World War I was finally realized, but before the disillusionment and cynicism [. . .] had set in."[13] To the artist Gino Severini, Matisse's wartime work was "an architecture of the will," an edifice of color "ever more spiritual and abstract, almost independent of the real objects."* Matisse's painting is a monumental image of "stoicism and mute witness," as much a symbol of the war of 1914-1918 as Picasso's *Guernica* would be to the rise of the Nazi menace.[14]

Like *Bathers by a River*, *The Moroccans* is dark toned and organized as if "in chapters."[15] The longtime art critic for the *Washington Post*, Paul Richard, describes a tomb and round forms that could be watermelons or faceless supplicants kneeling in prayer before their leader. *But the third chapter?* "There is no way to be sure . . . The right third of the painting," he admits "cannot be deciphered." Parts of the painting, Hilary Spurling agrees, "remain almost indecipherable."[16]

Matisse worked on *The Moroccans* during the Battle of Verdun in the first half of 1916. The target site in eastern France was cynically chosen by the German High Command not for strategic reasons but to bleed France white. For the French, the fortresses of Verdun were not to be lost, no matter the cost. Obligingly, 300,000 French soldiers trod *la voie sacrée*, "the sacred path," into the deadly trap of German artillery. Was anything as illogical as a continent killing off a generation of young men for mere meters and ruined villages here and there?

---

* Curator Stephanie D'Allesandro describes *Bathers by a River* as "chilling and beautiful"; a painting reminiscent of a phrase from Shakespeare: "gorgeous tragedy." "The artist who feels deeply the horror [of war] will be more apt to translate his reaction into familiar, everyday things . . . The result is not a battle picture, but a deepened and broadened interpretation of the surroundings and of his relation to them." Edward Alden Jewell, "Art in a Time of War," *The New York Times*, March 13, 1943.

This was the context for Henri Matisse's third important work from 1916: a painting that tells us much about Matisse as a father to his sons, Jean and Pierre: *The Piano Lesson*. It is another painting of Issy: a spacious living room, the garden outside represented by a triangle of green. The subject is Pierre, age 16, "barricaded" behind a Pleyel piano. In the right background sits a faceless oval-headed figure: his piano teacher, her hands folded in her lap, as she listens to the boy practicing his scales. The seated figure is a reworking of *Woman on a High Stool*, but in this work the figure is even further elongated, more androgynous, an almost extraterrestrial apparition, not unlike the gray-skinned figures in *Bathers by a River*.[17] The painting is "a severe, unnerving comedy" of the interior of family life.[18]

The austere geometric shapes are dominated by a brooding color scheme anchored by battleship gray. Matisse depicts his second-born son with a deliberate flatness—pruned to an essence beyond that of Amélie in *Woman with a Hat*. In the words of John Elderfield, "It is as if the fabric of the paint itself has all but absorbed its human subject, blurring outlines, merging forms, [and] deconstructing."[19] The metronome atop the piano sits "like an instrument of torture."[20] Further restrictions to the boy at the keyboard are the hourglass and iron grill across the window.

Elderfield was not alone in interpreting these restrictions as reflecting Matisse's parenting style. As a father (and northerner), Matisse was prone to visit upon his sons the "routine humiliations" he had suffered from *his* father.* "He's a nervous artist," observed his sister-in-law, Berthe Parayre, "he can be a bit of an authoritarian."[21] Matisse valued

---

* The senior Henri Matisse was a seed merchant imbued with the hard practicality of northern France. He had seen his son abandon the law for a painting career and witnessed the fallow years that followed. When Matisse was forty and had finally bought the suburban villa at Issy-les-Moulineaux, he had his parents for a visit. Taking his father out to see the flowerbeds, then in full flame, Matisse waited for a kind word from his father—perhaps the overdue congratulations for turning an avocation into a successful career, or for making the surname *Matisse* one celebrated around the world. "Why not grow something useful, like potatoes?" asked his father.

an economy of words: "What is not necessary is harmful!" was an aphorism he applied to his art and to his interactions with his sons.[22] Matisse's frugality with words was in keeping with his worldview.*

"Approximations don't attract him," said French writer Francis Carco. "The habit of reflection, of logic, of analysis, leads him to formulate each one of his thoughts or his impressions with all the clarity and rigor one could wish for."[23] To the eminent painter, "skill was just a matter of determination and hard work," so if his sons failed to reach the first-chair at the symphony or sell out at a first-rate gallery, they just weren't working hard enough.[24] While some of their letters are full of "profound mutual affection and concern," in-person, father-son exchanges were often "harsh and grating."[25] "You have no idea how much I detested those piano lessons," Pierre Matisse later admitted.

Seen in the context of the war, there is a more poignant interpretation. Matisse may have been refused his request to join the French Army, but his sons would soon be old enough to be conscripted.†

---

* Perhaps Matisse's reluctance to convert his canvases and sculptures into sentences came from an episode early in his career. In *Notes of a Painter* from 1908, Matisse described his aim as creating balance, purity, and serenity. The kind of art that for a "businessman or writer" would be an "appeasing influence," like a "good armchair in which to rest from physical fatigue." He may as well have painted a bullseye on his chest for his critics (and even friends) to take aim. The description of art as a "good armchair" dogged Matisse during his lifetime and beyond. "For you Matisse is a saint who can do no wrong," Picasso yelled at Françoise Gilot in a tantrum of jealousy, "but let me tell you one or two things about the armchairs!" Matisse's eagerness to please the eye, Picasso went on, was proof he was a bourgeois making merely decorative art. Once during a visit with Matisse, Françoise Gilot asked, "Isn't painting the art of silence?" Matisse paused, then glanced at her approvingly. See Gilot, *Matisse and Picasso*, 90, 149.

† In *Matisse: His Art and His Public*, Alfred Barr, who knew the Matisse family, says Madame Matisse dated *The Piano Lesson* after its companion piece, *The Music Lesson* (mid-1917). Matisse claims he finished the abstract work of Pierre *before* the realistic *The Music Lesson*, but Barr seems to doubt this as Matisse's abstracts usually followed his more realistic studies. If this is the case, *both* paintings—one abstract, one realistic—would have been painted at the time the

What father wouldn't wish to keep his artistically minded son out of the trenches? The piano and the iron grill keep Pierre put; he is where he belongs, in the comfortable family home, with the green garden beckoning, improving himself. With the hourglass, it is as if Matisse knew this state of domestic tranquility was not to last. The metronome keeps time—*tick . . . tick . . . TICK*—like the thud of bombs getting closer and closer to Paris, and to Issy-les-Moulineaux.

Matisse may have wanted to improve relations with his sons, but by the war's third year it was too late. In the summer of 1917, Jean was called up by the French Army. The emerging young sculptor was soon translating his hands-on talent as a military airplane mechanic. It was a season of desertion and mutiny as the heralded offensive under General Robert Nivelle ground to a halt within days of its launch. "They live like pigs," Matisse complained to Amélie upon seeing Jean and his regiment in the mud, forced to wash but once a week in a cold stream.[26] "It's a prison camp," the artist reported to his friend André Rouveyre.[27]

The next summer, the family, sans Jean, took refuge in Nice, as the German Army's last offensive of World War I advanced to within shelling distance of Paris. It was there that the sand finally drained from the hourglass. Faced with the drudgery of piano or violin practice, and without the company of his Paris friends, on his eighteenth birthday, Pierre ran off to the station and boarded a train bound for the threatened capital. There he enlisted in an army desperate for soldiers as it prepared for the decisive Second Battle of the Marne.[28] As he was preparing to be sent to the front with an artillery regiment, Pierre fell ill with a near-fatal bout of Spanish influenza. He later recounted how his wartime travails seemed nothing compared with the airless environment under his father's roof. "I was saved by the war," Pierre told Rosamund Bernier.[29]

Matisses' eldest son, Jean, was inducted into the French Army. See Barr, *Matisse: His Art and His Public*, 193.

After the British Army liberated Bohain on October 8, 1918, Matisse was one of the first civilians to enter the devastated village of his youth. Another returning son described its skeletal buildings and cratered streets as "the death of the earth itself, a landscape of the Last Judgment."[30] Matisse's mother and brother survived this hell on earth, as did Jean and Pierre, but for four years, Matisse, like millions of French parents, worried about the fate of France and the price his sons might have to pay for *la patrie*. Matisse's letters express his powerlessness and frustration, but the roiling emotions in his core are revealed more by his Great War masterpieces, subconsciously imbued with senseless violence. They took decades to decipher, but with the passage of time came clarity: Matisse's wartime canvases were a mobilization of the intellect, a silent howl for a Europe passing through a terrible portal into a new, modern world.

CHAPTER FIVE

Flanking Maneuvers

"*Most men resemble great deserted palaces: the owner occupies only a few rooms and has closed off wings where
he never ventures.*"

—FRANÇOIS MAURIAC

EARLY IN 1939, JUST AFTER his sixty-ninth birthday, Henri Matisse
wrote to Pierre in New York. He and Amélie were at the new Cimiez apartment, he reported; the rooms were finished and decorated,
and the workmen who had so often squabbled with Amélie had, at
long last, vacated the hilltop premises. "We live way above the fogs,"
the father told his son. "Let us hope that this will continue."[1]

Despite his hope for clear weather, a marital storm was gathering
strength. In their large apartment, Pierre's parents were essentially
separated. They saw each other only at mealtimes, which were quiet,
icy affairs. The return of Madame Lydia as an ordinary daytime em-
ployee had failed as a compromise. Like the lawyer he had once
trained to be, in his letters to his son Matisse made several arguments
trying to bring Pierre to his side.

His first appeal was health related.

*My dear Pierre, for more than a month we have not known
how to go on living. Your mother must never know I told
you this. My doctors were very much disturbed at the state
of cerebral tension that I had got into. They told me I might
have had a stroke. That meant nothing to her. She was like
a woman possessed.*[2]

Matisse continued with a tone of indignation.

*I swear by all that I hold sacred, that my conscience is clear.
My relations with Lydia are strictly and honestly those of
artist and model.*

Then he took the artistic angle.

*At my age, inspiration is fragile . . . And given the poetical
nature of my work, she is essential to me.*

Then the practical argument.

"Your mother knows," Matisse continued in his letter, "that without
Madame Lydia [it is difficult to work]. I need her to set up the studio,
to keep it clean, and to be ready with the colors I need, hour by hour.

I count on you to back me in that."

On March 6, 1939, Henri Matisse awoke to find his wife, her luggage, and her nurse gone. On the table was a letter.

Dear Henri,
   I am leaving for the reasons you know of.
   *I . . . hope . . . that you will be able to pursue your work
in peace and quiet.*
                      —A Matisse

Amélie Matisse never returned.

Independent of Matisse after many years, Amélie seemed to re-gain her edge. "Your mother has been spreading as much scandal as she can," Matisse complained to Pierre. "In London everyone says I have run off with my secretary. I don't know what they're say-ing in America, but they'll get on to it soon enough."[3] The allegation that he'd been unfaithful also echoed closer to home: "Everyone in Paris knows it."[4] Hurling more verbal grenades, Mat-isse went on. "In wartime, given my age . . . your mother's behavior will be catastrophic," Matisse predicted to his son. She "thinks only of revenge," he said. "What she has really done [is] monstrous . . . she will destroy us all."[5]

In this atmosphere of "deep-seated and long-lasting rancor," the warring couple each sought an ally. For Madame, it was Marguerite, who was living with her in Paris after she discovered her husband Georges Duthuit's infidelity. Meanwhile, Matisse worked to bring on Pierre as his transatlantic confidant and to become closer to Jean and his family.

Pierre and his American wife, Alexina, were raising their three sons in New York. His gallery was doing well, and the son was able to report to the father that *The Dance I* was in a place of honor in the enlarged Museum of Modern Art.[6] In New York and while vis-iting France, Pierre acted as an intermediary. "I have tried in every way," he told his father, "to persuade Mama not to sue for divorce. I also believe that she has hired a lawyer in Paris. And I only hope that he is intelligent and understanding."[7] The lawyer was smart enough to know Henri Matisse owned valuable possessions from artwork to real estate—all of which could be considered marital property.

After Amélie served Matisse with a Deed of Separation, demand-ing fifty percent of all his possessions, Matisse opened safes, weighed gold, counted U.S. dollars, and took inventory to the last piece of furniture. Madame Matisse wanted to know how many of her hus-band's paintings were with Pierre in New York and whether there was a bank account there. The signing of the final accounting of the marital ledger was scheduled for Paris the following May.

Relations between Matisse and his eldest son, Jean, were never as close as those with his other two children. Marguerite remained an active correspondent with her father in the aftermath of her husband's unfaithfulness. Pierre drove a Bugatti along the canyons of skyscrapers in New York City, owned an apartment in that city, and counted great artists and collectors among his friends. Jean chain-smoked pungent French cigarettes, was married to a struggling sculptor, and was chronically behind on his rent.[8] If Pierre's was a cool personality, his brother's was not. "I shall take every possible precaution," Matisse told Pierre, "to avoid touching [Jean] on the raw. What a character!"[9]

Both sons could find it difficult to communicate with their father, but where Pierre could mollify that by regular correspondence, Jean was no writer. Nor was he much of a painter. For all the museum visits and discussions of painting, the absence of commercial viability for Jean's work came as a "crushing disappointment" to his father. Jean Matisse's painting career had ended on the realization that he would only mimic his father's comprehensive greatness. "I have to force myself not to fall back on turning out *Matisses*," he said. His father had "seized the essence . . . so thoroughly, you end up stupid and discouraged."[10] Even Marguerite, who was the most gifted artist of the three Matisse children, felt suffocated by the comparison. Upon hearing a mistaken comment that a few of *her* paintings were "Matisses," she destroyed them. Always mechanically inclined, however, Jean eventually found his artistic calling as a sculptor. "I'll never forget the sight of Jean, chisel in hand, cutting into the wood of his statue," marveled his brother. "It seems as if he was born for it."[11]

Despite the tension, the paterfamilias did what he could to support Jean's family. When Jean's wife, Louise, and their son, Pierrot, paid a visit to Matisse, the former painting teacher treated the

budding eleven-year-old artist to an impromptu lesson.* In an interview many years later, Matisse's grandson recounted the
experience:

> So, I came to my grandfather with a big box full of color
> tubes I had purchased with my own money . . . He foraged
> through the box taking out tubes of vermillion, ultrama-
> rine, yellow, and white [and] said "From now on, paint
> with these four colors—*rouge, bleu, jaune, et blanc* . . .
> Now go and paint. *C'est tout.*"†

Though his grandfather and father had difficulty connecting
emotionally, Pierrot recognized the similarity of their work habits.
Standing before a sculpture, Jean was entranced. "Whatever the medium—marble or wood—his eyes are sure. His hands firmly
holding the chisel . . . He has to have absolute mental concentra-

---

* Pierre H. Matisse was sometimes referred to as Pierrot, and to avoid confusion
  with Henri Matisse's second son Pierre, I will use Pierrot for Matisse's grandson.

† Pierre H. Matisse. *The Missing Matisse: A Memoir* (Tyndale-Momentum, 2016),
  xii-xiii. Pierre Henri Matisse writes in this memoir he was raised as the grandson
  of Henri Matisse. As to this episode, Pierre remembers this meeting in the
  summer in Nice. Other sources indicate Matisse was not in Nice until November.
  Much of this unique memoir is written from the perspective of an adolescent-
  teenager, the age of Pierre Henri Matisse, born in 1928, during the Occupation.
  The title alludes to the question of his paternity. When he was 12, Pierrot was
  told to answer to the name Leroy rather than Matisse. Later, he resumed using
  the name Matisse. From *Publisher's Weekly* review: "At age 12, Matisse was informed by his mother, Louise, that his name was legally Pierre Leroy. He sensed
  a shameful secret but didn't learn the details until years later: while married to
  Camille Leroy, Louise had an affair with Jean Matisse—Pierre's birth father. She
  and Camille divorced just after Pierre's birth, but Camille bitterly insisted on
  keeping the boy linked to him. Recreated dialogue and present-tense narration
  enliven the high-action scenes of the war years." See also Lisa Bartelt, "Art, War
  & Resistance: A Review of the Missing Matisse by Pierre H. Matisse," Jan. 27,
  2017. https://lisabartelt.com/2017/01/art-war-resistance-review-of-the-missing-
  matisse-by-pierre-h-matisse.

tion."[12] Like his father, Jean required a small ration of cigarettes while he worked.

Jean's family's visit to Amélie that summer in Beauzelle was rather more fraught. In secret, Jean referred to Amélie as the Queen Mother, and holding a cane in her right hand like a scepter, the handsome, formidable Madame Matisse ruled her court. In the inner circle was the "inseparable" Marguerite, with her son, Claude. The lesser nobles included her son Pierre, whom she called "*l'Américain*" in a "cold and loveless voice," and Jean, of whom she said, "Give [him] a piece of wood, a hammer, and some nails, and he will leave you in peace the whole day."[13] Jean's wife, Louise, a divorcée, was outside the castle walls, as was Pierrot. On the verge of his teen years, the boy had not been easy on his parents: at boarding school he suffered from lice, bullies, and was the target of administrators. His clothing was "a hodgepodge of hand-me-downs" that he quickly outgrew. Pierrot was more adept with his hands than with academic pursuits; he'd rather make a few francs raising rabbits than reading books.[14] Banned from his grandmother's royal table for insolence, Jean's son thereafter ate with the servants. A Pekinese played the role of court jester.

ON THE LAST day of August 1939, Henri Matisse arrived at the offices of *Verve* magazine, located at 4 rue Férou, in the sixth arrondissement of Paris, the bell tower of Saint-Sulpice in the distance. There, Matisse delivered to his friend and publisher Stratis Eleftheriades, known as Tériade, his cover design for the latest edition of the respected publication of literature and art.

Tériade's magazine had been born in "times of anxiety . . . times of grave crises," and the publisher wanted artists, poets, writers, and printers who were "ripe for action."[15] Matisse delivered. *Symphonie Chromatique* was composed of stylized fleurs-de-lys Matisse had assembled by cutting shapes from saturated sheets of heavy paper—a process called découpage. The artist's heraldic flowers were a riot of color, a true chromatic symphony, requiring twenty-six passes through the printer. Matisse placed his fleur-de-lys, the ancient and enduring symbol of France on a uniform black background, a hue he used "as a force," imagery meant for the moment.[16] At four o'clock the next morning, German panzer divisions crashed over the Polish frontier. Two days later, Great Britain and France were at war with Nazi Germany.

The outbreak of war caused a panic in the French capital. Posted everywhere was the *Ordre de Mobilisation Générale*. Men from their late teens to their forties scurried about reporting for military service or were already in uniform. Civilians able to do so fled the city by train, bus, or cars, often with mattresses tied to their roofs. "Those who are left rush about like black rats with their gas masks," Matisse reported to Pierre. "One shop in twenty or more is open."[17] Being *éternellement chic*, the Paris "shopgirls [wore] large silk bows tied to their masks."[18]

In the melee, the director of the French National Museums, Jacques Jaujard, having anticipated the need to safeguard France's most important cultural and historic artworks, assembled a staff of curators, museum guards, and art students to carefully pack and inventory the jewels of the Louvre. In a matter of days, several centuries of France's artistic treasures were heading by truck convoy to sites far from the city.[19]

Joining the throngs fleeing the city, Henri Matisse and Lydia stopped at Rochefort-les-Yvelines and waited, fearing a German attack that never came.* Staying at the village inn, the famous old painter and his young companion were both aware they were the

---

* Regarding the unsuccessful suicide attempt, after pulling the trigger, Lydia Delectorskaya realized she was unhurt; she fired the weapon out the window to see if it worked; it did, but she didn't have the nerve to turn the gun on herself again. When she awoke the next morning, she boarded the tram at Galleries Lafayette, exited at *Les Arènes*, walked across the street to the Hôtel Régina, and quietly resumed her duties for the Matisse family.

subject of town gossip.[20] "You are young," Matisse told Lydia. "You have your entire life ahead; a whole road stretches before you."

"A road leading where?" she wanted to know. "To what?"[21]

Perhaps attuned to their flight, and the dangers that lurked ahead, at Rochefort Matisse drew a portrait of Lydia in a hooded cloak—a depiction she later said made her recall the Russian folk tales she'd heard as a child. The traveling garb was appropriate, for Lydia decided at Rochefort that her future was with Henri Matisse, wherever he may go. "It was there that our collaboration for the future was agreed . . . I barely hesitated. I was alone [with] no ties."[22] Matisse made her believe her life could still be useful.[23]

After the initial shock over the outbreak of the long-feared war, an uneasy calm descended over France. For weeks, then months after Poland ceased to exist—having been carved up by the Germans and the Soviets—nothing much happened. There were no massive troop buildups at the border, there were no aerial bombardments to soften up targets for a ground offensive. Perhaps the sense of stillness came from knowing France possessed the largest land army in Europe; an army dug in behind the impregnable Maginot Line—the series of fortifications along the French-German border. In these months, the English-speaking press began referring to the war as the Phony War. In France, it was *la Drôle de Guerre*, in Germany, *Sitzkrieg*.

Henri Matisse, after having tried to make peace with Jean's family, arrived in Nice with Lydia in October. In preparation for the division of marital property, the apartment was stripped to its essentials. The imposing Greek *kouros* stood a lonesome sentry on the patterned marble floor. The studio—a large and airy space of 900 square feet with high ceilings—was decorated by nothing more than bountiful philodendrons. Between that and the living area was a tiled room used as an aviary, the birds often Matisse's only companions. The dining room was as forlorn as the bedroom formerly used by his wife. Lydia decided to stay in the small quarters reserved for the staff four floors above. "I always wore an apron," she explained

later, "to make it perfectly clear I was doing a job."[24] The apron was
not merely a prop: for the duration of their relationship Lydia used
the formal *vous* when addressing Matisse, her *patron*.

It might have been called the Phony War, but in Nice, there were
signs that the expanding conflict was very real. There was a company
of French Moroccan soldiers quartered in the grand dining room of
the Hôtel Régina.[25] Restrictions on travel within France meant that
Lydia, a Russian émigré, required a travel permit, which Matisse procured by calling in a favor from a government minister, an old
collector of his work.[26] No government minister, however, could
prevent the drafting of Matisse's sons. Jean had been conscripted
into the French Army, and by the following spring was stationed at
Moissac, north of Toulouse. As for Pierre, who was then in France
visiting family, his failure to file paperwork excusing him from service as a father of three children meant he was drafted as well. Both
Matisse sons, 39 and 38, were drafted into the so-called Series B reinforcements, second-line units that the government hoped would
not need to be thrust into combat at a critical moment.

Pierre had dutifully complied with his mother's requests to determine marital assets in New York, but now Matisse saw a chance
to get closer to his son. He offered to help Pierre get an exit visa
back to the United States, and suggested he wear his army decorations from the previous war to his physical. Chalking up Pierre's
efforts on behalf of his mother as "absentmindedness," Matisse said
he was glad there was "no barrier between us." Dispensing fatherly
advice and perhaps chastened by illness, Matisse warned against
"hot baths" too late in the evening and drinking too much wine before dinner. "Remember your liver, too—if you abuse it, it'll play
hell with you later."[27]

In October, Pierre met with the authorities and was exempted
from military service, allowing his return to New York.[28] The next
month, Matisse's budding alliance with Pierre suffered a setback,

when Pierre wrote his father requesting the return of Matisse's cherished watch. "My mother would be glad if you would send back the watch chain that had belonged to her mother. You have apparently worn it for a long time. You have only to send it to Marguerite at my mother's Paris address." Matisse's response was volcanic. Asking for the watch chain back was "an act of pointless and excessive cruelty," and having to make a response made his "heart bleed." Of his son, the father asked, "Have you any idea how deeply you have wounded me?"[29]

Perhaps it was also dismaying to Matisse that his children did not mention Madame Lydia in their letters. To them, writes Hilary Spurling, Delectorskaya was a "grasping, manipulative schemer" who did not warrant a mention in letters to their father.[30] Delectorskaya was ten years younger than Matisse's sons and fifteen years younger than Marguerite. To all three Matisse children, their surname had been "as much a burden as a benefit." They had lived in the glow of his genius and in the shadow of his inscrutability, and now they lived with the fact he was a divorced older man with a young companion. To Matisse, on the other hand, Lydia, who once was to him just "the Russian who looks after my wife," had become indispensable, both poetic and practical, his manager and muse.[31]

Despite the jarring changes to his circumstances, Matisse emphasized the positive in a letter to his old friend and fellow artist Pierre Bonnard, just after Christmas 1939: "A number of things have happened to, or rather against me, in the past year. Still my health is not too bad."[32] He also maintained hope for normalized relations with his family. To Albert Marquet, he wrote, "You always come back to the family as you do to the land."[33] But there was no family home to come back to; they were scattered: Pierre in America; Jean on a dusty army base; Madame Matisse, Marguerite, and his grandson Claude in Beauzelle or entrenched in Paris. The war promised further destabilization. To Matisse, whose life was his art, even throwing himself into a new project could not salve the pain of his emotional exile. "What would be left to me in my life—*my work. But all the same, that is not enough for me...*" (emphasis added).[34] It was a surprising admission from the man who told Amélie forty years before, "I shall always love painting more."

CHAPTER SIX

Flight from Paris

"The fight has ended. A new order begins."
—MARSHAL PHILIPPE PÉTAIN, JUNE 17, 1940

"Whatever happens, the flame of the French resistance must not be extinguished and will not be extinguished."[*]
—GENERAL CHARLES DE GAULLE, JUNE 18, 1940

THE BANSHEE WAIL OF STUKA dive bombers and the rumble of panzer divisions heralded the end of the Phony War in April 1940, when Hitler moved against Denmark and Norway, conquering both with a minimum of losses. At dawn on Friday, May 10, German troops crossed into the low countries. By Tuesday, May 14, the Netherlands had fallen, and shockingly, German armored units were crashing through the Ardennes Forest on the French right flank. The Battle of France had begun.

---

[*] "Quoi qu'il arrive, la flamme de la résistance française ne doit pas s'éteindre et ne s'éteindra pas."

The German High Command's plan of attack, *Sichelschnitt*, was an offensive operation shaped like a question mark curving north-westerly around the German border with Luxembourg, France, and Belgium. Just as they had done in 1914, the French and British sent their best troops north to meet the enemy. But in 1940, the plan's real thrust was not at the end of the curve, but southeast—the dot at the bottom of the question mark. Steeply hilly, the Ardennes Forest with its fast-flowing rivers and poor road network was thought by the French high command to be impenetrable. When the panzer corps broke through and crossed the Meuse River, the Germans proved otherwise. "They took no account of the roads," wrote Marc Bloch, the French historian pressed into military service. "They were every-where."[1] Seventy-two hours after entering the forest, German General Heinz Guderian and his armored vanguard were in the open French countryside at Sedan—behind, or rather underneath, the helpless allies. "We were through the Maginot Line!" General Erwin Rommel noted in his diary on May 17, 1940, "It was hardly conceivable."[2]

It was still conceivable that France could save itself. The panzer thrust was, to borrow the simile of historian Ernest R. May, like an arrow: the armored divisions at the westerly end, with their nimble tank commanders and battle-hardened troops, were the iron arrow-head; the procession behind—the less-experienced troops, the refitted tanks, and horse-drawn equipment—made up the wooden shaft of the arrow.[3] An attempt to snap the shaft never materialized. The French Series B troops[4] lacked initiative, and their tactics were outdated. With tanks spread out in twos and threes and lacking radio communication with each other (some French tank crews re-sorted to signal flags raised from open turrets to communicate with their comrades), French armor offered only scattered resistance.[5] Two days after reaching Sedan, the tanks, trucks, and troops of the Third Reich made up a "Panzer Corridor" hooking northwest in the general direction of Paris. Meanwhile, the right flank of the German Army Group from the north was engaged with the British Expedi-

tionary Force from the channel to Belgium. By the time French staff
officers pinned their map markers fifty miles from Boulogne and Ca-
lais, it was too late. Hitler's divisions were bypassing Paris and seizing
control of the ports along the English Channel. The British Army
would be doomed in an untenable pocket—the channel their only
escape hatch. Brussels had fallen, as had Amsterdam. Paris lay virtually undefended. Operation Sickle-Cut had worked brilliantly;
France was cut in two.

Politically, things were collapsing. The government in Paris,
headed by Paul Reynaud, was making plans to evacuate to Bordeaux. Rather than stiffening Reynaud's spine, the Cabinet, replete
with "fatalists, careerists, opportunists, and I-told-you-so's," timidly
followed suit.[6] The unfolding debacle unleashed a flood of refugees
from metropolitan Paris and northeastern France. Everything with
wheels that hadn't left in the panic of the previous September was
leaving Paris: tourist buses, ice-cream trucks, fire engines, street
sweepers, their brushes still attached, and butcher's carts.[7] Trains
were booked to overflowing, so families from the capital, Île-de-
France, and Rouen took to the roads with their belongings on their
backs, on carts, or on bicycle panniers. The strafing by the Luftwaffe
left the roadsides littered with broken-down, bug-like Citroëns and
dead horses. Disorganized bands of French soldiers wandered the
countryside. Looking down from his aircraft high above the unfolding chaos, it seemed to Antoine de Saint-Exupéry that an anthill
had been stomped on. His fellow citizens were reduced to "ants on
the march."[8] For the two million French who'd survived the German occupation of 1914–1918, of ten *départments*, including major
cities like Lille, one half decade of impoverishment and humiliation
was enough for one lifetime. They were leaving their homes, heading south or southwest, away from the enemy and toward an
uncertain future.

Émigré writers and artists in Paris or elsewhere in France were
caught up in the *l'exode*. Vladimir Nabokov was loaned money by

the composer Sergei Rachmaninoff to buy a ticket on an ocean liner
bound for New York; Surrealist painters Salvador Dalí and Man
Ray followed him; James Joyce was making his way to Switzerland.[9]
Maneuvering against this human river was an ill seventy-year-old
Henri Matisse and his companion Lydia *returning* to Paris. Though
he was "stunned by what was going on," Matisse had forty years'
worth of paintings and artworks to safeguard and a separation to
finalize.

While there, Matisse stayed in Île-de-France at the Hôtel Ven-
dôme[10] when one night he suffered a stomach pain so acute he
summoned a doctor to the hotel (the doctor found nothing amiss).
For several days Matisse met Marguerite at Banque Nationale pour
le Commerce et l'Industrie to catalog the artworks—his own as well
as the family's two Cézannes and a Renoir—in his vault.[11] On his
way to the bank one morning, Matisse came face-to-face with his
friend and rival, Pablo Picasso, who bitterly remarked on the utter
ineffectiveness of the French leadership.[12] "I was rather stunned by
what was going on," Matisse reported. "The days seemed to last a
long time. . . ." The situation became untenable on May 19, 1940.
Matisse "running with sweat" was in the vault when he heard the
peal of air raid sirens. Minutes later, he and Marguerite were in a
cold damp bomb shelter packed with other Parisians. Dreading an
attack of "bronchial pneumonia, I decided that this was no life for
me. It was time for me to get out of Paris."[13] Marguerite returned
to the Paris apartment on rue de Miromesnil that she shared with
Amélie. Matisse and Lydia, amongst the throngs of those fleeing the
French capital, booked a train for Bordeaux.

The first night in Bordeaux, as scores of other Parisian refugees
slept in parks or in their Renaults and Citroëns, Matisse and Lydia
found a room at a *maison de passe*, a brothel, where an enamel plaque
affixed to the bidet advised how to avoid venereal disease. One night
was enough. "I left at six A.M. to take the train to Saint-Jean-de-
Luz," Matisse reported to Pierre in a letter from the town of Ciboure,

the birthplace of composer Maurice Ravel, in the Basque region.[14] The painter rented a house near the estuary, and next door to the church. Hearing the same church bells as Ravel gave Matisse "a feeling of peace and tenderness," and the views of the harbor seemed to take his mind off the Battle of France and the major offensive operations within his own family.[15]

> When I look out, I can see the little steamboats that come and go. They are all painted a pure ultramarine blue with a little chimney that is painted pure vermilion. They bring back sardines, anchovies, and mackerel.[16]

Back to practical matters, Matisse reported that his grandson Claude was out of harm's way with a family friend. As for Marguerite, "She could have left Paris," Matisse told Pierre, "but she preferred to stay there... This probably suits the banked-up ardor that is within her. She says that at last she is alone and can do what she likes...

"Marguerite wants to make herself useful."[17]

Matisse and Lydia held on in Ciboure from May 22, 1940, until June 27, 1940, as refugees poured into the vice between advancing Germans and Spanish border guards. In that time events moved with disorienting speed. On May 27, 1940, newspapers in Nice and elsewhere published an order requiring German nationals to present themselves at the internment camp at Gurs, just sixty miles from Saint-Jean-de-Luz. French officials feared a "fifth column" of Hitler's agents, though the German nationals in France—including thousands of German Jews—had fled Nazi persecution. Nevertheless, they were ordered to the westernmost concentration camp in Europe. Among the thousands taken by train to the barracks at Gurs was Charlotte Salomon, a young art student and admirer of Matisse who'd fled Berlin, Germany, for the refuge of her grandparents' home on the French Riviera.[18]

As the German Army raced toward Paris, Tériade rushed Matisse's *Chromatic Symphony* to print.[19] On Saturday, June 1, 1940, *Verve* was published, its cover the symbolic lilies against a foreboding background matched by the blackout paint that now covered the streetlamps and Métro stations of the French capital.[20] Matisse didn't see his cover before the German invasion caused him and Lydia to join the flight from the capital.[21] Paris, left undefended, was declared an open city just days later.

On June 10, 1940, fascist Italy declared war on a reeling France. Mussolini's Italian Army attacked the southeastern corner of France and ignited the Battle of the Alps. The Italians' goal was Nice, whose strategic value led the Greek settlers to call it *Nikaia*—Victory City, after the Greek goddess *Nike*. The battle cry was *Vive l'Italie! Vive Nizza Italienne!* But Nice, the hometown of the hero of Italian unification, Giuseppe Garibaldi, proved an unattainable prize.[22] Italian Alpini troops were checked by the French Armée des Alpes at each mountain pass, including the one protected by Fort du Chaberton— "the battleship in the clouds."[23] Though the invasion was blunted before the Italians reached Nice, Mussolini's gambit won him the French border city of Menton, and signaled to the belligerents that the Mediterranean Sea was to become one of the major theaters of the war. The cynical opportunism led to an outburst by American President Franklin D. Roosevelt: "The hand that held the dagger," he said, referring to fascist Italy, "has struck it into the back of its neighbor."[24]

On June 16, 1940, the new British Prime Minister Winston Churchill arrived at the Quai d'Orsay in Paris to meet with the stunned French political and military leadership.

Looking at General Maurice Gamelin, Churchill asked about the strategic reserve.

"*Aucune*," said the general with a shake of his head.

"None."

Outside in the garden of the foreign ministry, clouds of smoke rose from large bonfires, as government officials poured wheelbarrows of state papers, from secret battle plans to mundane memoranda, onto them.[25]

On June 22, 1940, Marshal Philippe Pétain announced the armistice in a radio broadcast. "I would rather die with weapons in my hands," said a stunned Marguerite, "than hear such things!"[26] Three days later, the Third Republic was dead. Nazi Germany took over the north, including Paris, the channel and Atlantic coasts. Southern France, including the Mediterranean coast, remained unoccupied but under a pro-German local administration. Fearing the Germans would take control of the French navy, the RAF (the British Royal Air Force) attacked the fleet at dawn on July 3 while at anchor at Mers-el-Kébir, Algeria, killing over a thousand French sailors. British Prime Minister Winston Churchill saw no alternative to destroying the fleet of Britain's ally, a task he described as "odious" and "inhuman."[27] Besides metropolitan France and French colonies in North Africa, there was another zone: a wedge of land between the Rhone and northern Italy. As part of the Franco-Italian treaty ending the Battle of the Alps, the contested land was declared a "demilitarized zone." Nice, its largest city, became an island of freedom in Axis Europe.*

Having barely escaped to London, General Charles de Gaulle was the leading figure of the government-in-exile hoping to someday return to power in Paris. (He did so under a sentence of death from a court-martial for joining a foreign power.) Pétain, the hero of Verdun in the Great War, the leader who'd encouraged the soldiers in horizon blue uniforms with the cry, *"On ne passe pas!"* ("They shall not pass!") was the head of the government at Vichy, where Nazi puppet masters were free to come and go as they pleased.

---

* Despite changing hands so often over the centuries, the postcard-perfect beauty of Nice and the sweetness of its climate made it a port of relative tolerance and diversity. One millennium after the Greeks and Celts shared the area, in 1793, leaders of the French Revolution in Paris sent a guillotine to Nice for use in the Alpes-Maritimes. Finding no use for it, the device was shipped to nearby Grasse, where it was employed on dozens of unfortunate souls.

The foreboding mood of the *Verve* issue Matisse called "the war number [issue]" had become shockingly real. As a cognate to Matisse's visual art, the poet Louis Aragon, in his poem "The Lilacs and the Roses," tried to verbalize the tragedy unfolding under the glorious summer sun in mid-1940:

> *O months of flowering*
> *months of metamorphosis*
> *May without a cloud and June lacerated.**

To the poet Aragon, to Henri Matisse, and to much of France itself, the unthinkable had happened. Paris, *La Ville Lumière*—the City of Light—had been extinguished, and France was in the first days of "the darkest and longest fifty months of her long existence."[28]

The Germans would soon occupy Ciboure, and Matisse knew from the scars left on his boyhood home that it was imperative to evade the advancing army. For the second time in less than two months, Matisse and Lydia loaded their belongings into a taxi on June 27, 1940, and drove out the southern end of town just as German units probed the northern edge. "I've been in Saint Jean-de-Luz," he wrote Pierre Bonnard. "I left Bayonne by way of Toulouse. And at the same time the Germans entered by the road from Bordeaux. What luck? . . . As soon as traffic can resume, I'll go to Nice."[29] After using up the tankful of petrol on the choked roads heading east, the pair found themselves at Saint-Gaudens in the foothills of the Pyrenees. The stabbing pains that had mystified the hotel doctor in Paris in May returned and befuddled the village doctor. "I

---

* In May-June 1940, lilacs were "showered" on the French troops in Belgium as they expected a quick Allied victory; the roses were in bloom everywhere as soldiers retreated and civilians fled to the south of France. The poem also includes the poignant line, *On nous a dit ce soir que Paris s'est rendu* ("We were told tonight that Paris surrendered."). M. Adereth. *Aragon: The Resistance Poems* (London: Grant & Cutler Ltd., 1985), 16.

could have died like a rat in a trap," Matisse later said of his time in Saint-Gaudens.[30] On August 3, the artist and his companion were offered a car ride to the imposing medieval town of Carcassonne, where they stayed for another two weeks while waiting to book passage on a train bound for Marseille.

Matisse and Lydia found themselves in the "busy, dirty Mediterranean port" teeming with sailors of all nations as they ferried goods from North Africa, the Near East, and through the Suez Canal. It was a city where corruption flourished. "You could make a deal, a *combine*, as the French called it, about anything," said the American Mary Jayne Gold. "Smuggling was an honorable trade. [French] girls for the brothels of North Africa slipped out illegally and cheap labor from the whole world slipped in."[31]

As it turned out, someone else had slipped into Marseille. On that first morning, while at the port, Matisse was surprised to run into Marguerite. The encounter was more bittersweet than happy, as she was there to send her eight-year-old son, Claude, to live with his father Georges Duthuit, who was on the lecture circuit in the United States, having been among the thousands of intellectuals who fled France for safety. Her half brother Pierre would act as a sort of godfather. There, amidst the sulfurous odor of decay, Matisse took the brief opportunity to sketch his favorite grandson, who he regarded as "a little David Copperfield."[32] As Claude walked up the gangplank, both mother and grandfather must have wondered when, and if, they'd see him again. The emotional scar of sending her little boy away to live with her unfaithful husband, for Marguerite, was as hidden as the scar on her throat. After Matisse bid Marguerite adieu, she headed back to Paris to "make herself useful." After a few nights' rest in Marseille, Matisse was well enough for the last stage to Nice.

From the day he left the damp air raid shelter in Paris, Matisse had been on an odyssey lasting 100 days and traversing three sides of the hexagon-shaped nation of France. In the chaotic flight, the international press lost track of the great artist.[33] Throughout the ordeal Matisse carried in his vest pocket a visa for Rio de Janeiro, Brazil. On his return to Nice, doctors diagnosed the recurring abdominal pain as enteritis and commenced treatment that lasted until the end of the year. As he rested, Matisse corresponded with his friends Pierre Bonnard and Raymond Escholier, curator at the Petit Palais Museum in Paris. "I find myself again within walls in which I have known outside peace. I must also say that I am close, *very close*, to restless neighbors who could occupy Nice at the drop of a hat" (emphasis added). For the third time in Henri Matisse's lifetime, France had been attacked by its neighbor to the east. Unlike the Franco-Prussian War, with its reliance on the horse, or the war of attrition in the trenches between 1914 and 1918, the Germans slashed into French territory with alarming speed. The Germans occupied three-fifths of France, and as Matisse alluded in his letter, Italian dictator Benito Mussolini was puffed up with imperial ambition; *Il Duce* was braying for his piece.

On September 1, 1940, one year after the beginning of the Second World War, Matisse sat down to write a long letter to Pierre. The frontier between occupied and unoccupied France had been closed for a month, and it was rumored sixty million letters were already blocked at the border. If Italy invaded again, the situation would deteriorate even further, making transatlantic communication with Pierre nearly impossible. He shared news of Marguerite and Jean and complimented Pierre on the new placements for his paintings. It seemed that the ill and weary father had softened. "I am delighted that . . . *Music* has found such a good home, as has . . . *Quai Saint-Michel with Lorette*, which is a picture of which I think very highly indeed. People say that all my best paintings are in Moscow, but this one is an exception." He also expressed gratitude that *Romanian Blouse* had been purchased by the Cincinnati Art Museum.

Turning to the situation on the Côte d'Azur, he wrote of the "day-to-day anxieties we have here—we might be occupied, on no matter what pretext."

Before signing off, Matisse explained why he had not used the visa. "It seemed to me," he told his son, "as if I would be deserting."

"If everyone who has any value leaves France, what remains of France?"[34]

CHAPTER SEVEN

Scoundrels and Martyrs

By princes, by kings you are loved,
And also by emperors.
　　　—"LA NISSARDA," TRADITIONAL SONG OF NICE

You see fops on bicycles . . .
You see girls who are led astray
You see the feet of orphan children
You see the backs of cabaret singers
. . . And life rushing pell-mell by.
　　　—"*Fêtes Galantes*" (A POEM ABOUT NICE), LOUIS
　　　　ARAGON, 1941. TRANSLATION BY RICHARD
　　　　STOKES, FROM A FRENCH SONG COMPAN-
　　　　ION (OXFORD, 2000)

Fᴿᴏᴹ ɪᴛs ᴍᴀɪɴ ʀᴀɪʟ sᴛᴀᴛɪᴏɴ, Nice flows downward toward the
French Mediterranean coast; behind it are hills and perched villages, and beyond those, the sharp, snowy peaks of the Alps. De-
scending from their trains, refugees from Nazi-occupied Europe
found a city of ochre and rose, baroque churches, and sumptuous

hotels. The maze of alleys in the old quarter offered the relief of shade, as did the market tents, but in the plazas, by the fountains, and in the parks, the Riviera sun was relentless despite the tall palms that stretched overhead.

The arrivals fanned out into the narrow streets into a sea of vendors. An old woman at the vegetable stand looked over her crates of plump tomatoes, Cavaillon melons, and red, gold, and white onions; the fishmonger had oysters and octopus on ice and fish so fresh their eyes still shined with life; whole chickens and large dried sausages hung next to a shop selling linens and basketry. Waiters and salesgirls headed to work among the men in suits and hats, and women shopping for flowers. The clack of heels, the squeaks and groans of bicycles, and the screeches of trams mixed with people greeting, shouting, flirting, and cursing. The fragrance of *socca*, the local crêpe of chickpea flour and olive oil, mixed with the saline air and the heady scents of exotic tropical foliage. Among this bounty, few could guess that a regime of rationing (and worse) was in store.

"History is a mighty *dramos*," wrote Thomas Carlyle, the nineteenth-century Scottish historian, "enacted upon the theatre of times, with suns for lamps and eternity for a background."[1] Carlyle might have been writing about Nice. Characters, a set both sunny and shady, and drama—Nice had it all. There is a theatricality to Nice, where so much life is lived *en plein air*, and appearances and attitudes matter. "It's theater wherever you look," Matisse once remarked.[2]

The Second World War was the latest act in the story of the primeval port. In the enveloping quietude of conquered France, Nice was a sliver of noisy normality between the Vichy state and Mussolini's Italy. There were German soldiers, but they were on leave and wearing sunglasses. There were pro-Vichy thugs, but they were biding their time, yet to be unleashed. Even in wartime, *Nissa la Bella* was a combination of light and dark, the peacock-proud and the private—a cosmopolitan mix of artists and philosophers, writers and couturiers, the political and the perfidious. What was new was the influx of refugees from elsewhere in Nazi-occupied Europe. German Jews were among those pushed westward by the Nazi menace. Caravans of foreigners, looking as if they'd spent "too many days in the same clothes and too many nights in different little hotel rooms," wiped their brows with handkerchiefs and stacked their piles of luggage in front of the city's numerous Victorian-era grand hotels: the Negresco, the Hôtel Roosevelt, the Westminster, and the Excelsior.[3] Other newcomers parked their bags in front of the seaside apartment buildings in the hope of an available flat.

One such refugee was Charlotte Salomon.

In her last days as a student at the Academy of Arts in Berlin, Salomon visited the traveling exhibition Entarte Kunst ("Degenerate Art"). From the time Hitler took power, avant-gardism was deemed an enemy of the state.* As the show traveled throughout Hitler's Germany, twenty thousand Germans per day, three million in total, were taught "contempt for the shapes and colors of the great expressionists."[4] They jeered the abstract, expressionist, Dadaist, and other modernist pieces, like Matisse's *Blue Window*, a cool-toned composition depicting his detached studio and gardens from the second-floor bedroom at Issy-les-Moulineaux.

The very works that inspired the young artist, according to the Nazi policy, "insult German feeling" by "confus[ing] natural form" and revealing "an absence of... manual and artistic skill."[5] According to the propagandists, Jews, of course, were behind the works that prevented the full flowering of the German people. Modern art was infected by a "syphilis of [Jewish] intellectualism." Hitler's stated goal was to stop the "hereditary transmission of such appalling physical defects." Those responsible for "cultural disintegration... will be picked up and liquidated."[6] It is the language of genocide.

---

* In the summer of 1937, propaganda minister Josef Goebbels organized a traveling exhibition of "Degenerate Art." The 650 works were removed from German museums, including those by Picasso and Matisse. Spotts, *Hitler and the Power of Aesthetics*, 163.

Charlotte Salomon examined the paintings—purposefully hung in a chaotic manner with denigrating "notes"—not to ridicule, but to revel in the modernist works she so admired.[7] "We had no access to modern painters," she said, "but we had a beautiful library which I used a lot."[8] While a refugee in the Côte d'Azur, Salomon's boldly colored paintings revealed "a wide knowledge of art and visual culture from Munch, Matisse, and Van Gogh to Michelangelo's Sistine ceiling." She had painted her friend Barbara as "a languid Matisse Madonna" after her enrollment at the prestigious art school was annulled on account of her being a Jew.* Her mistreatment and the "For Aryans Only" signs on every park bench, movie house, and library portended the violence yet to come. After her brief internment at the Gurs camp with other German women refugees, Salomon returned to live with her grandparents in Villefranche, a medieval seaside town next to Nice.[9]

Along the Côte d'Azur, Jewish refugees from Berlin and Vienna lived largely free from persecution. Many of the city's hotels remained open to them, and unlike anywhere else in German-controlled Europe, Jews in Nice mingled freely in the cafés along the Promenade des Anglais, shopped where they liked, and were allowed to worship. Jewish artists held showings in the city's galleries. "Things were bad in all the other places," said one Jewish woman of her years in Nice during the war, "and we were the fortunate." Yiddish could be heard along the streets by people who "never once sewed on a yellow star." Of her new home, Charlotte Salomon said, "While there were battles everywhere, we stayed tranquil enough on the Côte d'Azur."[10]

A few kilometers and a world away from the sumptuous Belle Epoque hotels was the garage of Joseph Darnand. Dark-haired and

---

* Felstiner, *To Paint Her Life*, 65. After the Degenerate Art exhibition passed from Berlin, Salomon won first prize in a blind art competition, but when the professor discovered who had won, the award was given to one of Salomon's classmates. Salomon's biographer, Mary Felstiner describes how this incident presaged the annulment of Salomon's enrollment at the school.

heavy-jawed, the stocky forty-five-year-old Darnand wore a thin moustache and the floppy beret called the *bonnet de chasseur*. In the First World War, he'd shown uncommon bravery by going behind enemy lines and capturing over two dozen of the Kaiser's soldiers.[11] His exploit made him a national hero. Denied a commission by his superiors, Darnand transformed after the war into a modern-day Iago, Shakespeare's villain who turned to murder after being passed over as Othello's lieutenant. Darnand turned to far-right politics, becoming a prominent member of the *Cagoulards* ("Hooded Men"), an underground terrorist group that organized bombings, assassinations, and stored arms in depots across France.[12] To pay the bills, Darnand ran a shady trucking firm that smuggled Biretta semiautomatics from Italy, wrote bad checks on his mistress's account, and filed "fraudulent bankruptcy" three times.[13]

As Darnand became ever more pro-Nazi in his politics as the leader of a far-right paramilitary, Allied intelligence opened a dossier on his activities, calling him "a kind of [French Heinrich] Himmler." Another entry in the file warned: "Subject should be handled with care, [he's] a damned good fighter." Darnand's curdled reputation had even made its way across the Atlantic, to the American press. *TIME* magazine called him "the new bully on the block," and feared he would prove a potent figure in German Europe.[14]

While Darnand stewed in his oily garage, a quiet, elegant figure was installing himself at the fashionable center of Nice, not far from the pastel-pink dome of the Negresco, at 22 rue de France. The storefront was under construction, and old newspapers covered the windows like curtains. A sign noted the upcoming grand opening of La Galerie Romanin. "Romanin" was the *nom d'artiste* of Jean Mercier, whose papers indicated he was born in Péronne; he was a professor at the International Institute of New York; and he permanently resided there in an apartment on Fifth Avenue. His new gallery, free from the censorship faced by gallerists in Paris, would house his modernistic watercolors of scenes from the South of France, as well as works by Raoul Dufy, Maurice Utrillo, and Henri Matisse.

WHEN HENRI MATISSE returned to Nice via the circuitous trip after the Fall of France, his circumstances and those of the city were different from before the war. He had been a resident of Ville de Nice for fifteen years; as much as anywhere, it was his home. The loneliness he'd felt in previous stays in Nice was tempered by Lydia's companionship. His claustrophobic hotel rooms were a memory, and he'd been able to move from the Cours Saleya market to a luxurious suite in the Hôtel Régina. Perhaps it was better to be on the hill above *Vieux Nice*. The foxtrotting, Casino-going of the old days was replaced by a city vacated by holidaymakers and gripped by malaise. That fall, the rumors persisted that Nice would be taken by the fascist army of Benito Mussolini, which remained keen to return the Mediterranean jewel to Italian rule even after being thwarted in the Battle of the Alps.

At the eastern terminus of the bus route from Nice was Menton, an idyllic seaside town of pastel buildings and turquoise surf. Menton was the one prize won by Mussolini in his Machiavellian scheme against France, and its experience under fascist rule alarmed the citizens of Nice. The weekly parade of black-shirted youths called the *Avanguardisti* caused fights in bistros between the Italians and French youths. Broken glass littered the streets, and doors lay ajar. Promenade du Midi was renamed Passeggiata Mare Nostrum ("Our Sea"). Menton's city hall no longer bore the sign *Mairie*; it was *Municipio*. The darkest day might have been when vandals toppled the bust of Marianne, the symbol of the French Revolution, in Menton's central square.[15]

Il Duce was no Julius Caesar, and his army reminded no one of the invincible Roman Legions two thousand years earlier. Still, fascist militants were not satisfied with one border city; they called for Nice's capture with cries of *"O Nizza o morte!"* ("Nice or Death!") and *"Nizza fino alla morte!"* ("Nice until death!").[16] Henri Matisse was keenly aware that his city was in the path of invasion, should the Italian dictator heed the cries. So was his son Pierre. In early October, Pierre wrote his father to report that a visiting professorship was open for him at Mills College in San Francisco. Like the chance to sail to safety to Rio de Janeiro, Matisse declined.[17] "Every moment now seems precious," he said in his response to Pierre.

"And the future? I'm waiting for it ... I have lived through terrible times ... but at my age I am not going to put down roots somewhere else."*

"I have decided not to leave Nice," he repeated to his old friend, the painter Pierre Bonnard in a letter on October 17, 1940. "I don't see myself starting over again somewhere else ... I've been invited to San Francisco to teach in an art school. I refused [...] I cannot see myself fleeing France at this time."[18]

Remaining in France was a risk for the ailing and elderly painter, but for Jewish artists and gallerists, the danger was immediate. In October 1940, Matisse ran into Georges Bernheim, the cousin of the Bernheim *frères*, Gaston and Josse, who ran the venerable Bernheim-Jeunes gallery. His old friend's misery over the recent death of his wife was compounded by the fact that his son, Claude, was being held in a German prison camp. Because he was Jewish, Bernheim lamented, he may never again gaze upon the paintings that had been a significant part of his life. After the distressing encounter, Matisse and Bonnard provided official testimonials on behalf of the Bernheims in order to "ward off persecutions."†

---

* Henri Matisse to Pierre Matisse, Oct. 1940; Russell, *Matisse: Father & Son*, 195-197. There were other reasons for Matisse not to go. "I could not go with my secretary-nurse," he told Pierre, because it would cause "gossip and calumny." Because he was providing money and furnishings for Jean's family and for Marguerite, "I am really a prisoner in France."

† See Pierre Bonnard/Henri Matisse correspondence of Jan. 28, 1941, in *Bonnard/Matisse*, 95. In 1941, the Bernheim-Jeunes gallery at 28 rue Duquesne, "home to much of the most avant-garde art of Europe for half a century," was sequestered, paintings confiscated, and their buildings sold. Gaston Bernheim fled

The threat of Nice becoming a battlefield sapped Matisse's normal capacity for work. Gone was the prodigious output of previous working seasons. In yet another letter to Bonnard, who spent the war years in nearby Cannes, "Each one of us must find his own way to limit the moral shock of this catastrophe . . . I am trying to distract myself from it as far as possible by *clinging to the idea of the future work I could still do*. If I don't let myself be destroyed" (emphasis added). Immersing himself in his painting had acted like a pressure-release valve for Matisse in previous crises, but with his nation two-thirds occupied, he was disconsolate. "Utterly beaten down, totally discouraged. I am paralyzed by some element of conventionality that keeps me from expressing myself the way I would like to in painting. My drawing and my painting are separating."[19]

Nearly seventy-one, Matisse remained the "professorial paterfamilias," with his gold-rimmed glasses, closely trimmed beard, waistcoat, and tie.[20] Still time had taken its toll. "My hair and my beard get whiter," he wrote Pierre. "There is a new hollowness about my features. My neck is scrawnier, and so on."[21] As 1940 drew to a close, Matisse's health seemed to deteriorate on a number of fronts. "I've been in bed since Friday," he wrote Bonnard, "[with] a head cold that I'm afraid may take a turn for the worse."[22] Worry over his eyesight was the subject of numerous letters to Bonnard, and also to Pierre: "My eyes are better. But my inside isn't."[23] Mired in creative doldrums, Matisse was left to dream "of future work." Perhaps he sensed that whatever time he had left was to be dictated by his health, and by the mysterious stabbing stomach pains he had suffered on his odyssey from Paris to Nice.

In November 1940, Bonnard tried to allay his friend's fears. "I've heard a rather reassuring tip about Nice, supposedly from the

---

to Monaco, and his brother Josse to Lyon. Josse Bernheim died in March 1941 in Lyon of natural causes. Claude Bernheim de Villers, Georges' son, was arrested and deported to Auschwitz on convoy no. 64 on December 7, 1943.

prefect, that the city will remain French. Let's hope so, while we wait for details."[24]

"Let's just wait," Matisse agreed. "It's what we're accustomed to do right now."[25]

Wait.

In this timeless city of sun and rock, sea and sky the mighty *dramos* of history's next act was being staged. Near the rail station and the port, families languished as they sought papers—legitimate or forged—for safe passage from Nazi Europe. In the scrubby pine hills above the city, the rebel groups known as the *maquis* prepared for their opportunity to shelter a spy, or to cut a rail line.[26] Militia leader Joseph Darnand schemed for a promotion from Vichy or Berlin. Romanin prepared for the opening of his art gallery and perhaps for other tasks. And, as he had done for so many seasons before in Nice, Henri Matisse would abide. Despite worries about his health, he would wait: to again see his son Pierre and his grandson Claude; for Marguerite to come around to his way of thinking rather than her mother's. He'd wait for the Occupation to end, for the fever of fascism to break, and to wake up one morning inspired to conjure the contours and colors of the future.

Until then, there was nothing left to do but wait.

—➤

CHAPTER EIGHT

Brush with Death

"Give me the three or four years I need to finish my work."

—HENRI MATISSE TO HIS SURGEONS

LYON, FRANCE
JANUARY 1941

The visitor stepped off the train at Gare Perrache and into the cold and cavernous hall. The final exhalations of smoke rose from the resting train engines, mixing with the breath of scurrying passengers. There were no German soldiers in field gray and no "blood banners," with the swastika on a red background, as the invaders had retreated north of the Demarcation Line after the armistice. But the new *police nationale*, purged of officers who refused to swear an oath to Pétain and the Vichy regime, strutted about in their all-black uniforms trimmed in silver or smoked Gitanes in groups of three or four. The young woman, aware she was under the threat of arrest and internment by the Vichy authorities as an enemy alien, was careful to avoid meeting the glances of the uniformed men.

The flat winter light coming through the station's three massive arched windows did nothing to alleviate the heavy grayness. Even the familiar red, blue, and white of the French *tricolore* were joyless. To the crowds passing underneath it, the message was an abasement of France's republican motto—*liberté, égalité, fraternité*. Instead of freedom, equality, and brotherhood, they exited under the Vichy command: "Work, Family, Fatherland."

Walking briskly in the cold, the caller headed north up the peninsula. The crosswinds whipping from the Saône River on the west bank across to the Rhône stung like the eye-watering cold she knew from her girlhood in Siberia. She passed the Hôtel de la Croix-Laval and the Textile Arts Museum housed inside. By the time she reached Place des Cordeliers, named for the corded belts worn by a local sect of Franciscan monks, she'd generated sufficient body heat to gird herself for crossing the Pont Lafayette. She checked her pocket and felt for her travel papers.

The man she was there to see—if he was still in a condition to be seen—was the descendant of weavers who had spent his boyhood in a Picardy town renowned for the artistry of its handlooms. He would have known the heritage of Lyon. In Roman times, Lyon had been the capital of Celtic Gaul—*Lugdunum*. Situated at the confluence of two rivers, for two millennia the city was a hub of coin minting, printing, and silk-making. Jacquard loomers labored to weave silk fabrics with intricate patterns and designs; with them, Florentine financial princes adorned themselves and their chateaux.

While no longer the capital, Lyon in 1941 retained its strategic importance: it was in the middle of a France cleaved in two by the shocking success of Hitler's invasion in May and June 1940. Not far from the Demarcation Line that separated German-occupied northern France from the southern Nazi puppet state, Lyon was, in a way, the seat of power in the distressed middle of France, between the *Zone Occupée* and the *Zone Libre*. If the Resistance had a capital city, it was Lyon.

This the Germans knew. The following year, across the river from where Henri Matisse convalesced, SS Lieutenant Klaus Barbie would take command of Gestapo headquarters. He was sent to Lyon because it was the nexus of the Resistance, where the various secret armies— *Combat, Libération*, and *Franc-tireur*— would likely try to unify. General Charles de Gaulle would send an agent to do just that, and Klaus Barbie would be waiting. There, in the basement of the stately Hôtel Terminus, Klaus Barbie would earn his nickname, "The Butcher of Lyon."

The woman crossed to the east bank of the Rhône, and from there took the gravel path through the city's botanical garden, dormant in winter. At last, she arrived at the Clinique du Parc. Like all hospitals, it was both quiet and busy; a combination of strong medicinal scents and the familiar pungency of the bodies being tended to within its walls. A sister in a black habit asked the visitor to sign in on the visitor's log. The woman took off her gloves, warmed her hands with a few breaths, took the pen, and signed in a delicate hand, *Lydia Delectorskaya*.

"Venez, s'il vous plaît." A nurse motioned Madame Delectorskaya to the door of the patient she was there to see. The nurse knocked, and an old man's gravelly voice responded. *"Entrez-vous."*

The nurse pushed the door open, its hinges creaking.

Sitting up in the bed, peering over the top of his gold-rimmed spectacles, was Monsieur Henri Matisse; his blue eyes were alert, but his face was gaunt, lacking its usual healthy glow from the Mediterranean sun. The room was sparse, save for a nightstand with notebook, pencils, and a few books, and a cross on the wall. In the corner was his daughter, Marguerite, in her trademark tailored suit, black hair, and ribbon around her neck. Lydia had not spoken to or seen her for nearly two years; now Matisse's grave illness brought the two women to an uneasy truce. Matisse wore a woolen toque hat and a silk scarf. Who could blame the great artist for his desire for comfort in the winter chill?

After all, he was dying.

While in Nice in early January, the stomach pains that had plagued the artist for nearly a year worsened to the point Matisse had to be hospitalized. From his hospital bed in Nice, he wrote Pierre Bonnard, "I am at the Saint-Antoine clinic suffering from intestinal troubles. A diverticulitis. Cimiez was too inaccessible for the doctor, who hasn't enough gasoline. A little operation may be necessary..."[1] In fact, the only chance of saving his life was a major operation requiring a team of doctors in a larger city. On January 7, 1941, Marguerite intervened. A twelve-hour wintertime journey north toward the German occupiers was not the best medicine for a dying man, but it had to be done. Marguerite had to get him to Lyon, where he was to be operated on for intestinal blockage.* "I have slipped out of the hands of the Nice doctors," he told Bonnard.[2]

Prior to the procedure, Matisse tried to put his affairs—financial and emotional—in order. Next to his hospital bed sat a box of documents, including a letter, to be delivered upon his death, making peace with Amélie. The farewells to his friends, among them Pablo Picasso and Bonnard, his art dealer, would be taken to the post in the morning, as would a letter to his son-in-law, Georges Duthuit, letting him know exactly what Matisse thought of him following his separation from Marguerite.

To his son Pierre, Matisse set forth his wish that his estate be divided into three equal parts, one for Jean, one for Marguerite, and one for Pierre. "I love my family," he wrote with uncommon emotion, "truly, dearly and profoundly." He had been far from perfect as a husband and father. But now it was time to say goodbye. He ended the letter by leaving his latest painting, *The Dream*, to the City of Paris, and with a poignant request to the wartime postal censor:

---

* His underlying medical issue is often described as duodenal cancer, but Hilary Spurling suggests the blockage was related to a hernia Matisse suffered when he was younger.

"As I am about to undergo a surgical operation it may be my last letter to [my son]."[3]

In two stages, on January 16 and January 20, 1941, surgeons removed part of Matisse's intestine. A pulmonary embolism two days later nearly killed him. "I am not a wounded man," he wrote Pierre after the colostomy, "I am a mutilated one."[4] His diminished state was such that Marguerite allowed Lydia to accompany her at her father's bedside. The ordeal left Matisse in "the foulest possible temper," and his outbursts caused the two women to "each go off in a corner of their own and cry their eyes out."[5] On March 3, Matisse suffered a near-fatal blood clot in his lung and his wound became infected. To his doctors and nurses, the end seemed at hand for the seventy-one-year-old artist.

With Lydia and Marguerite trading shifts, Matisse lay in a state of delirium for eight days, hovering between lucidity and a dream-world. As he lay there "in a faint lull of horrible suffering," Matisse asked himself, "would you rather be in the cold of a tomb or here?"[6] In a series of letters to his friends, he answered his own question. To André Rouveyre, he wrote: "I saw the interior [of a] very dark, slightly greenish cellar without a door (there was no coffin, it was the walls of my room which had moved closer): No, no I still prefer to live."[7] To Bonnard, he professed no fear at dying, and to Henry de Montherlant, he expressed a sense of peace come what may. In "my long night of insomnia, it comes back to me that I wrote to you about the extraordinary serenity I feel.

"I wait! I wait for the hour like a traveler in a station waits for his train."[8]

The destination was unknown, but Matisse always knew what he sought. "I live only for the light," he had said, "and in search of its subtleties, I have been to the ends of the earth."[9] Matisse rubbed his tired eyes. His eyes had been the conduit through which he had taken in the cacophony of color in the Moroccan casbah, the cold light of Manhattan, and the fiery flora and fauna of Oceania. His eyes had been washed by saltwater lagoons and had squinted into the Mediterranean Sea toward Africa, ever in search of a light, a painterly light, an artist's light. When he found what he was looking for, the results were "like squinting into sunlight . . . as if he were painting the inside of his eyelids, capturing on canvas the paradise that flickered halfway between the imagined and the seen."[10]

Reconciling the imagination and the natural world was Matisse's modernist imperative. Referring to the Impressionist landscape artist Alfred Sisley, Matisse once said, "A Cézanne is a moment of the artist, while a Sisley is a moment of nature."[11] Matisse clearly wanted to follow the path of Cézanne, but not to the point of abstraction. Even if his was a "tenuous and distant reliance on the real," it still meant that to paint, Matisse needed models and flowers, vases and violins.[12]

"Why do you paint?" a critic once asked.

"Why, to translate my emotions, the feelings, and the reactions of my sensibility into color and design."[13]

If harmonizing the objective with the subjective, synthesizing the imagined and the real, was Matisse's knottiest problem, travel helped him work out a solution. "Having worked forty years in European light and space," Matisse explained, "I always dreamed of other proportions which might be found in the other hemisphere. I was always conscious of another space in which *the objects of my reveries evolved*" (emphasis added).[14] Indulging his own sort of Cartesian mind-body dualism, Matisse took himself to exotic locales to give his dreamworld something new to work with.*

At each stop, the artist added to his "theoretical arsenal." Color and light were the first arrows he added to his quiver. "He went abroad to experience different light effects and native colors," in the phrase of one commentator, booking trips "the way Pablo Picasso

---

* To Descartes, the immaterial mind and the material body, while distinct, worked together. In Matisse's case, he took his body to places to see things that his mind could add to its dream vocabulary.

changed mistresses."[15] After spending time in Ajaccio, Sicily, Toulouse, and Andalusia, Matisse left the northern grays and muted
colors of his early work behind much as he had quit Bohain for Saint-
Quentin, and Saint-Quentin for Paris. By the time he was in North
Africa, his use of color and light was becoming revolutionary.

"Tangier is known as 'the white city.' Its whitewashed domes and
walls are bathed in blazing sunlight," observed *Washington Post* art
critic Richard Paul. But the Tangier of Matisse is "ruled by blues . . .
The gleaming domes, the minarets, the garden paths, the trees seen
from his hotel room, and the shadows of *The Casbah Gate* are all
washed with cooled-down greens and blues."[16]

Or, as Matisse himself put it with characteristic economy:
"When I paint green it doesn't mean grass; when I paint blue, it
doesn't mean sky."

As he ventured further from representational art, Matisse unlocked the metaphysical power of colors on a flat surface. He
"discovered that color was structure," said Françoise Gilot, herself a
colorist. Hues "define positions in space if they are used in comple-
mentary couples. Warm colors naturally proceed, while cold colors
recede. A bright yellow appears to be on the first plane, while a purple seems further away."[17] Gilot goes on:

> Each tone had its own natural power of expansion,
> which was larger for warm tones than for cold ones . . .
> Matisse saw how he could use the arabesque to prevent
> neighboring colors from swallowing each other. The ara-
> besque was the charmer; it was natural, it moved, it was
> musical.[18]

During one long sojourn, Matisse wrote the French art critic Raymond Escholier that he was "unconsciously storing up many
things."[19] With every trip to see Russian icons, Persian miniatures,
African masks, and lacy Moorish designs, Matisse's intellectual jour-

ney took him further from the coastline of representative western art. Screens, tapestries, rugs—drawn from real life and not merely abstractions—allowed Matisse to incorporate an eastern vocabulary into the language of European art he had learned from the Sienese primitives to Paul Cézanne. Matisse's "virtuosity in combining Eastern decorative patternizing with Western traditions of pictorial depth and directional lighting" resulted in *The Checkerboard and Music.*[20] Instead of juxtaposing, Matisse harmonized his sweeping arabesques and crosshatched motifs just as he balanced purple with green. The effect, in the words of art historian Jack Flam, was "to extend the energy within individual things beyond their physical boundaries."[21] If Matisse's *Moorish Screen* had been painted in the nineteenth century, the two women figures in that painting would be shaded to appear in the foreground, and the room décor the background. Matisse, however, elevates the background and flattens the figures, in doing so Matisse synthesizes east and west while giving the decorative arts, like the handloomed textiles of his boyhood, equal billing with fine art. "For me, the subject of a picture and its background must have the same value," he wrote.[22]

In 1930, when he was sixty, Matisse was in Papeete, French Polynesia, where he described an "ash-blue sky alive with stars," a rising sun "crimson purple," waters running "glaucous green like the rivers of France," with a surface "the texture of black grape-skins."[23] He marveled at "the undersea light which is like a second sky" and the island's "pure light, pure air, pure color . . . diamond, sapphire, emerald, turquoise."[24] But it wasn't the interplay of color and light he was storing up this time, it was the humble plumbline. "I got fed up there in the end," he said, "but I had learned the meaning of the horizontal and the vertical from the shoreline and the coco palms." His 1931 painting *The Yellow Dress* is "a hymn to the horizontal and the vertical."[25]

AFTER EIGHT DAYS in a state of "lucid delirium" brought on by his embolism and infection, the fever broke. Henri Matisse's condition slowly began to improve. As the chilly April turned to May, he was able to go through the botanical garden using a cane, a walker, and a cart. Afterward, with a writing board across his lap, Matisse wrote a letter to Bonnard "in a jerky, almost illegible hand."* "It is all in bloom," he began. "There are some extraordinary greenhouses, *where you could dream you were in another world* when a sunbeam strikes . . . camellias of pink and red, hemstitched dog roses . . . there are also animals: elegant and majestic llamas, and a brand-new, beautiful lioness.

"As if on the first morning of Creation" (emphasis added).[26]

On this most modest voyage, outdoors in the middle of France in springtime, Matisse found a world once again in bloom, an Edenic paradise at the center of a continent at war. What the rest of the Occupation would mean for Henri Matisse and his family was unknowable, but the artist had made it through the twin crises of national defeat and near death.

The man the nuns called *Le Ressucité* ("The Resurrected One") was back to life.

---

* *Bonnard/Matisse*, 12. Previously, on the first of April 1941, he wrote Pierre Bonnard. Happiness, he told him, was defined by Rodin as living to seventy and pursuing with passion what he loves. By then spring was in the air: "From my room, I saw the leaves bud on the plane trees along the Rhône."

CHAPTER NINE

Paris Under the Swastika

"Whenever I hear the word culture, I release the safety-catch of my Browning!"
—GERMAN ESSAYIST HANNS JOHST

H E HAD BEEN A FAILED watercolorist in Vienna, but on Sunday, June 23, 1940, Adolf Hitler was a triumphant dictator astride a prostrate Paris. The Führer stood on the steps of the Trocadéro with the Eiffel Tour as a backdrop, then took in the splendor of Sainte-Chapelle, within the medieval residence of the kings of France. After touring the Louvre, Hitler remarked to his adjutant that he now understood why so many artists loved the city.[1] He and his entourage walked to Les Invalides and in a photograph taken there, Hitler, wearing a white double-breasted suit as if on holiday, gazes down reverently at the magnificent tomb of Napoleon.

The Kommandant of *Gross Paris* took over the Chamber of Deputies in the Palais Bourbon and worked with an efficiency equal to that of the panzer divisions that carved through the Ardennes. Hermann Göring and his Luftwaffe moved into the Luxembourg Palace; the Gestapo settled into 74 avenue Foch—named after the heroic

French general of 1914-1918; and the *Sicherheitsdienst* (the SD security forces) requisitioned the luxurious Hôtel de Crillon. The Vichy government opened an embassy at Matignon, formerly the prime minister's residence. Ten kilometers west, on the far side of the Bois de Boulogne, was Fort Mont-Valérien, commandeered by the Germans as a prison and execution site. To the south a similar distance was Fresnes Prison, with a similar purpose. By mid-summer 1940, the swastika hung along the boulevards of the city, over its municipal buildings, and on both sides of the Seine.

Parisians observing the jackbooted Wehrmacht officers reading newspapers at the café tables in the sunshine might have momentarily hoped the occupation would be bearable. But when the sun went down, loudspeakers announcing the curfew—in German—quickly revealed the stakes.[2] "The German High Command will tolerate no act of hostility towards the occupation troops. Every aggression, every sabotage will be punished by death."[3] A young Parisian named Jacques Bonsergent, accused of insulting a German soldier and executed by firing squad, became the first example of this ruthless new edict. "Officers passed by in their puffed-up caps," reported American expatriate Mary Jayne Gold:

> with the golden eagles and swastika pinned in the middle. Underneath the neat patent leather brim the calm, proud eyes looked back, and on every face the look of victory. God, how I hated them![4]

After subduing Paris, Hitler launched "a second blitzkrieg," in the words of scholar Frederic Spotts, "with the intention of making Germany as supreme culturally as it was militarily."[5] On one front of this offensive was the attempt to erase the rich and complex cultural life found in the French capital city. Two thousand titles deemed offensive to the Nazi regime were removed from its libraries: histories; biographies; classics like *All Quiet on the Western Front*;

works by the Communist poet Louis Aragon; and by Jews, including Albert Einstein, Sigmund Freud, and Thomas Mann.[6] Writers Albert Camus, Antoine de Saint-Exupéry, and Georges Simenon were among those who faced censorship. "Politically," complained the feminist writer Simone de Beauvoir, "we found ourselves reduced to a position of impotence."[7]

Before a gallery could mount a show, approval was required from the German Propaganda-Abteilung, installed in offices on Avenue des Champs-Elysées. A *referat* from the bureau would then attend the live show to act as a spy, ensuring compliance.[8] As if to prove the magnificent treasures within Paris now belonged to the German dictator, the statue of Great War French hero General Mangin—which outraged the Führer—was destroyed.

A simultaneous assault was waged on private art collections and public museums. Nazi bureaucrats entered each bank and inventoried the contents of safes, strongrooms, and vaults. Once cataloged, items were confiscated with typical Teutonic efficiency and sent to Germany or liquidated for Hitler's war effort. Foreign stocks and bonds, precious metals, and fine jewelry were of particular interest to the Germans. Valuable paintings looted mainly from prominent French Jewish families and characterized as "ownerless" were warehoused in the German Embassy, the Musée de Louvre, and the Jeu de Paume.* By 1944, the Special Staff for Pictorial Art could gloat over 21,903 stolen artworks, including masterpieces by Gainsborough, Goya, Rembrandt, Van Dyck, Velázquez, and Vermeer. "This collection can compare with those of the finest European museums. It includes many works of the foremost French masters,

---

* That many of these works were later returned to their rightful owners is due to the brave efforts of Rose Valland, the conservator of Jeu de Paume, who maintained a secret inventory of the pillaged works. See the recent book by Michelle Young, *The Art Spy: The Extraordinary Untold Tale of WWII Resistance Hero Rose Valland*, New York, HarperOne, 2025. Also taken were sculptures, textiles, fine furniture, and antiquities.

who up to now have been only inadequately represented in the best German museums."[9]

Some French cultural treasures remained beyond the reach of the Germans. Nearly a year had passed since national Museum Director Jacques Jaujard ordered priceless artworks and *objets* crated and carried away. At Loc-Dieu Abbey, seventy-five miles north of Toulouse, the local curator uncrated the seventeenth-century paintings of Nicholas Poussins to check on their condition. A group of children and farmers approached the paintings, which were set against haystacks in the late-summer sun. One of the children began to clap; then all of them; the farmers tossed their spades to the ground and joined in. "Follow me," said the curator, overcome with emotion. He took them inside the abbey, where they stood before a simple wooden crate with three red dots and the words "Musée Nationale." He lifted the lid to reveal Leonardo da Vinci's *Mona Lisa*.[10]

The Old Masters were not the only target of the occupiers. When a Nazi task force plundered the gallery and apartment of noted art dealer Paul Rosenberg, they made off with several Matisses, including *Woman Seated in an Armchair* and *Girl in Yellow and Blue with Guitar*.[11] As if driving the Jewish art dealer from his home and looting its contents were not enough, the Nazis then transformed Rosenberg's gallery into the office of the Institute for the Study of the Jewish Question, using the space to organize *Le Juif en France*, one of the largest anti-Semitic exhibitions in history,* an act of

---

* "Exhibition Reveals Lost Stories of Works of Nazi Looted Art." The Jewish Museum, May 25, 2021. *Daisies* and *Girl in Yellow and Blue with Guitar* were transferred to the Musée du Louvre and then to the Jeu de Paume gallery, both of which had been converted into Nazi storage depots. On November 27, 1942, *Girl in Yellow and Blue with Guitar* was part of a four-painting exchange with German art dealer Gustav Rochlitz acting on behalf of Hermann Göring. *Daisies* remained at the Jeu de Paume and was also restituted after the war. Both works were sold by Rosenberg and belonged to several private collectors before entering the collection of the Art Institute of Chicago, *Daisies* in 1983 and *Girl in Yellow and Blue with Guitar* in 2007.

grotesque irony. For Parisian Jews in 1941 and 1942, these thefts were compounded by a cascade of other degradations, including the loss of distinguished positions at the Sorbonne, in banking, science, and medicine, with more devastation to come.

Woman Seated in an Armchair and *Girl in Yellow and Blue with Guitar* were chosen for the personal collection of Reichsmarschall Hermann Göring, Nazi Germany's second-in-command, who had "carefully vetted" the stolen Matisse works.[12] A photo from December 1941 shows a seated Göring at the Jeu de Paume ogling two more Matisses set before him by his aids: *Daisies* and *Odalisque with a Tambourine*. That the artist was in the collections of Jewish-American families, such as that of Gertrude Stein, did not dissuade the Luftwaffe chief from adding a fifth Matisse to his collection, *Woman in Blue in Front of a Fireplace*. As he gazed upon the profile of the handsome woman in a blue ruffled dress, Göring could not have known the model was Lydia Delectorskaya.

There were also Matisses in the two dark storerooms in the Jeu de Paume set aside for "Degenerate Art," in addition to the crates bound for Reichsmarschall Göring, but something vastly more valuable was at risk: Henri Matisse's private collection. Much of his life's work, as well as pieces by Cézanne, Courbet, and Renoir, were in his vault in the basement of Banque Nationale pour le Commerce et l'Industrie located on Boulevard des Italiens. "I know what refined and robust removal men the Germans can be," Matisse worriedly wrote to Pierre.[13]

Amélie Matisse and Marguerite were living just a short distance from the bank in an apartment on rue de Miromesnil. Amélie had refused to leave the capital, declaring "there may be something for me to do." She had been "a semi-invalid" by the end of her marriage, but with the war she acquired "a new charge of energy and self-reliance. It was almost as if she were in training for an active, and quite possibly a dangerous, life."[14] The resourceful Madame Matisse, who had once run her world-famous husband's art career, again had a cause: the defense of Paris and its treasured artworks.

While Matisse and Lydia were en route to Nice, the German removal men paid a visit to Banque Nationale pour le Commerce et l'Industrie. The "technicians" were two German soldiers, who demanded of the bank manager to be taken to the huge circular subterranean chamber so they could begin the inventory. There were three vaults for artwork; Matisse owned one. Whenever possible, vault owners raced to their bank to be present for the process, lest their cherished valuables go missing. Would the bank manager—a friend of Matisse—alert the family members in time?

As the two soldiers descended the elevator to the three art vaults, escorted by the bank manager, neither Madame Matisse nor Marguerite was present. Instead, the Germans would be led through the vaults by the owner of the other two. Pablo Ruiz Picasso.

THE RELATIONSHIP BETWEEN Henri Matisse and Pablo Picasso had, in part, been shaped by war. In the years prior to the Great War, they had both been flowers in the creative hothouse of Montmartre. The outbreak of war scattered the international art cohort. The Germans disappeared; some, like the Expressionist August Macke, who was inspired by Matisse, died for their Kaiser. Georges Braque and André Derain donned the horizon blue of the French Army. The Spanish artists, Picasso and Juan Gris, continued their work in France. But for all of them, according to Françoise Gilot, life was never the same. "The arguments, the companionship, the rivalries, the sense of humor, and the hope and enthusiasm for the avant-garde were over. From then on, each painter had to fend for himself."[15] For Matisse, this meant a move to the southern light of Nice to wage his artistic battle with himself. For Picasso, it meant the evolution of Cubism.

In the mid-1930s, the Spanish Civil War between the fascist forces of Franco and the nationalists was a harbinger that a second general European war lay just over the horizon. At this moment, the friendship between the two giants deepened. They were recognized

leaders of an artistic movement denigrated by Nazi leadership as
Marxist-Jewish decadence. Their opposite numbers in Germany, like
Paul Klee, fled Nazi Germany or stayed and suffered, like Felix Nuss-
baum.[16] Instead of experimental modernism, the work favored by
the Nazi regime was "the exaggerated musculature of warriors and
athletes . . . middlebrow descriptive art extolling the virtues of young
SS athletes and or fair-haired women producing babies" for the
Third Reich. In Mussolini's Italy, it was a modern replay of the
Roman Triumph, but instead of victorious legions carting conquered treasure, it was "flaccid Fascist statuary."[17]

In this artistic front of war, Matisse and Picasso were on the same
side. They had passed from the *fin de siècle* through the portal of mod-
ernity that was the Great War. Theirs had been a guarded cordiality,
but now, "they shared the same fate of being attacked and often denounced."[18] "A deep emotional bond was sealed. After all, no one
could understand them as they did each other."[19] For all their differences in background, temperament, and approaches to art, Matisse
and Picasso both venerated Cézanne, Delacroix, Manet, and van
Gogh. They exchanged paintings with each other and paid homage
to each other with works including elements of the other's style. Picasso's sculptures seemed, to Gilot, to be "blown-up, radicalized
replicas of Matisse's own [earlier] work."[20]

They were allies against a common enemy, but the two men were
vastly different artistically, and temperamentally. Twelve years older
and speaking from the perch of propriety he'd learned early in life
in Picardy, Matisse at first frowned on the Andalusian's "rebellious
attire and extravagant behavior." Matisse dressed the part of a British
gentleman and gazed at his conversation partners with a serenity that
bordered on a trance. Picasso was the "fierce bull," his large head
and shoulders bent forward, his feet stamping the floor.[21] While Matisse harbored an almost spiritual "global vision of the universe as
permeated by love," Picasso "was possessed by the desire to know,
to analyze, to discover, even if it meant to destroy or to divide."[22]

There was a vibration and luminosity somewhere out there to Matisse; to Picasso there was a latent malignancy. "As complimentary as red and green, as opposed as white and black," the two developed a "mutual respect" and an "appreciation of each other's greatness."[23] Matisse, sober in mind and appearance, with sonorous, albeit economic French. By contrast, Picasso's "erratic pronouncements" filtered through his imperfect French and his "romantic aura" became "enticing enigmas." Friendly but formal, the two men waged an elegant and knightly war with each other over artistic ideas—what the French call *la guerre en dentalle*," a lace war.

Far from a knightly war, the German advance in 1941–1942 against France was a dirty one, with thieving of private property and menace against civilians. As an enemy of the Spanish fascist Franco, Pablo Picasso was persona non grata in addition to being an artistic enemy of the Reich. He was taking a considerable risk by being in the bank vaults with the two soldiers.

In the basement catacomb, Picasso rushed the two inspectors "from one room into the next, pulling out canvases, inspecting them, shoving them back in again, leading the soldiers around corners, [and] making wrong turns." Muttering in his Spanish-inflected French, Picasso gestured to paintings of angles, planes, and fragmented forms. Trying to keep up, the two Germans scribbled in their notebooks, but "they were all at sea"; they "didn't know what they were looking at," which Picasso exploited. "Germans always have a respect for authority, whatever form it may take. The fact that I was somebody everyone had heard of and I came there myself and gave them exact details of sizes, values, and dates—all that impressed them very much. And they couldn't imagine anyone telling them a story that might cost him very dear if he had been found out."[24]

Thoroughly confused in the unfamiliar world of Cubist shapes and Surrealistic phantasmagoria, the soldiers stepped into the dark hall and stood in front of Matisse's vault.

"Oh, we've seen these," Picasso said.

Satisfied, one of the soldiers asked in French: *Alors, que valent toutes ces choses?* (Well then, how much are all these things worth?)

Picasso looked up the circular column to the lights of the bank lobby above, as if doing calculations in his head. In the three vaults were the treasures of the best-known modernist painters in the world, works that might one day adorn the walls of great collections and conservatories.

"Huit milles francs."

One of the soldiers looked from Picasso to his notebook, and jotted down the figure, repeating as he wrote: *huit... milles... francs.*[25]

Picasso's figure must have had the intended effect, because the two soldiers had no desire to crate and carry away the contents—not for $178.

By remaining in France during the Occupation, both Matisse and Picasso were taking a risk. Matisse would have his own encounters with the Germans in the south, but Picasso, who remained in Paris at his apartment and studio at 7 rue des Grands Augustins, was a ready target for harassment.[26] Every few weeks, three or four Germans in suits and fedoras would appear at his entryway.

"This is where Monsieur Lipchitz lives, isn't it?"[27]

"No," replied Picasso's secretary, Jaime Sabartés. "This is Monsieur Picasso."

"Oh, no. We know it's Monsieur Lipchitz's apartment."

"But, no," Sabartés would insist. "This is Monsieur Picasso."

"Monsieur Picasso isn't a Jew, by any chance?" said one of the men.

The men well knew Lipchitz was in the United States, and Picasso was not Jewish, but it didn't matter.

"We're coming in to search for papers."

The disorder of Picasso's studio was an invitation to them to rummage through his paintings and belongings, leaving behind tipped-over works, pulled-out drawers, and papers on the floor. "They insulted me, called me a degenerate, a communist," Picasso told his friend André-Louis Dubois after one of the episodes. Once, the visitors stole the bed linens; on other occasions, they threatened further damage. "They kicked the canvases. They told me they'd be back."[28]

The first Nazi official to visit Picasso during the war became part of an often-told story that may be apocryphal, but which was nonetheless related by Alfred Barr, Matisse's first biographer. Not long after the conquest, so the story goes, Otto Abetz, the infamous, though cultivated, German agent, called on Picasso. Picasso received him coldly, refused his offer of fuel, and showed him the door. On his way out of the studio Abetz noticed a photograph of *Guernica*. "Ah, Monsieur Picasso," he said, adjusting his monocle, "so it was you who did that."[29]

"No," replied Picasso as he closed the door, "you did."

While it had not been bombed to rubble like the martyred Spanish town of Guernica, life in the French capital had also been violently upended by the Germans. Around the corner from Picasso, on the ground floor of 21 Quai des Grand Augustins, lived twelve-year-old Colette Chauvelot. After spending the first two years of the war in Nice, and struggling for food, Colette's mother and aunt were desperate. In the south, they had subsisted on bread made with dried corn, sunchokes, and *betterave à vaches (fourragère)*—the hard, misshapen beets used to feed cows. When they tired of having to barter cigarettes for the occasional egg, the two women took jobs in Paris, and enrolled Colette in a Catholic girls' school.

Trying to study in Occupied Paris wasn't Colette's only responsibility. The nightly siren, then the curfew orders, were her signal to go to sleep. In the predawn hours, Colette would slip out onto the deserted streets and alleys just across the River Seine from Île de la Cité, anchored at one end by the Cathédrale Notre-Dame. The clack of German boots dictated which route she would take to the corner of rue Gît-le-Coeur and rue des Arts. She was breaking curfew, and risking arrest, but her mission on behalf of her household was worth it: she was on her way to the *boulangerie* owned by a woman whose act of resistance was providing loaves of luxurious white bread to hungry families.[30]

During the Occupation, every *citoyen*, whether a celebrated modernist, a Parisian baker, or young schoolgirl, faced a *crise de conscience*. Not everyone handled this moral dilemma in the same way. In contrast to Matisse and Picasso, other figures in the world of art and literature saw the Nazi takeover as an opportunity. Addressing a "ridiculous rumor" that Picasso was in an "insane asylum," Matisse wrote to Pierre in New York, "[Picasso] leads a dignified life in Paris. He works, he doesn't want to sell, and he makes no demands. *He still has the human dignity that his colleagues have abandoned to an unbelievable degree*" (emphasis added).[31] Matisse *père* was referring to a disheartening episode in May 1942 when André Derain and Maurice Vlaminck, old friends of his going back to their days as originators of Fauvism, attended a banquet in Paris for Arno Breker, the official Nazi sculptor who was making a lucrative career transforming the Aryan ideals of *Übermenschen* into bronze for Hitler. Derain's acquiescence, at a time when imprisonment, torture, or deportation was the outcome for patriotic French in all walks of life, wounded Matisse.* In the early Fauve days, Derain's parents threatened to put an end to his career. Only an appeal by Matisse, older and conservatively dressed, changed their minds.[32]

"Our 'guests,'" Matisse continued bitterly to his son "have made a great thing out of this Breker exhibition . . . [there was] pomp, ceremony, and a big official banquet . . . at the Ritz. Everyone sang the praises of Breker, the great traditional sculptor."

---

* Derain mixed in society, and not always successfully: a Russian princess likened him to an "eel." According to the writer Francis Carco, Derain "goes out a lot and becomes infatuated with all sorts of people."

Arno Breker stands as a prime example of the type of opportunistic mediocrity given positions of influence by strongmen to fulfill their fascist fantasies. Like others of this ilk, he seemed to be oblivious to his shortcomings to make room for his overstuffed self-importance. Breker's studio included a full-sized pipe organ and two live horses, who served as models for his sculptures of racially pure Aryan supermen on their charges. In Paris, he made a second home in the luxurious apartment vacated by cosmetics magnate Helena Rubinstein (but only after demanding it be "Aryanized").[33] The statues of Hitler's official sculptor are classical but curdled, lacking the Greeks' "moderation, simplicity, and proportion." Breker's bronzes of men holding daggers and swords are "stilted and brutish," says one art historian, "shoulders too broad, hips too narrow. . . with faces grim, arrogant, ruthless." One can almost hear the *Ride of the Valkyries* looking at Breker's works, "hypertrophied in proportion and Nazified in intent." Breker had not only avoided military service but had been gifted with professorships and accolades for his bronze busts of Richard Wagner and Adolf Hitler. The Führer, of course, deemed Breker's figures "among the most beautiful ever created in Germany."[34]

A newsreel cameraman was at the spectacle at the Paris Ritz in May '42 and when he tried to shoot André Derain, the artist hid behind the genitals of one of Breker's gigantic bronze horses.[35] They couldn't hide the fact that this was not the first time Derain and Vlaminck had feted the fascists' favorite artist. One tactic of Hitler's artistic blitzkrieg was to induce respected French artists to travel to the Third Reich to pay homage to Breker. During Vlaminck and Derain's two weeks in the Third Reich, they toured Breker's massive studio in Berlin (where the workers included French prisoners of war who specialized in foundry work) and Hitler's new Chancellery in Nuremberg.[36] According to Picasso, Vlaminck willingly played along with his hosts, denouncing the Spanish modernist as a "Jew-ish degenerate."*

These colleagues of Picasso and Matisse had allowed themselves to be pawns on the board where checkmate wasn't merely German prevention of political freedom of France, but the stealing away of its cultural soul, Paris. André Derain and Maurice Vlaminck were not the only cultural elites who raised champagne flutes in toasts with their National Socialist overlords; there were other artists, writers, and entertainers who sullied themselves, but Matisse was especially wounded by the treacherous acts of men he once consid-ered his allies in the revolution of Fauvism. After Vlaminck's vicious attack on Picasso, Matisse refused to exhibit alongside his former mate.[37] "Some of them have had the time to take trips by invitation," Matisse wrote Pierre. "What a crew! It was lamentable and now that it's turned out badly for them . . . some of them claim they were forced into it. A likely tale! . . . They went off to Germany together, by the time they came back, they looked pretty ghastly."[38]

* Alfred H. Barr. "Picasso 1940-1944: A Digest with Notes." *The Bulletin of the Museum of Modern Art* 12, no. 3 (1945), 2-9. Picasso was not in a forgiving mood when it came to the collaborationist duo of Derain and Vlaminck, telling friends Derain should be "shot."

CHAPTER TEN

Zone Nono

"In the countryside nothing changed, everyone just waited. They waited for the war to end, for the block-ade to be lifted, for the prisoners to come home, for the end of winter."
—IRENE NEMIROVSKY, *Suite Française*

"We can't live anymore like birds on a branch."
—PIERRE BONNARD TO HENRI MATISSE

I T WAS THE SILENCE ONE noticed more than anything.
Under the Occupation, the hustle-bustle of the French capital had become muted. Elegant buildings with their stone façades and ironwork were marred by boarded or blacked-out windows (to avoid air raids). Engines and car horns went silent; automobiles were banned except for doctors and midwives. Overnight, the only sounds were enemy trucks, black Citroëns of the prowling Gestapo, and the hobnail boots of the five-man German patrols.[1] Parisians walked and bicycled about in a "silent chaos of defeat."[2]

Paris, Bordeaux, Rouen—three-fifths of France comprising two-thirds of its population and three-quarters of its industry—were in the Occupied Zone, known as *Zone Occupée*. In the middle, south, and southeast, the city of Toulouse and port of Marseille, lay the nonoccupied zone, *Zone Non-Occupée*. Though the often-used phrase is "free zone," *Zone Nono* was a fiefdom of proscriptions and privations. Given absolute authority during the death throes of the Third Republic, Marshal Philippe Pétain directed his state, Vichy France, backward, to a pre-republican France, where the Roman Catholic clergy and the monarchy shared power, and the peasant and the soil he tilled was mythologized: *Travaille, Famille, Patrie*. "I hate lies," the marshal exclaimed, "they have done you so much harm in the past. But the earth. The earth does not lie."[3] Echoing the Nazi motif "blood and soil," Pétain saw the ideal France as purer and more virtuous. He also parroted Nazi Germany's catalytic cycle of fascism: where a "sense of overwhelming crisis" and "a belief in victimhood" justifies the aggrieved group to act out "without legal or moral limits" against enemies within and without.[4] To Pétainists, France's defeat in 1940 could be pinned on the liars: Jews, Communists, Freemasons, and modern liberal ideals. When the old war hero shook hands with Adolf Hitler at Montoire in October 1940, any shroud of autonomy was torn away: Vichy France was to be the junior partner of Germany's National Socialism.

Lawmakers in Vichy went on to draft prohibitions against divorce and to make abortion a capital offense. Pétainist officials censored the press, opened mail, and listened in on phone calls.[5] There was "a sort of indifference," reported a prefect, "[people] are retreating into their shells."[6] As one citizen described it, "You didn't listen to the news, you didn't read the newspapers; you wondered where your next meal would come from . . . you just got on with life."[7] So-called undesirable teachers were cashiered, and critics of the government were imprisoned. If the whir of Paris was muffled, the silence of the largely rural *Zone Nono* was medieval.

Like their Nazi underwriters, the Pétainist regime came with its own set of symbols and performances. Uniforms of some sort or another were worn everywhere in the nonoccupied zone. Blue beret-wearing teenagers in the pro-Vichy Compagnons de France marched signing *"Maréchal, nous voilà!"* (Marshal, we are here!). Older men who had served in the world wars joined the right-wing Légion Française des Combattants.* Whether in khaki or black, members often used the stiff-armed Roman salute.[8] Instead of the logo of the Third Republic, the *police nationale* bore the insignia of the *fasces*, a bundle of rods tied around an ax, symbolizing the power of Roman magistrates to issue sentences of flogging or death. The Gallic modification to Mussolini's fascist icon was to depict the ax as the *francisque*—the double-bladed battle-ax of the ancient Franks.[9]

In town halls, schools, and public places, busts of Marianne, personifying liberty in her red Phrygian bonnet, were replaced with busts of Marshal Pétain. Under a képi or with his bald pate, the painted plaster-cast Marshal hardly called to mind "eternal France." Marianne was not the only Frenchwoman to be removed from public spaces. "We have to think twice before educating girls," wrote an education official in 1941. "A girl must first and foremost be the double of her mother, in the home and in the family."[10] Children and adolescent boys were also indoctrinated through books, posters, and board games to see athletic prowess as preferable to intellectual or cultural achievement. *A woman's place is in the kitchen* was essentially official government policy, as was *children should be seen and not heard.* In the occupied zone, Jewish businesses were required to post "Jewish Enterprise" on their shop window. In *Zone Nono*, this was not required, yet non-Jewish shopkeepers were urged to post *"Enterprise Française,"* as if French Jews were not French at all.[11]

---

* Stephen Cullen. *World War II Vichy French Security Troops* (Osprey, 2018), 6-10; and Delphine Manzoni. "Maintenir l'Ordre à Lyon, 1940-1943," paper for Université Lyon, 2007. In this paper, the Vichy Interior Minister wrote of nationalizing the police force as early as December 1940; the law was passed in April 1941. The Third Republic insignias had been ripped off and replaced with l'État Français.

In keeping with its other reactionary aspects, Vichy devalued modern art. To the extent fine art was admired, it was paintings like *Interior* by Alfred Giess, a product of the conservative Beaux-Arts who presided over the jury of the Salon des Artistes Français. His oil painting of three women in a tranquil domestic scene, like his mother and child work entitled *Maternité*, was conservative in its subject and conjured by techniques in use since the Renaissance. "The theme is secular and mundane; the subject matter is immediately recognizable; the perspective, contours, colors and shades have been carefully worked out so that the image comes close to photographic exactitude."[12] Whether landscapes, nudes, portraits, or still lifes, the culture of Vichy wanted not a transcription of the artist's emotion in the presence of what is seen, but a transcription of what was seen; not the artist's voice, but the artist's mimicry.[13]

Much more common in *Zone Nono* were arts and crafts like woodcuts, sold in the thousands, showing the grandfatherly Marshal Pétain as a Christ-like figure. The objects created under the rubric *l'art Maréchal* often veered into kitsch, like those pairing Pétain with Joan of Arc, the marshal in knight's armor, or his likeness on crystal vases, cutlery, and pocket flasks.[14] In posters and popular art, men were depicted as warriors or field workers, women as mothers or domestic workers. Imagery of knights, swords, lances, axes, and warriors completed this vision of a reinvented past.

The artists and dealers considered "decadent," "degenerate," "Judeo-Marxist," or guilty of "cultural Bolshevism" had been scattered by the Fall of France and subsequent flight, but as the frontiers between the zones closed for good, they were settling in. Pablo Picasso had been in fact in Royan (near Bordeaux), and rumored to be in many other places, but he was now in Paris. Matisse was in Nice, but he was hardly the only member of the art world along the Côte d'Azur: Georges Rouault was in Golfe-Juan, west of Antibes; Charles Camoin was in Saint-Tropez; André Rouveyre was in Cannes; gallery owner Gaston Bernheim was in Monaco; and Matisse's art school friend Simon Bussy was at Roquebrune, where he lived with his wife and acidic daughter, Jane.[15] In the *village perché* of Gordes, perched in the hills north of Marseille, Marc Chagall was keeping a low profile; for him and other Jewish and Masonic artists, the ports and frontiers of the south offered at least a chance of escape should one be necessary. Whether they were under German or Vichy dominion, Picasso spoke for his fellow artists when he described life during the Occupation: "There was nothing to do but work, struggle to find food, see one's friends quietly and look forward to the day of freedom."[16]

As Henri Matisse recuperated in his apartment in Cimiez from his near-fatal operations, he was mired in a state of artistic stagnation and personal isolation so deep that American newspapers referred to "the late Henri Matisse."[17] He was the most renowned artist in the nonoccupied zone, but unlike Picasso in Paris, he couldn't walk or bicycle to see a friend and he hadn't an entourage. The distances, gasoline shortages, and absence of taxis made seeing one's friends and family nearly impossible. Pieces of the puzzle of Matisse's own life, too, remained scattered about. Amélie was in Paris on rue de Miromesnil, not far from the cache of looted artwork at the Jeu de Paume and not far from the Paris headquarters of the SD security service. With her was Marguerite, unburdened by the duties of motherhood and doing something "to make herself useful." Pierre was in New York, but maintaining lines of contact as best he could with artists like Chagall and others trapped in Nazi-occupied Europe.[18] He saw little of Jean, who was passing the Occupation in his usual peripatetic and private ways, with sojourns to the Paris suburbs, Montauban, and now Nice. Even though Jean was nearby, he didn't visit, so Matisse may have wondered why he'd moved to be near the coast, and why he'd been careful to rent a villa with a cellar.*

---

* In June 1941, Jean Matisse and his family were living in Nice, in a little house among the pines, with a view of the snowcapped Alps. They could see the Régina

Confined to bed for hours each day after highly invasive surgeries, Matisse neither kept abreast of the art world nor socialized. Lydia was his only human touch. His white doves his only company. Ill, deeply frustrated, and in a city run by authoritarians and threatened by fascists and Nazis, painting still gave him reason to rise with the sun. He had barely made it through 1941 and his doctors were unsure if he'd make it through 1942, as each day was a "daily duel between physical suffering and artistic creativity."[19] When he made it to the easel, Matisse, as always, waged a war within himself.

During this period, Pierre Courthion, who met with Matisse several times for a proposed memoir, observed that Matisse "lives only in function of the next picture to be done." It was an evaluation corroborated by the artist himself: "I am chained to my canvas," Matisse crabbily confirmed.[20] But twenty-five miles west along the coast was another lonely artist in his seventies and in declining health, Pierre Bonnard. "I'd like to see you," Bonnard told Matisse, "since material concerns and worries about the future are troubling me a lot."[21] Matisse responded, "I need to see someone, and you're the one I want to see."[22] They set about trying to find each other.

Matisse and Bonnard had exchanged letters since 1925, but their correspondence was inconsistent and the contents often just a few lines on a postcard.[23] The war changed that; the two artists commenced an exchange that reveals not only the travails of living in a defeated France, but the life of the working artist, the indignities of aging, and the specter of death.

"Our constant anxiety," Matisse wrote, "disturbs the unconscious work that customarily occupies us when we are no longer in front of an easel." Rather than thinking (or dreaming) about painting, thoughts turned to food and fuel. "We had some real problems with

---

in the distance. With the good telescope, Henri Matisse could almost have peeked into their living room, though not down to the basement, in which Jean was later to harbor sticks of dynamite for the French Resistance.

food," Bonnard wrote, "having received only a part of our ration cards. Shortages are starting to be noticeable. Ten days without meat or cheese."[24] Bread, sugar, and pasta—a staple in the Italian-influenced Côte d'Azur—had been rationed first, followed by meat, cheese, butter, and eggs.* A people whose heritage was the bounty of France's fields and farms waited listlessly in interminable queues for their monthly egg, ran their tongues over bleeding gums, and scratched at irritated skin. People could only dream of getting their hands on BOF—slang for *beurre, oeufs, fromage* (butter, eggs, cheese).[25] Instead, there were beans: black beans, white beans, brown beans. *C'est la fin des haricots!* became "the most feared doomsday expression."[26] People ate horse sausage, and carrots, always a role-player on the French table, became the star. "Normal life slowed down to wasted time, black market and night hunger."[27] "Although gardeners pulled up flowers and replaced them with vegetables, the yields were less than modest. Nothing grew."[28] "Workmen and their families are literally starving, as the Alpes-Maritimes is possibly the most denuded department in the whole of France."[29] Unlike the north, hunting was allowed in *Zone Nono*; but the artist Bonnard was no hunter. "Painting is no longer the question," he concluded one letter to Matisse, "eating is."[30]

The French genius for improvising—*le système D*—found other outlets, like milling flour in coffee grinders and trapping pigeons in city parks.[31] To alleviate the dull ache of hunger, families reared rabbits and guinea pigs in balconies and bathrooms.[32] Instead of rich dark coffee, one drank *café national*, brewed from chickpeas and roasted acorns. The *tabac national* was a disappointing mélange of dried artichoke petals, nettles, corn silk, and oak leaves. Even the venerable old artist Henri Matisse benefitted from *le système D*: a young printer, Aimé Maeght, saw Lydia Delectorskaya scouring

---

* According to Mary Jayne Gold, the monthly ration was 1/2 pound of pasta, and weekly meat ration was 10 ounces. The weekly fats ration was 4.5 ounces, equal to about one stick of butter. Gold, *Crossroads Marseille*, 233.

the alleys and plazas of Nice in search of fresh vegetables, to better aid Matisse's recuperation. Attracted to Lydia, the young man devised a plan.

"My father had secretly bought a cow, so my sickly brother could have fresh milk. I would take some to Matisse every morning."[33]

Working (or trying to) helped pass the days. "I got back to work right away," Matisse reported, "to regain my equilibrium, but there is such a funk here . . . that my work is difficult."[34] Bonnard, installed at Villa Le Bosquet near Cannes, also found it hard to concentrate. "I'm afraid that painting may abandon me because of a lack of mental freedom."[35] And with no access to a car, Bonnard found himself "virtually a prisoner of my mountain"; a predicament that applied to his friend at Cimiez as well.

Health was a consistent refrain. "I've not been in good health these days," admits Bonnard in one letter, and calls himself "this old carcass" in another.[36] Matisse was "in bed since Friday," with "sensitive bronchi," "sore throats," and "tormented by liver attacks." Matisse also bore the indignity of the "special belt" of metal and rubber he wore after his colostomy—and the ever-present fear of infection. Lungs, kidneys, and livers were fretful subjects, but for both artists, eyesight was a particular and profound concern. Bonnard thanks Matisse for his "painter's solicitude for my eyes . . . I still continue with the salve and the ointment." Matisse responds, "I started with [eye] drops and changed to hot-water compresses twice a day to avoid the spasms in the artery of the eye."[37] Matisse's obsession with his eyesight appears again later: "My eyes are clouding over."[38]

The persistent cold due to heating fuel shortages exacerbated matters. It was "the kind of cold that jars and weakens," Bonnard complained to Matisse in a letter. When the worst of winter passed, the worries continued. "I don't dream of moving an inch," Bonnard told Matisse, "having worries enough about heat for next winter (already), but we can't live any more like birds on a branch."[39] Perhaps a visit could be arranged. "We have hotels that are somewhat heated,"

Matisse remarked laconically in a letter inviting Bonnard to visit Nice or Villefranche.[40]

The lack of transportation added to the misery. In Vichy France, driving was allowed—if you could get your hands on a can of petrol. "The shortages," Pierre Bonnard reported to Matisse, "start with gasoline."[41] "Gas for private cars," echoed Jean Matisse's son, Pierrot, "[was] out of the question."[42] The vehicles that were on the roads— buses and trucks—were often powered by huge contraptions, like outboard motors on a boat, attached to the rear (or top) of the vehicle. The unsightly contraptions were called *gagozène* by the French, and converted firewood and coal into the essence that ran the vehicles.[43]

In peacetime, the Côte d'Azur is for the young in summer, and the old in winter. The war years were like a long winter, and mortality cast its shadow over many of the letters between Matisse and Bonnard. "I have had a great loss," Bonnard says, relaying news of his brother's death in Algeria. "I reacted by working."[44] "I've heard from Paris that Paul Klee, a German painter of rare sensitivity, has died."[45] Their mutual friend Josse Bernheim had died of natural causes in Lyon. When people died during these years, they died quietly. When Pierre Bonnard's wife, Marthe, died of cardiac arrest, he buried her in a small-town cemetery in Le Cannet and told just a few intimates, including Matisse.[46] Too ill to visit Bonnard in the wake of his loss, Matisse invited his friend to Nice.

> We'll spend the afternoon together and you will sleep at
> my house. If you're tired in the afternoon, you can lie
> down a bit. If you like, bring your dog; you have to buy
> a [tram] ticket for the pooch.[47]

On the same hill where Romans had once talked of peace and war, posterity and mortality, and man and gods, the two painters spent an afternoon in the golden light.[48] There is no record of what they discussed, but if face-to-face they expanded on their letters,

Henri Matisse and Pierre Bonnard spoke of wartime disorders, the frailties of old age, and absent and lost loved ones. Matisse may have mentioned the interview he gave to the art critic Gaston Diehl, who asked, "What matters most to you?" Matisse responded by trying to describe the difficulty of creating art based on a real object but that speaks to a greater universal.* Or the interview he most likely felt compelled to give to the Vichy-sanctioned radio, when he dared to criticize the academic Beaux-Arts system so favored by Pétainist art critics as a useless "mutual aid society... [that was] deadly for the young artist."[49] Bonnard would have fully appreciated that this relatively mild condemnation was all Matisse could risk so as not to imperil Lydia Delectorskaya or members of his family.[50] Matisse was not interviewed again.

They likely discussed their painting, as they often did in writing. "A painter," Matisse wrote, "exists with a palette in his hand and he does what he can." Bonnard agreed: "The painter's only solid ground is the palette and colors."[51] Perhaps, too, they spoke of the magnificent works of art before which they both stood in wonder. It was Bonnard who told Matisse of the paleolithic frescoes discovered by four French schoolboys in a cave complex in the Dordogne village of Lascaux. "It is very fine—what drawing!" For a brief moment, the world's attention shifted away from the war to the hunt scenes of oxen, deer, and horse in the sanctuary being called the "Sistine Chapel of Prehistory." To Matisse, it was the frescoes of a later epoch—the Renaissance—that transcended time itself: the miraculous blues of the Arena Chapel in Padua, Italy. "For me Giotto is the summit of my desires, but the road leading to an equivalent, in our age, is too long for one lifetime."[52]

---

* In asserting that by sitting for an interview on Vichy-sanctioned radio, Matisse was giving his approval to the regime, Michèle Cone flatly concludes that "current events "find no place in Matisse's comments." Yet as art historian Frederic Spotts says, "the liberation of France" would have no doubt been taken for granted by the two men.

One lifetime. In some ways, nothing had changed: Matisse's first letter to Pierre Bonnard, written on a postcard from Amsterdam in the summer of 1925, reads:

> *Long live*
> *Painting!!!*
> *In friendship.*

In other ways, the passage of time had left marks like striations on an ice age boulder scraped across a continent by a retreating glacier. The lifetimes of the two contemporaries were bookended by war. The Prussians on horseback in 1870, the trenches of the Great War in 1914, and now the Germans, toting cameras instead of rifles while on leave along the beach at La Croisette. Invaders who had broken a nation, leaving two celebrated artists in their seventies in a France that was like "a puzzle that had fallen off the table and onto the floor."[53]

CHAPTER ELEVEN

Escape to New York

"We came to the harbor of New York. I will never forget it. It was like I came from death to life"

—JACQUES LIPCHITZ

"My enemy forced me to take the road of exile."

—MARC CHAGALL

"Men in exile feed on dreams of hope."

—AESCHYLUS, *Agamemnon*

ON THANKSGIVING WEEKEND 1942, hundreds of New Yorkers
braved the chill to stand in line at the Hollywood Theatre on
Broadway and Fifty-First Street to see a popular and timely new
movie. Tickets in hand, they entered the Art Deco lobby, walked
through an office building, and emerged in the low-lit theater, a
dreamland of red and gold with stylings of French Baroque and Rococo. As the theatergoers unfolded their plush red seats, the lights
dimmed. Before indulging their two hours of wartime escapism,
they took in the newsreel of the events on far-flung battlefields of

the Second World War. The spinning black-and-white globe and tri-
umphal music gave way to a newsman's stentorian voice: "Rommel's
Africa Corps defeated on the sands of Egypt." Images flickered by:
British General Bernard Montgomery atop a Matilda tank; American bombers in the clear skies above the smoking wreckage of
Rommel's supply train; U.S. troops wearing sand goggles entering
Oran, Algeria. "This is the opening phase of a second front," said
the voiceover, "the American occupation of North Africa may prove
to be the turning point of the war."

The feature started where the newsreel left off. As the Warner
Brothers crest faded to a map of Africa, the up-tempo music herald-
ing the studio's new film changed key to a snaking Arabic melody
punctuated by tom-toms. As the names of the stars swept across the
screen, the Middle Eastern instruments gave way to the rousing "La
Marseillaise," the French national anthem. When the map tightened
focus to wartime Europe and North Africa, another voiceover described a "tortuous roundabout refugee trail." The outcome of the
war was unknowable in late 1942, but escaping Nazi-occupied Europe
was imperative for enemies of the Third Reich like the artists, writers,
and intellectuals on the Gestapo's hit list. For Jewish artists, it was a
matter of life or death. The New World was the goal, but before they
boarded ships in Lisbon, those fleeing the Nazis first had to get out
of Paris, and to places like Marseille, the Pyrenees . . . or Casablanca.

Shot and produced during the ongoing war, *Casablanca* tells the
story of Rick Blaine, the tough-skinned American played by Hum-
phrey Bogart. Rick's life is interrupted when his former lover, Ilsa
Laszlo, arrives in the French Moroccan seaport now under Vichy
control. Earlier in the war, Ilsa and Rick spent a romantic month together in Paris when she believed her husband, a Resistance leader,
had been killed. When a very alive Victor Laszlo appears with Ilsa
at Rick's Café in Casablanca, the drama hinges on whether Rick will
bury his feelings for Ilsa to help the couple escape Vichy territory for
safety in Lisbon.

Partly a propaganda picture, the film's politics are never in doubt. When a German officer commandeers the café's piano to lead his men in "Watch on the Rhine," the outraged Victor orders the house band to play "La Marseillaise." The bandleader looks to Rick, who nods his assent. Many in the Hollywood Theatre wept along with Yvonne, played by the young French actress Madeleine Lebeau, as the exiles and refugees, continentals and colonials, lovers and Resistance fighters drowned out the Germans with their own patriotic song. *"Vive la France!"* cries Yvonne at the end, *"Vive la democratie!"*

The audience may have come to Times Square to see what reviews were calling an "entertaining adventure story," but what they didn't realize is there was a deadly serious drama playing out in the real world; one that included a young American flying to France on a Pan American Clipper, harried exiles and daring women, secret messages hidden in toothpaste tubes and shoeshine tins, and a roundup of "the usual suspects." This real drama had its own Rick's Café, a place where those driven from home felt at ease—and that sanctuary was just six blocks away.

Pierre Matisse's Gallery, a showplace for modern art in a city that had yet to embrace contemporary styles, was more than a waystation on the timetable of those fleeing Europe; it was the last stop of an underground railroad. It was a place where French was spoken rather than English; a piece of the Paris art world in the New World, offering "taste, refinement, superb food, and intelligent conversation."[1] If *Casablanca* had a sequel, it might have started with shots of the ocean liner steaming out of Lisbon and, a moment later, sailing past the Statue of Liberty. Then an overhead shot of New York City, the emerald rectangle of Central Park, then to its southeastern corner: 41 East 57th Street, the Fuller Building.

But instead of a film crew, there was Henri Matisse's second son, now forty-one, working alone on the Sunday. That he would work on the day of rest was not surprising. The gallery was "his empire, his spiritual or corporeal domain . . . his idea of a perfect Sunday was to be in the gallery by himself [hanging] the next exhibition."[2] He would step onto the ladder, hang the painting, climb another rung or two, adjust the spotlight just so, and examine the work in the context of his sanctum.

Like his father, Pierre was of medium height with a compact built. He had his mother's fine facial features and complexion, brown eyes, and dark eyebrows. Pierre liked well-made clothing—woolen double-breasted suits, silk socks, and fine leather loafers—and combed his prematurely thinning hair straight back. He didn't like to appear too American, but he had no choice but to wear the rather more colorful patterned ties in New York's men's clothing boutiques. He was married to an American, but in his choice of car, he chose European elegance: a Bugatti. If New York, as Pierre told his father, was a city where "gigantic monuments turn into a vast theater set," then his gallery in the forty-story Art Deco skyscraper that towered over Central Park and the Ritz Hotel was among the props.[3] There, in the sunlit space on the seventeenth floor, the reticent and reserved Pierre took his work as seriously as his famous *père*, even if he lacked his father's artistic exuberance. The distances of the Atlantic Ocean and a decade and a half could never change who he was fundamentally. Pierre Matisse was, like he always signed off in his letters to his father, *votre fils devoué* (your devoted son).

On the morning of Sunday, March 1, 1942, the elevator door opened, and Pierre Matisse stepped into his gallery and turned on the lights. The Madison Avenue traffic below was a muffled hum. He hung his jacket over the back of a chair and began to work on an exhibit that would reverberate long after the war was over. "I stayed in town," he wrote his father, "to hang the exiles' show... there is [Amadée] Ozenfant, whom I knew in the last war, [Ferdinand] Léger, of course, and [Marc] Chagall, [Jacques] Lipchitz, [André] Masson, [Ossip] Zadkine, [Yves] Tanguy, André Breton... and [Piet] Modrian. They number fourteen in all." Born with the privilege and the burden of his world-famous surname, this was the second-born son's moment to emerge as his own person. By mounting an exhibit of émigré artists who formed the avant-garde, Pierre Matisse was helping desperate men and their families settle in a new home while at the same time setting the stage for New York City to become the postwar capital of modern art.

For these figures of the Continental avant-garde, it was a new life; one with gigantic automobiles, shining skyscrapers, and garish neon. If they were disoriented, they had a gallery whose seven letters—M-A-T-I-S-S-E—were as familiar as a strong cup of *café* and a pack of Gauloises Bleus; it was their "safe house, clearinghouse and coffeehouse."[4] Unlike the temporary reprieve under the low-lit Moorish archways of Bogart's unsavory tavern, 41 East 57th Street was an establishment of permanent safety, a literal New World free of pogroms and camps; New York was the terminus; this was the future.

They would help make it so.

But first, the endangered artists had to escape a Europe in flames.

Taking on this mission was the New York–based Emergency Rescue Committee. The ERC came into being in the immediate aftermath of the Fall of France when it became clear the "hopelessly encumbered immigration policy" of the U.S. government was not going to provide enough visas for refugees pouring into the port of Marseille.[5] Time was short, money was a consistent headache, and American neutrality complicated matters.

To act as its agent in Marseille, the ERC sent Varian Fry. The thirty-five-year-old American was playing the real-life part of a Hollywood hero, with three thousand dollars taped to his leg and a list of artists, writers, and intellectuals who were in danger. Once in Marseille, Fry procured false documents; cut deals with black marketeers, forgers, and Corsican "businessmen"; and sent his "clients" across escape trails over the mountains to the Iberian Peninsula, where they embarked for ports of permanent safety.

Between Fry in Marseille and Pierre Matisse in New York was a transatlantic network of supporting characters. There was "the

La Famille Matisse: Matisse, Amélie, Pierre, Marguerite, and Jean, in front of the daisy-spotted painting of his daughter. "We were a family of artists," said Marguerite.

Henri Matisse and his wife Amélie in 1913. For many years Amélie posed and Matisse painted,
and these twin obsessions were woven together. Home was the studio; the studio was home.
Photo by Alvin Langdon Coburn. Courtesy of the George Eastman Museum.

When it came to their own artistic ambitions, Matisse's sons Jean and Pierre
found their famous surname to be a blessing and a curse.

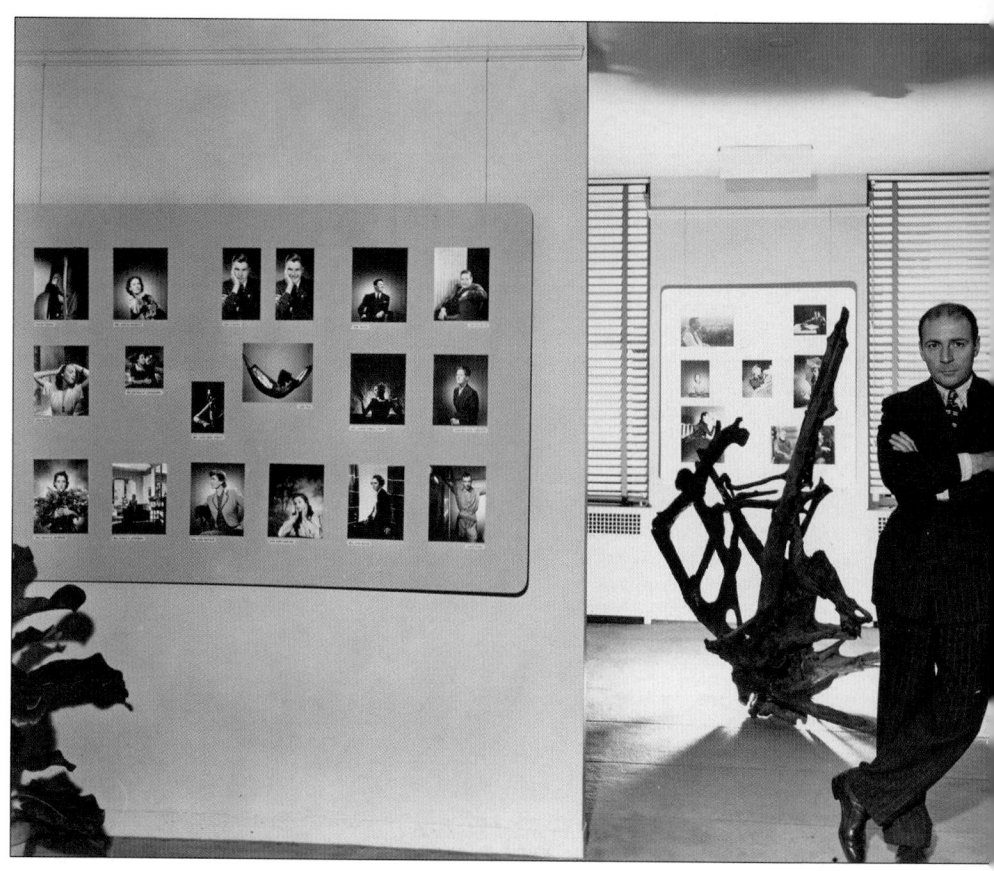

Among Matisse's three children, and despite the wartime censorship, Pierre was one of his father's [text cut off]
consistent correspondents during the war. Pierre Matisse at the New York gallery that bore his nam[text cut off]
The Morgan Library & Museum. MA 5020. Gift of the Pierre Matisse Foundation, 1997.

Henri Matisse was among the modernists derided by the Nazis. That did not stop them from stealing his art. At the Jeu de Paume Museum, Paris, Dec. 2, 1941 Reichsmarschall Hermann Göring (seated, lower left) ogles two paintings by Henri Matisse and stolen from dealer Paul Rosenberg. *Archives des Musées Nationaux.*

Matisse's first permanent residence in Nice, at the end of the busy Cours Saleya.
Photo by author.

"Don't move," Matisse told Lydia Delectorskaya one day in 1934
as she was taking a break from domestic chores. The resultant painting,
The Blue Eyes, was the beginning of a remarkable two-decade partnership.

Lydia was Matisse's constant companion during the war years.
Here she sits opposite Matisse in a photo by Henri Cartier-Bresson,
who visited Matisse at Villa Le Rêve while on the run from a German labor camp.
© Henri Cartier-Bresson/Magnum Photos.

Casualty of war. A paratrooper killed in action during Operation Varsity.
Courtesy U.S. Army.

Poet Louis Aragon, a friend of Matisse, said that the star-shapes in **The Fall of Icarus** stood for "bursting shells." Archives Henri Matisse, all rights reserved.

"Whatever happens, the flame of the French resistance must not be extinguished and will not be extinguished." ~ General Charles De Gaulle.
Creative Commons.

To many wartime observers, Matisse's cut-out **Monsieur Loyal**
resembled the profile of General Charles de Gaulle.

Woman Reading at a Yellow Table is a wartime work of hope.
The model, Annelies Nelck, is portrayed as a modern-day Marianne,
that ancient symbol of France. In a blouse the color of spring and regeneration, she cradles a book
Note Matisse's subtle use of the patriotic tricolor in the flower vase at right.
Courtesy the Matisse Museum, Nice, France.

The hopefulness of *Woman Reading at a Yellow Table* is absent in **The Wolf**.
To Riva Castleman former chief curator of the Museum of Modern Art in New York,
this was "a symbol for the threatening Gestapo."

Just a few years after she appeared in ***Marguerite with Black Velvet Ribbon***,
Matisse's daughter expressed fear about the future war with Germany. "The future looks like the abys

The Allied invasion fleet readies
for its landing on Southern France.
Courtesy of the U.S. Navy,
National Archives
Identifier 80-G-59468

Germany, April 1945,
General Dwight D. Eisenhower,
Supreme Allied Commander,
accompanied by generals
Bradley and Patton,
inspects the art treasures
stolen by Germans
and hidden in salt mine
in Merkers, Germany.
One stolen wartime Matisse
was not returned until 2015!
National Archives Identifier: 540134

Even in poor health during the Occupation, Henri Matisse was driven to create.
Here, he sits in bed at Hôtel Régina in September 1942 with his brushes in hand.

gawky American heiress" Peggy Guggenheim who used her wealth and sexual insatiability to collect art as well as artists. "During the dangerous days before and just after the Fall of France, Peggy Guggenheim made it a point of honor to buy a painting a day from working artists, which was certainly good for the Guggenheim collection, but also saved a great many painters." One newspaper piece credited her with saving "art treasures for the post-war world" even as "old cities crumble."[6] Guggenheim saved people, too: her efforts helped Max Ernst, Marcel Duchamp, André Masson, and André Breton escape Nazi-occupied France. In New York she was a celebrity, a kingmaker of reputations and of financial success. Along the way, from her many male companions she "demanded everything I had seen in Pompeii Frescoes."[7]

Less dramatic but no less effective were the married couple Alfred H. Barr, Jr., the first director of the Museum of Modern Art (and a friend of Pierre Matisse), and his Italian-born wife, Margaret, known as "Marga." "Phone calls and letter-writing were only one part of it," Marga Barr explained of their efforts back in New York, "because Alfred and I were constantly anxious about the fate of the artists, most of whom we knew personally, some of them trapped in the occupied zone, others wandering from place to place . . . often with no firm address." The Barrs not only identified those targeted by the Nazis, but they handled the logistics of emigration. Marga secured affidavits vouching that the person is in imminent danger and would not pose a threat to the United States; she proofread biographical sketches and requested letters of reference. It was a full-time job she said was:

> particularly difficult because, not only did you have to clear their papers, but also you had to find $400 for each one, and . . . guarantee that they would not become a charge to the state . . . [The artists] didn't have connections with collectors [or others] who would have helped them.[8]

To persuade potential donors to provide the sum that would save one refugee's life, the Emergency Rescue Committee printed pamphlets with such titles as: "Wanted by the Gestapo: Saved by America."

This was not an overstatement. When it came to modern artists, their styles had been denounced and their art destroyed by the Nazis beginning in the late 1930s. Following the Fall of France in June 1940, these enemies of the Reich were subject to being surrendered to the German authorities anywhere in France on demand. The need to leave was paramount to avoid internment, imprisonment, or worse. Of the fourteen émigré artists, those who faced almost certain death had they remained in Europe were the Jewish artists like Jacques Lipchitz and Ossip Zadkine.* If it had not been for the Emergency Rescue Committee, wrote the Marxist author Victor Serge from Marseille, "a goodly number of refugees would have had no reasonable course open to them but to jump into the sea from the height of a transporter bridge."[9]

One of the ERC's targets was Henri Matisse. But when Varian Fry made his case in person at the Hôtel Régina in December 1940, Matisse again refused to leave France. "In spite of the growing food shortages," Fry recalled, "and the difficulty he was already having in finding canvases and pigments, he said he preferred to stay in France." The occupied north of his childhood, and the capital of Paris, however, were off-limits: "I could never bear to live under the Boches," Matisse explained.[10]

---

* It was not only artists, of course, who were in danger. Among the imperiled were Jewish actors and artists, composers and critics, playwrights and philosophers. The German Jewish philosopher Walter Benjamin made it to Catalonia in September 1940, but local border agents decided to return his group to Nazi-occupied France. Benjamin committed suicide by overdosing on morphine pills. The German-Jewish playwright Walter Hasenclever, at the concentration camp Les Milles, near Aix-en-Provence, and art critic Carl Einstein in a lodging near the Spanish border, also took their own lives rather than falling into the hands of the Nazis. See Mary Jayne Gold. *Crossroads Marseille, 1940* (Garden City, NY: Doubleday & Company, Inc., 1980), 151.

Although they declined aid, both the writer André Gide and Henri Matisse signed on as "undercover operatives" of the ERC's *Comité de Patronage*.[11] Both men knew "full well the nature of the work and the ruthlessness of the enemy."[12] In this role Matisse provided scarce materials to artists by sending them some of his own supplies, but there was a hint he was doing more.[13] Matisse told Fry's assistant, Charlie Fawcett, that he "had a barn where he used to harbor refugees."[14]

As for refugees who made it to the Franco-Spanish border, they found one's fate could be determined by the recognition of falsified papers or the caprice of a policeman or a border guard. Max Ernst had been a German soldier in World War I before establishing his painting career in France in the interwar years. While Ernst was not a Jew, his Dadaist and Surrealist works were deemed offensive, an "Insult to German Womanhood."[15] After the outbreak of the Second World War, Ernst was imprisoned as "an enemy alien." He was freed but was later arrested by the Gestapo. Ernst escaped and with rolled-up paintings under his arm, he arrived at the Franco-Spanish border station of Canfranc lacking an exit visa.

"Your papers are not in order."

The border guard opened Ernst's suitcase and interrogated the artist about the paintings. Knowing he was "playing for his life," Ernst "spoke that day about painting as I had never spoken before."[16]

It worked.

"Monsieur, I adore talent," said the guard.

"You have a great talent. But I must send you back to Pau [occupied France]. There is the train for Pau. Here on the left is the train for Madrid [Spain]. Here is your passport.

"Don't take the wrong train."

When Ernst arrived in Lisbon via Madrid he packed his searing wartime work *Europe after the Rain I* in brown paper and mailed it addressed to himself at the Museum of Modern Art. Miraculously both he and his painting arrived safely.

Ernst was lucky, but for other artists considered enemies because of their avant-garde style or their religion, the doors were closing. Claude Lévi-Strauss described the port of Marseille as a pitiful way station for "the talent and expertise of Paris in her prime" now "hanging by slender threads ... reduced to the hunted, terribly tired men at [their] limit."

Among the hunted was Marc Chagall.

Born in Vitebsk, Russia, in the age of the tsars, by 1941 Chagall had witnessed pogroms against Jews, the First World War and Russian Revolution, and now the Nazi conquest of Europe. The storms of history were reflected in the somber hues of his early canvases; his colors were like a "banked fire" that spoke of a "resigned sadness." When he was twenty-one, he saw the paintings of Henri Matisse, still in his Fauvist phase. It was a style that had "turned its back on academic teaching ... and social vanities"; it was a new art, a purer painting, with "no class distinctions."[17] Seeing Matisse's riotous colors led Chagall to lighten his palette. His colors brightened further when Chagall moved from "potato-colored" Vitebsk to Paris in 1910. He found the City of Light as Henri Matisse had found Nice: a wonderland of "colors singing in the streets and in the sky."[18] After spending the years of World War I in Russia, Chagall returned to Paris in 1923, and the next year Chagall met Matisse's son Pierre. The younger man with the world-famous name was a novice art dealer learning from the older hands at Galerie Barbazanges-Hodebert. There, in December 1924, Pierre Matisse mounted Chagall's first exhibition in the art capital. "Matisse and Picasso ... came to my exhibition," Chagall wrote to a friend in Moscow. "What can I say about myself!"[19]

The fantastical paintings of Chagall that Pierre Matisse found "exhilarating" and possessed of a "wild side" were the work of a man who had seen too much.[20] "Timid [and] fearful," Chagall's "human relations [were] dominated by ... remembrances of humiliations, blows, and pogroms."[21] He had fled Russia for Paris, then Paris for the unoccupied zone. At first, he saw his French citizenship as a shield against persecution, but this sense of security was weakened in the spring of 1941, when the Vichy government passed further anti-Semitic laws. Stripped of French citizenship, the artist and his wife, Bella, fled Gordes for the Hôtel Moderne in Marseille. It was there that the real-life version of *Casablanca's* "round up the usual suspects" took place. When Vichy officials ordered the roundup of all foreign Jews in Marseille's hotels, Chagall was briefly taken into custody.[22]

He was aware of his fate had he remained in France. "The enemy was preparing a degrading death for me somewhere in Poland." Though he had been "born a second time in Paris" and lived as dual citizen of Russia and France, the war meant he was without a home. On May 7, the Chagalls were smuggled across the Franco-Spanish border. Four days later, they steamed out of Lisbon bound for New York City. "I took the hospitable hand of America," he said.

Providing "a link to the old world," Pierre Matisse met the Chagalls at the dock and provided a two-room apartment in the same building on 57th Street that housed his gallery.[23] Unable to speak English, Chagall got by with Yiddish and Russian on the Lower East Side, but with Pierre, no translator was needed. Handsome and curly haired, Chagall had a reputation for difficulty, but Pierre's friend and biographer John Russell says, "in his relations with Pierre he was easy, direct, affectionate and admiring."[24] The relationship between the progressive art dealer and the celebrated modernist was more than mutual admiration. "I grew up with painters," Pierre later explained. "I have always known that every painter, however successful, is haunted by what he believes to be the fickleness of the public."[25] Cognizant of Chagall's insecurities, Matisse supplied him with a monthly retainer of $350, "enabling him to bare his soul and psyche on canvas. A burst of creativity sprang from this remarkable partnership of master painter and master marketer."[26] In the phrase of Chagall's biographer, during a "bleak time" the backing of Pierre Matisse was "crucial."[27]

As he began his American odyssey, Chagall couldn't forget his homeland, nor the scars upon it. Even with its "fierce contrasts of colors," *The Crucifixion* is a painting of "unusual gravity and solemnity."[28] In *The War*, Chagall depicts a city in flames, "the burning red hair of a nursing mother," a corpse, soldiers, and a Jewish refugee. A horse with a rooster on its back burdened by a red-wheeled cart struggles to lift off from the flaming ruins, as if to transform the earthbound agony into "a dream of escape in Elijah's flaming chariot heading skyward."[29] To Italian art critic Lionello Venturi, "a vein of sadness runs through [Chagall's] joys."

But the sadness was the "shadow of a great light."[30] Chagall had seen the forms of Picasso and the colors of Matisse. "When Matisse dies," said Picasso, "Chagall will be the only painter left who understands what color really is."[31] But his compositions of Russian icons, farm animals, and the village life and Jewish ghetto of his childhood were *sui generis*. His "sentimental and naïve" paintings included "levitating oxen and horses . . . music, lovers, weddings, and births." In December 1941, Pierre Matisse introduced this imaginary world to the American public when he mounted the first Chagall exbibit in the United States—"Chagall Retrospective 1910-1941"—and it was a blockbuster.[32] "Not even the Japanese attack on Pearl Harbor [on December 7]," wrote John Russell in *The New York Times*, "could quote rob the exhibition of its impact."[33] Later during the war, Pierre Matisse printed a handsome limited-edition book with biographical details of Chagall's tempestuous life and several color plates. "The public is still slow to admit in painting the same freedom it admits in poetry," reads the text. "Time must pass before Chagall's work receives the mature understanding and full recognition it deserves." As the artist's sole representative in America, Pierre Matisse did all he could to accelerate American appreciation of Chagall. The exiled artist's paintings were soon added to private collections, as well as those of the Albright Art Gallery in Buffalo, the City Art Museum in Saint Louis, and the Museum of Modern Art in New York

City.[34] Pierre Matisse exhibited the artist sixteen more times over the next four decades.[35] Before fleeing France, Chagall had asked Varian Fry, "Will I have a subject in America? Will I be able to paint?" The dauntless young American couldn't answer that question, but the man at the other end of the transatlantic refugee trail could—and did. If the ERC had provided a lifeline to Marc Chagall, Pierre Matisse provided the livelihood.

IN NEW YORK the fortunate fourteen artists who had escaped Nazi Europe were disparate personalities. "Most of them didn't speak to one another when they were in France," Pierre Matisse told his father.[36] Not surprisingly, their response to the new circumstances differed. "These men did not really want to come here in the precise way they came, hurriedly and in flight, and with all the regrets and uncertainties that such a way of coming entails."[37] In the words of Mary Jayne Gold, who lived in Marseille and helped fund Fry's mission, "For an exile, no place is the right place."[38] Yet some adapted easily to New York. Peggy Guggenheim had fallen for Max Ernst, and the couple enjoyed homemade French dinners with the Ozenfants. Fernand Léger gave tours of the city, and others, like Piet Mondrian, created pieces that would have been unimaginable in the Old World, like *Broadway Boogie Woogie* from 1943. Some felt guilty for abandoning France. Max Ernst plaintively said of Paul Éluard: "He is my close friend and brother. He could have come, like we did [to] be safe. But he stayed."[39] Some of the artists wrestled with their new home and its materialism, commercialization, and paucity of culture. Others were nostalgic for their homeland while shuddering at its ethnic hatreds.

On Tuesday March 3, 1942, the curtain opened on Pierre Matisse's exhibition *Artists in Exile*. The fourteen artists each contributed a single piece in their contemporary modern styles: Dada, Surrealism, Cubism, and De Stijl. *The New York Times* art reviewer recognized the war's scars upon these works. There was Lipchitz's bronze *Rape of Europa*, Matta's "explosive" *Initiation*, and Masson's *Seeded Earth*, "violent enough to suggest direct relationship to the state of the world."[40] Still, there was a note of grace. The fellowship of Café de Flore in 1920s Paris was gone forever, but for the creative émigrés, many of whom would have been hunted to their deaths in Europe, the exhibition was the start of a second life for them and a new era of appreciation for their adopted country. The catalog accompanying the show was more of a manifesto:

> Here are fourteen artists who have come to America to live and work. They are a disparate group, but all belong to the rare company of those who have brought original- ity and authority to the art of their period. Their presence can mean . . . the beginning of a period during which the American traditions of freedom and generos- ity may implement a new internationalism in art, centered in this country.[41]

Seventeen years before his exhibition, Pierre Matisse was himself an exile in New York City, cast from France not by war but by a failed marriage and a murderous father-in-law. Perhaps, too, he was escaping the burden of his famous surname. With *Artists in Exile*, the devoted son was making his own name in his adopted home as "one of the century's most influential dealers in modern European works." In the words of one review, it had been the largest artistic migration since "the fall of Constantinople," during which each art- ist had brought with him into exile "a fragment of European thought."[42] Time would tell whether these fragments would fit into American life, but for Pierre Matisse, who helped these artists cohere in a new land, it was "diplomatic triumph."[43] Raymond Mason, an English sculptor whose works were championed by Matisse, said, "My most serious homage is this. When one said Pierre Matisse Gal- lery or even the Matisse Gallery, one did not think of the painter."[44]

BY THE END of the war, the Emergency Rescue Committee helped at least 1,500 refugees escape from France through Spain and provided aid to 2,000 more. For his role, Varian Fry was awarded the French Legion of Honor and after his death became the first American to be posthumously recognized as "Righteous Among the Nations" by the state of Israel. Pierre Matisse who was "no publicity hound" and "lacking in flamboyance" was content knowing he had put the spotlight on the very art the Nazis sought to destroy. Just eighty-five days after the Pearl Harbor attack, as a wave of anti-alien sentiment crested in the United States, Matisse's *Artists in Exile* was a powerful statement that art was an international language, not a nationalistic slogan. His show put the plight of exiles in American newspapers and national magazines like *Fortune*, *Newsweek*, and *The New Yorker* (though it would two years before the establishment of the War Refugee Board).

Pierre Matisse followed his *Artists in Exile Show* the next year with *War and the Artist*, which included works from his father. "At a time when a universal moral earthquake threatens," wrote one review, "it is heartening to come upon the spiritual fearlessness manifested in Henri Matisse's art."[45] Still later in the war, Pierre secretly planned to reverse the refugee trail and cross into fascist Spain to personally provide help to a desperate Joan Miró, whose art he had long championed. Pierre Matisse traveled to see Miró in October 1945 with $3,000 for the trapped artist inserted into a toothpaste tube. To prepare, he had spoken to his sister, Marguerite, who he said had "been in the Resistance and she knew all the networks." She put Pierre in touch with a *passeur* to help cross into Spain. Arriving at his hotel in Andorra, Pierre found four policemen waiting.[46]

"Let me show you how we make people talk," said the officer as a gendarme jabbed a baton into Pierre's gut.

In the end, the money was confiscated, Pierre was arrested, extradited to France, and spent three weeks in a Toulouse jail, where he was made to wax the oak floor every morning at six o'clock.[47]

Though he failed in his mission to help Miró, his other artists were grateful for the wartime efforts of Pierre Matisse. Back in France after the war, Chagall wrote Pierre. "I still think of High Falls [New York], where I was so wildly free." The sculptor Jacques Lipchitz found himself taking the Staten Island Ferry just to try to recreate the moment when he saw New York harbor and was granted a second life. "It's something I could not forget, I can't forget, and I can't describe."[48] Despite his nurturing, Pierre Matisse never claimed to have made anyone's career.

"My artists made me," he liked to say.[49]

CHAPTER TWELVE

Themes and Variations

*"And my song cannot refuse to be; because it is also a
weapon for the unarmed man."*
—LOUIS ARAGON

THE NEWS ACROSS THE FAR-FLUNG battlefields of the Second
World War was bleak in mid-1942, the third summer of the
Occupation. On the European continent the Wehrmacht was in the
ascendant, locking Leningrad under siege and driving into southern
Russia toward the strategic city of Stalingrad on the Volga River. In
the Pacific, Imperial Japan was at its zenith. After drawing the
United States into the war by its surprise attack at Pearl Harbor in
December 1941, Japan liquidated the last U.S. garrison in the Philip-
pines, pushed the British from Singapore, and now threatened
Australia. The seas, too, were a war zone, where German power
threatened America's ability to supply Britain. In June, Chief of Staff
of the U.S. Army General George C. Marshall wrote the "losses by
submarines off our Atlantic seaboard and in the Caribbean—now
threaten our entire war effort. I am fearful that another month or
two of this will so cripple our means of transport that we will be un-

able to bring sufficient men and planes to bear against the enemy."[1] In beleaguered London, General Charles de Gaulle represented the French government-in-waiting.

Neither de Gaulle nor any nation was coming to save France, not in 1942, and maybe not in '43. If the French wished to carry the fight to the German occupiers, it would be up to citizens—men and women—courageous enough to do so. In both zones, unknown numbers of men and women were clandestinely practicing the dark arts of resistance in grassroots organizations. In the north, there were assassinations of German soldiers and officials, sabotage of bridges, mixed-up road signs, and torn-up railway lines. Along the Riviera, brave souls performed reconnaissance, provided safehouses, and forged papers; they provided the *maquisards* with food and medicine. The long, craggy Mediterranean shore was an ideal place for discontent to turn into deeds.

Not everyone who resisted did so by hiding a cache of pistols or improvising explosives. In garages and root cellars, amateur printers mimeographed "newspapers" to counter the Vichy and German propaganda. Still others wielded the pen or the brush. As Resistance networks sprang up across *Zone Nono* in early 1942, an unlikely bond between a modernist poet and an ailing artist nearly thirty years his senior was forming in a grand apartment Nice's Hôtel Régina.

Even in the beau monde of Nice, Louis Aragon was like a Hollywood leading man. The forty-four-year-old Aragon was debonair in his double-breasted suits and robust head of hair. Tall and thin, he could appear as "something of a dandy," but the poet possessed a spine of steel. His wartime poetry was "a month-by-month record of the struggle," which had evolved from the "heartbreak" of 1940–1941 to "defiance and hope" in 1942.[2] It was at this moment he paid a visit to the "Casablanca of the Côte d'Azur." Behind his periwinkle eyes was a first-rate mind eager to know the man behind some of the world's greatest modern art.

Aragon's unflappable looks hid the fact that inwardly he was riled by concern for the safety of his friends and family. On his résumé were two things that made him an enemy of the authorities. Not only had he experimented with Dadaism, Cubism, and Surrealism; he was also an ardent leader of the French Communist Party, which had been outlawed after the armistice. Party members were a particularly tempting target for the Vichy regime, the south being more conservative than the north. "The Communist Party," decreed one right-wing newspaper, "had declared war on Marshal Pétain's national revolution."[3]

Throughout France, security forces conducted house searches, executed warrants, and discovered printing plants. The author of poems like "The Lilacs and the Roses" and "France Listen," Aragon was a target of the Germans and its puppet state. Able to voice his "anger with elegance," the rebel writer was at the same time an inspiring voice reflecting "the mood and the innermost feelings of . . . all those who resisted actively, or even passively." Aragon's writing, said journalist Monica Stirling, included all the emotions of war: "grief, patriotism, resolution [but never] despair."[4] Journalist and writer Alexander Werth declared that Louis Aragon, along with Paul Éluard "came very close to becoming the two national poets of France" during the Occupation.[5] During the war, Louis Aragon and Henri Matisse developed "an important relationship."[6]

Louis Aragon's wife, Elsa Triolet, like Lydia Delectorskaya had been born in Russia. The daughter of Jewish intellectuals, she emigrated to France and later became a novelist in that language. Her writing "was not propaganda, but literature." Still, her works revealed "her political emotions [were] as strong as her personal emotions." Talented, ardent in her convictions, Elsa was also beautiful. She had "thick . . . wheat-colored hair" that she wore braided, in the Russian fashion. She had "a delicate little nose that a Hollywood talent scout wouldn't spurn, a prettily obstinate mouth and chin, beautiful long hands, and a [trace of a Russian accent]," which gave her voice "an exotic element."[7] With Matisse, she spoke French; with Lydia, Russian. In her tiny hat with a veil and her "diaphanous silk stockings," Elsa Triolet could have played the mysterious European heroine in the war movies then being cranked out in Los Angeles.[8] Instead, she was playing that part in real life. In France, even during the war, she was the subject of many a love poem. "When duty and austerity were . . . in the air," observed journalist Monica Stirling, Louis Aragon, "a man in the greatest danger, [refused] to deny the importance of love."[9] Together, Aragon and Triolet were "the romantic heart of the French Resistance."[10]

After changing lodgings several times to evade the authorities, the charismatic couple found themselves in a dreary apartment above a restaurant on rue des Ponchettes, where instead of eucalyptus and roses, the air was redolent of salty odors from the fishmongers; but it was certainly better than their shelter of the previous months.[11] After the French signed the Armistice, Aragon—who fought during the Battle of France—fled with Elsa to Carcassonne before taking their chances back in Paris in March 1941.* There, Aragon was arrested by the Gestapo on May 6, 1941, but subsequently released. In June, he was arrested again, this time with Elsa; they spent three weeks in jail in Tours. Unable to determine their real identities, the authorities released the couple. Their release was just in time. The Nazi invasion of Soviet Russia that same month resulted in a deepening of the hostile relations between French Communists and the German and Vichy authorities. In August 1941, Vichy law decreed propagators of Communist propaganda would merit the death penalty. When Elsa tried to leave Aragon in 1943 "to reduce the chances of being caught" again, he refused; if arrested, they would suffer, and perhaps die, together.[12]

---

* Aragon was on the run as a Communist and because he was a demobilized French war veteran. He had fought the 3ème DLM (division légère mécanique) until the last day of the 1940 military campaign; a veteran of Dunkirk, Aragon was awarded two citations, a military medal and the *Croix de Guerre avec Palme*.

The handsome poet initially sought out Matisse in part to obtain illustrations for a friend's magazine. Aragon was not the first member of the literary *maquis* to approach the eminent artist. The writer Pierre Courthion was meeting with Matisse while he was contributing Resistance-themed poetry to the Swiss review *Lettres* and smuggling rebel leaflets to Switzerland.* For the editor Peter Seghers, another agitator, Matisse contributed drawings to *Poésie 42*, Nos. 1 and 5. Besides his budding friendship with Aragon, by lending his work to these journals, Matisse was "associating himself with other resistance-supporting writers like Robert Desnos, Paul Éluard, and Francis Ponge."[13]

That a fugitive Communist poet rumored to be high up on a Gestapo hit list would endanger his safety to seek out Matisse in the middle of the Occupation seems at odds with the notion by some critics that Matisse was personally guilty of "silence and abstention."† This narrative, as one-dimensional as it is persistent, can be traced from Clive and Quentin Bell in the 1920s, who interpreted Matisse's paintings as completely divorced from world events, to Michèle Cone in the nineties, who went so far as to claim "there is the possibility that Matisse . . . sided with the nationalism of the Vichy

---

* Courthion's wife worked for a British Resistance network. Thanks to his Swiss passport, Courthion was able to transport, at great personal risk, Resistance leaflets and other materials across the border between France and Switzerland. His project with Matisse did not come to fruition.

† Michèle C. Cone. *Artists Under Vichy: A Case of Prejudice and Persecution* (Princeton, NJ: Princeton University Press, 1992), 52. Cone's argument rests on a reed: in 1924 Matisse gave an interview to a Danish art critic in which he is reported to have said he did not find it desirable to have so many foreign artists in Paris. When evaluating Michèle Cone's assertion that Matisse was jingoistic, consider this: the eighty-three students in the Matisse Academy included seven Americans, five Hungarians, seven Russians, three Swiss, one Austrian, thirteen Germans, one Briton, one Icelander, twenty-six Swedes, sixteen Norwegians, and only three French. By comparison, the Salon des Indépendants in 1912 included 1,262 artists, 909 of whom were French. See Marit Werenskiold. *De norske Matisse-Elevene* (Oslo: Gyldendal), 197-198.

régime," and beyond.* A 1990 exhibition review called Matisse's art "wholly apolitical . . . two world wars and the Depression left no mark on his pictures."[14] Elaine Scarry's comment from 1998 that "Matisse never hoped to save lives" echoes this idea, as does David Carrier's remark in his 2004 paper that Matisse's works were "liberated from any vital connection with everyday life."[15]

If Matisse's painting was like Wordsworth's poetry, "emotion recollected in tranquility," critics like Cone chose to see only the tranquil aspects, without examining the turmoil undergirding the work.†

Those who lived under the Occupation and who knew Henri Matisse had a somewhat different take. Both he and Aragon had friends and acquaintances who had been hounded, whose valuables had been looted, who'd been jailed, or, in the poet's case, shot. Matisse knew of the persecution of his Jewish friends and in at least one case wrote a letter in their defense.[16] Matisse was "regularly harassed . . . by the local police threatening to arrest his companion, Lydia Delectorskaya, who was Russian" (like Elsa Triolet).[17]

Like Aragon, Matisse's respect for women was at odds with the Pétainist view that a woman's place was in the home and the Nazi fetishization of the male conqueror. Elsa's golden hair in his poem *La Diane française* is transformed into "the fire of approaching liberation."[18] The golden-haired young woman in Matisse's *Woman Reading at a Yellow Table* wears a blouse of spring-like green, signi-

---

* For a more nuanced take on Matisse, see David Marchese, "Marina Abramovic Thinks the Pain of Love Is Hell on Earth," *The New York Times*, Oct. 26, 2023. In this interview there are echoes of this notion: "I was also thinking how interesting it is that in war, when everybody was making art that reflected what happened, *Henri Matisse was painting flowers.* I finally understand that. The way to fight is not to reflect horror and put your spirit down. It's to create something with beauty that gives you hope" (emphasis added).

† Matisse himself said something very similar: "The idea that an artist feels an experience or an emotion and then sits right down and expresses it is far from the truth, of course. First, that emotion must undergo a period, frequently a very prolonged period, of gestation."

fying hope.[19] On her reading table sits a vase of red flowers, against a blue wall, illuminated by a patch of white—the French tricolor.* Like a modern Marianne, that national symbol of liberty and wisdom, Matisse's woman doesn't hold the book so much as cradle it.

Both the writer-on-the-run and the "degenerate" modern artist knew this was not only a war of national liberation but a struggle against a reactionary foe willing to violently turn the clock back on social and political progress. Another common theme was their patriotism. Matisse steadfastly refused to leave France and saw no reason to offer an apologia for his decision. Aragon was as verbose as Matisse was taciturn, and spoke for both when he said, "[I]n spite of its dangers . . . We see emigration [. . .] as desertion. This country, my country, must not be abandoned at such an hour."[20] When Aragon found himself in England in 1940 after the Dunkirk evacuation, he was grateful to be alive; still, he wrote the line, "Land, but not the land where you were born."[21]

While Aragon saw language "as a weapon" in the military and cultural battle against Nazi Germany, for Matisse it was enough to heed the call he'd first heard in the Great War: "to continue to paint well."[22] The very act of painting—whether a vase of flowers or *Guernica*—"upheld the values of humanism." Remembering the war years, Françoise Gilot explained how the young people were sustained by the poetry of Louis Aragon and Paul Éluard, and how they were encouraged in the knowledge that neither Matisse nor Picasso had fled.

---

*   Matisse's message is similar to *La Bête Est morte!* where it is not the French flag carrying the blue, white, and red, but clothing, bird feathers, festoons, and flowers (see Nayak-Guercio, "The Project of Liberation" dissertation). In *Artists under Vichy*, Michèle Cone recounts when German authorities ordered Francis Gruber to remove the red, white, and blue bouquet in his 1942 painting *Hommage à Jacques Callot*, Gruber painted over the brush strokes, then replaced them with red, white, and blue pointillistic dots, which evaded the censor's eye. French observers during the Occupation would have recognized the deliberateness of Matisse's works.

*Culture had to be upheld like a flag against Hitler's totali-
tarian empire,* against his cult of superhuman Nietzschean
values. *[Hitler] was waging war against civilization as most
understood it . . . [T]ruth had to supersede the unleashed
forces of darkness* (emphasis added).[23]

What appeared to a handful of latecomers as Matisse's noncha-
lance was during the Occupation deemed a steadfastness to live and
work during a national tragedy that made the white-haired artist "a
beacon of hope for the young."[24] Matisse, who considered "the con-
tinuation of culture a patriotic response in and of itself," was a
symbol to the French people that their distinctive heritage could be
extinguished by no enemy.[25]

The refusal of both Matisse and Picasso to flee during the war is
often cited as having an encouraging effect on the French people.
Even though the Spanish-born Picasso was conspicuous in Paris, his
wartime home, it was Matisse's solidarity that was perhaps more mean-
ingful. Intellectuals and artists in France had a great influence on
public opinion and were called *maîtres à penser*, master thinkers. This
was especially true if they were French. As Jennifer Farrell, a curator
at the Metropolitan Museum of Art in New York, notes, Matisse was
"a symbol of France in a way Picasso wasn't; he had a weight that no
one else had."[26] According to his first biographer, Alfred Barr, Matisse
was conscious of this perception, assuming "a public prominence as
a repository of 'French' values during the Occupation."[27]

The importance of Matisse, Picasso, and the Resistance poets remaining in France to hold up the flag of culture is more remarkable
when one considers the actions of other artists. The two most celebrated poets of the war years, Paul Claudel and Paul Valéry, "staked
everything on the German horse."[28] Claudel even penned a syrupy
ode to Pétain with the lines "hold France in your arms and reassure
us with your deep voice."[29] Robert Brasillach, who edited the far-
right *Je Suis Partout* with his poison pen, was astonishingly frank

when he said, "During these years, the French have all more or less been to bed with Germany, and whatever quarrels there were, the memory was sweet."[30] Many of these *grands collaborators* would face consequences after the war, but during the war, the pro-Vichy intellectual elite seemed to outnumber the resistors. This is perhaps not surprising: the choice was to play for safety or risk your life.

Louis Aragon, who had been honored with the Croix de Guerre for his courage in the doomed defense that ended at the beaches of Dunkirk, saw Matisse as "one of the few ramparts still standing among the ruins of civilization."[31]

In their "mute, humiliated country," Henri Matisse didn't need to pull the pin from a grenade or paint *The Charge of the Light Brigade* to have an encouraging effect. "It was not in his nature to be a bomb-thrower," says Jennifer Farrell, "he didn't need to be."[32]

Whether in his paintings or in interviews, Matisse was never going to be a sloganeer. Unlike Picasso, there would be no "skulls and so on" to signify the "tragedy of war."[33] Like the pristine lines he painted, shorn of all that was extraneous, Matisse was known for his thrift with words. Pierre Matisse once explained that his father was from the last generation of French adults who considered it a virtue to communicate with strict economy. This was especially so as a painter. "But what do you want me to say?" Matisse once asked American journalist Dorothy Dudley. "The painter should have nothing to say. His painting speaks for him." To his students he said the same rather more severely: "You want to be a painter? First of all, you must cut out your tongue because your decision has taken away from you the right to express yourself with anything but your brush."[34] The French people knew where Matisse stood. As Aragon stated at the time: "It simply seemed to me that the time had come to be aware of the national reality of Matisse...because he was of France, because he was France."[35]

Matisse provided the illustrations to Louis Aragon as he'd been asked to do, but he also presented the poet with a greater opportunity:

Would he write a preface for a book of drawings Matisse was keen to publish directly to readers, without a gallery's participation? Over the first quarter of 1942, Aragon set his observations of Matisse down on paper while the artist made dozens of sketches of his interviewer. Day after day, in the line of Matisse's "blue hunter's gaze," their roles reversed. "He, whose portrait I thought I was drawing, had started to draw mine," Aragon said.[36] If Louis Aragon was haunted by the security forces out to find him, Henri Matisse was haunted by daily pain and the mortality it portended. Aragon was moved to write about the pain as the "invisible third party always present at their interviews... at the back of the studio."[37] At the end of March, Matisse described to him a physical breakdown. "My dear friend, I am still where you left me on your last visit—namely, in bed." What followed was a catalog of ailments so severe it left the artist unable to hold his pencil: hidden pleurisy, incipient otitis, dizzy spells, and a temperature of 38.5. "I have a little 'volumetto' that I want to send to Elsa; I should like to decorate it, but I'm too exhausted at the moment.[38]

Making matters worse, Matisse was beset that spring by the liver and stomach pains he had described in letters to Pierre Bonnard. In May 1942, Aragon and Elsa were forced to flee Nice. As he left the city, Aragon sensed the death of his friend was near. "The stranger was nipping and snarling silently in the shadows."[39] As the courageous couple made their way to a safehouse in Villeneuve-lès-Avignon, Matisse lay bedridden, eating nothing but purées and vegetable broth, and unable to paint. His Nice doctors took X-rays but feared a further operation would be fatal. Lydia did what she could to comfort him. "Since 1942 he had had a night nurse," Lydia told a friend:

> But when it was too hard for him, he sent her after me.
> If asthma medications did not help, I sat down by his
> bed, took his hand and simply, but persistently asked,
> what 'back thought' bothered him. He usually denied,

but ended up finding some restless, relentless thought.
We 'bit it through,' and I instantly proved to him that
none of it was disturbing.[40]

In July 1942, on hearing the news of the gravity of her father's
condition, Marguerite Matisse-Duthuit took the train from Paris
and installed herself in Cannes. She was close enough to supervise
her father's care yet far enough away from what was essentially
Lydia's household. Their common task did not resolve the differences between the two women. Individually, they were "magnificent
human beings" possessed of a "grandeur of spirit" and a "total dedication to Henri Matisse . . . but that they could have any kind of
rapprochement was out of the question."[41] The tension in the room
was both personal and medical. The ensuing consultation of doctors,
including one down from Paris, determined it was gallstones, not
cancer as feared. Still, the doctors' prognosis remained dire.

On September 26, 1942, Monique Bourgeois, a twenty-one-year-
old nursing student, held the strap on the crowded tram as it labored
its way up the steep hill away from the port and its breeze. Once in
the exclusive Cimiez neighborhood, the abundance of trees would
provide welcome shade, but until then the warm early autumn sun
baked the tram's tin roof. Mademoiselle Bourgeois had seen an ad-
vertisement at her nursing school placed by Lydia: "The painter
Henri Matisse is looking for a young and pretty night nurse." "I'm
certainly young," she had told the head nurse, "but I'm not so sure
about the rest."[42]

Monique Bourgeois's lack of assuredness was hardly surprising
given her upbringing. Her father, seriously wounded in the Great
War a generation earlier, had been unable to provide for his family.
He nevertheless barked orders to his wife and daughter like an officer
amid a German trench assault. By the Second World War, Monsieur
Bourgeois was dying in a military hospital, and young Monique's
dream of attending art school was dying with him. "The war had

completely ruined our family," she said.[43] Her mother had no income and no veteran's benefits. At nineteen, Monique was given a waiver to commence nursing school early, which she did despite not having fully recovered from "a tubercular lung."[44] When her father died, he left her a legacy of timidity and a deficit of confidence. The young woman needed to help her widowed mother survive—"the situation was critical"—so she accepted the night nurse position.

Unlike Louis Aragon, Monique Bourgeois had no idea what she was getting into.

After a moment to revel in the cool of the Régina's marble lobby, Mademoiselle Bourgeois took the elevator to the seventh floor and rang the bell. Madame Lydia opened the door. "Tall, and very beautiful," she recalled. "Blond, almost white hair." Lydia addressed the woman with formality. Where once the door to Matisse's world had opened for Lydia, now it was she who opened the door for a younger woman. The imposing Russian beauty and the imperious hotel were not the only shocks. There in the front parlor stood the colossal six-foot-tall *kouros*—a ancient Greek statue of a young man, quite anatomically correct. "The penis—POOF—right in my face!"[45] Holding her nurse's jacket over her arm, Monique awaited her instructions. "The patient needs a great deal of care," Lydia began, "the bandages will need changing. At night you will stay close to him and read . . . And then he will tell you himself what you have to do."[46]

Then Mademoiselle Bourgeois was shown into the sickroom.

In the dimly lit bedroom, on an old painted iron bed was "a rather stout gentleman [in] an apple-green nightcap" that sat askew on his mostly bald head. Monsieur Matisse adjusted his gold-rimmed glasses and fixed his eyes on his new caregiver. Monique donned her nurse's jacket. That first night, the patient didn't say much other than to order her to the library to fetch a book. Unfamiliar with the contents of Matisse's library, she pulled the first book she found. "No, that one's not good for you. Go put that back where you found it," he ordered. Finding the second book acceptable, Matisse had her read to him into the small hours of the night, until at last he fell asleep.[47] In time a nightly ritual was formed. Monique would feed the painter warm milk and wheat germ, change the dressings on his abdomen, and bathe him. Over the ensuing nights, as Matisse struggled to sleep, tossing, sighing, and mumbling, the pious young woman would read from books she knew better: the Bible and St. Thomas Aquinas. Finally asleep, Matisse would "raise his hand as though he was drawing and then, dreaming he had made a mistake, [he would take] his left hand as if to erase what he had done."[48]

That autumn they grew more comfortable with each other. In his well-timbered voice and with his economy of words, Matisse "talked about his travels to Russia and Tahiti"; he showed her old photographs of his parents, of himself and Amélie when they were young—before they "no longer saw eye to eye."[49] He told Monique about his children and grandchildren. Matisse asked Monique about her life. When he learned she painted, he asked to see her work.

"Monsieur, why are you looking at my drawings upside down?"

"If you want to see the strength of the lines, the force or depth of the strokes, it's good to turn a drawing upside down."[50]

Prevented from art school by her family's poverty, Monique Bourgeois was soon studying perspective from one of the western world's greatest artists. One day Matisse took her into the small marble room, surrounded by his paintings.

"What do you think of them?"

"Excuse me, sir, I like the colors, but the forms are terrible."

Appreciating her candor, Matisse often repeated her comment.

Slowly, Matisse's strength improved. The stomach muscles that had been severed in the surgery the previous year in Lyon healed to the point Matisse would walk assisted by Monique across the street to the Roman ruins. Sensing that it exhausted Monique as much as it did him, Matisse rented a car and Monique drove him around.

One day Matisse telephoned.

"I want you to pose for me."

"I didn't know what to say," she later told filmmaker Barbara Freed, "when I was a child my parents told me I was ugly."[51] *Why did you choose me?* she asked Matisse. "I have a nose like a candle-snuffer and a mouth like a holy water basin."[52]

Days later, Monique, who had never worn makeup in her life, was being dressed by Lydia in a sleeveless chiffon frock and festooned with costume jewelry.

"Sit down," said the artist.

"Not bad, not bad at all." Matisse began to paint.

Like Amélie Matisse many years before, when Monique saw the finished painting, she was disappointed; she told Matisse so.

"If I wanted something that captured reality," he replied, "I'd take a photograph."[53]

As with the nightly routine, the painting sessions evolved into a pattern. "I had to sit there for two or three hours erect, without moving ... absolutely silent. During the sessions I saw nothing but the back of the easel."[54] On breaks, Matisse would tell stories, repeat curse words he'd heard Lydia mutter, "that Cossack," he'd say, "that Bolshevik." He gave the young woman bread ration tickets, bags of sugar—a wartime luxury—and life advice.[55]

"You know, Monsieur Matisse, I don't consider you merely a patient. You're like a grandfather for me. I never knew my own, but I picture them like you."[56] That "simple sentence," Monique later said, "touched him deeply."[57]

She, too, was touched by Matisse's friendship. In his company, Monique Bourgeois was free of the weight she had borne since "the mockeries I had endured as a child."[58] "The days I spent with him were wonderful," Monique said. "I gradually shed the feelings of inferiority ... I really blossomed during that time."[59] Matisse loved her long dark hair, and in his drawings and paintings, the timid country girl became statuesque, her head held high, her bare arms conveying strength and elegance. The young woman who knew only impoverishment looks as if she belongs in the expensive gowns and jewelry.

As with other models, Matisse did not "depersonalize" his subject but "allowed himself to be led on by the singularity" of the sitter.[60] In an armchair, against a red-checkered background, the black-haired woman wears a robin-egg gown clasped at the shoulders by medallions. Wearing a gold necklace and bangle, she could be a woman of power in ancient Alexandria or modern Paris. "To be Matisse's model," said Lydia Delectorskaya, "is to mediate between the artist and the dream."[61] Monique Bourgeois was no longer hanging on the strap on the bus, self-conscious of her appearance and unsure of her place in the world.

She was *The Idol.*

The Idol was the second of four Matisse paintings of Monique Bourgeois; the others are *Monique in a Grey Robe, Monique in Green Dress and Oranges,* and *Tabac Royal.*[62] "It was Monique, more than any other model," Lydia told biographer Hilary Spurling, "who renewed his determination to push forward once again as a painter into unknown territory." In *Interior with Bars of Sunlight,* the "most radical canvas of the whole sequence," the model is left unpainted. Amid the geometric bars and rectangles is "a young-woman-shaped space of bare canvas." It was as if Matisse had a metaphysical sense that his sitter was unsure of her place in the world; that she perhaps knew it was not posing in an armchair in a grand apartment of a modern artist; and that her soul would be filled in elsewhere. "His real feelings came out in his paintings," Monique said.

MONIQUE'S PRESENCE DURING the night and her inspiration as a model during the day was the prescription for a return to artistic vigor. By the time Matisse had helped secure a scholarship for Monique to return to her nursing studies—when he should have been convalescing in bed—Matisse had instead produced 158 drawings for *Dessins: Thèmes et Variations.* Using charcoal, India ink, black Conte crayon or pencil, Matisse's themes featured women and still-life subjects. The subjects were not new, but the technique had achieved a new level of elegance. "The physical touch of the pen," wrote Matisse authority Jack Flam, "is as carefully modulated as a violinist's work with his bow." The finest of the drawings, according to Flam, combine a "breath-taking virtuosity" and a "heightened emotional pitch."[63]

Rather than ranking drawing with pen and pencil as a lesser art, Matisse considered such work a predicate to his goal as an artist. In "Notes of a Painter on His Drawing," Matisse recounted how line drawing was "the purest and most direct translation" of his emotion because it was a purified medium.[64] As Monique Bourgeois noted, Matisse could go months without an artistic inspiration. In the long months of his convalescence, he had been inspired by a rebel poet and a reluctant model. His art soared free once again, but his body remained mostly bedridden. If *Thèmes et Variations* were to be his last work, Matisse seemed at peace with this. "For a year now," he wrote Pierre, "I've been making an enormous effort in drawing. I say 'effort' but that's a mistake, because what has occurred is a 'floraison' after fifty years of effort."[65]

When Matisse and Louis Aragon submitted *Dessins: Thèmes et Variations*, the publisher objected to the long preface being written by an avowed Communist. Titled "Matisse-en-France," the poet's preamble praised the painter for bravely remaining in France. Together with Matisse's images that "proclaimed his continuing aesthetic proclivity in the face of challenge," the book was "a work of barely disguised defiance."[66] Aragon refused to publish under a pseudonym. The publisher gave in.

"I consider it an honor," Louis Aragon wrote Matisse:

> that this text should appear alongside your drawings, and particularly these drawings which have been this year a large part of my life and thoughts, and practically the only human consolation for the life of horror that now surrounds us.[67]

CHAPTER THIRTEEN

A Measure of Sovereignty

God forge us a peace, that's my desire!
Then I'll be quickly refreshed for one,
Wiped clean of the stain of unhappiness,
In France again, there, taking the sun.
—CHARLES D'ORLÉANS[1]

"Our military defeat should not admit by extension a
general rout of all the best things our civilization has
produced."
—JEAN BAZAINE[2]

DESPITE THE PREDICTIONS OF TWO local doctors that the winter of 1942 would be his last, Matisse continued his productive run.[3] The next source of inspiration came from Matisse's friend, André Rouveyre, who suggested a new *livre d'artiste*, a project the artist could work on while sitting in bed.* Matisse had previously il-

---

* "Artist's books" were not simply illustrated books. They included original engravings, etchings, woodcuts, or lithographs and were printed under strict supervision

lustrated the poems of Stéphane Mallarmé and provided etchings related to Homer's *Odyssey* for a limited American edition of James
Joyce's *Ulysses*. Instead of a wandering hero on a decade-long odyssey,
the subject of this new artist's book was a fifteenth-century imprisoned aristocrat, Charles de Valois, duc d'Orléans.[4] *The Poems of
Charles d'Orléans* would include select poems of the duke written in
Matisse's hand complemented by the artist's illustrations.

Matisse's interest in the ill-fated royal might have seemed an odd
choice given his strong republicanism. But as he studied the poems
of Charles d'Orléans, he felt a keen kinship, and his outlook brightened. "I inhabited his poetry. I was with him . . . the spirit, the life
comes from the poetry itself."[5] Perhaps destiny played a role in Matisse finding secours with an ancient poet, as he had in his friendship
with the contemporary French poet, Louis Aragon. Perhaps what res-
onated with Matisse was the historical similarity of his time with the
duke's era. Half a millennia before German panzer divisions cleaved
France in two, another invader, England's King Henry V, crossed
into France and won a shocking victory through masterful battlefield
tactics.[6] On a rain- and blood-soaked field at Agincourt, in October
1415, English longbowmen exacted a gruesome toll on the French
knights whose mounts, weighted down by armor, floundered in the
mud as arrows rained down. The victorious king and his men seized
lands and killed and imprisoned civilians and warriors alike.

No prize taken by the English on that muddy field was of greater
value than the Duke of Orleans, the nephew of King Charles VI, and
a *prince du sang* who was in the line of succession for the French
throne. For the next quarter century, this valuable "blood prince"
languished in a succession of English prisons, including the Tower
of London. Charles spent his time in captivity learning English and

---

in limited numbers—usually fewer than 300. These were luxury items that gar-
nered good money for artists who did them, including Braque, Ernst, Miró, and
Picasso, to name a few.

becoming a notable medieval poet in English and a symbol of resistance for the French. *In the Forest of Long Waiting*, Charles's melancholy rumination on captivity, he feels himself lost in a maze of "diverse paths," trapped physically and mentally in the "room of his thoughts." Five hundred years later, Pierre Reverdy, the Surrealist poet, used a similar metaphor in his book of poems *Chants des morts* to describe the feelings of loneliness and entrapment in occupied France, where people were "hostages . . . in exile within the borders of their own country."[7]

> *All my blood like vinegar*
> *I've taken my measure*
> *On the knotted rope of hard luck*
> *And now I sleep until the next alarm*
> *In the tunnel riddled with false exits.*[8]

By the time Charles d'Orléans returned to France as a middle-aged man, he spoke "better English than French."[9] His ignominious capture at Agincourt and subsequent ransom was in time eclipsed by his ballads, chansons, and rondels, which are still read today. His trove of poetic jewels—"*fleurons* on the crown of immortality"—was not all Charles left to posterity: on May 27, 1498, at Reims Cathedral, his stepson received the unction of chrism and oil from the Holy Ampulla, put on the silk hose, satin tunic, and velour cloak decorated with fleurs-de-lys, and was crowned King Louis XII.

Sitting up in bed, wearing a sweater over his pajamas, and balancing a board across his knees, Matisse jotted down his ideas.[10] For his first illustration, Matisse sought a poem that would serve as a "declaration of sympathy between [Charles d'Orléans] and myself."[11] Matisse and Rouveyre picked the rondeau "Il me Pleust Bien."

> *It well pleases me*
> *(In this journey)*

> *I wake to see*
> *It was all mine.*

The simple rondeau, as art scholar Rodney Swan points out, serves as an acceptance by Matisse of the poet.[12] There is also the sense in these four lines that even in exile—even as a hostage—there is a self-direction of the spirit; something that cannot be taken. This notion is supported by Françoise Gilot, who said that despite being "in exile within the [his] own country," Matisse held that "a measure of sovereignty was still within each individual."[13] Matisse's sense of unity with the aristocratic poet is summed up in a line from another letter to Rouveyre: "I am hooked on to this Charles."[14] Illustrating these carefully selected poems with his "colorful borders, ornamental arabesques and scrolls" was liberating both physically and artistically, for he could work notwithstanding his illness and express solidarity in the very choice of his subjects.

As Matisse worked and convalesced, conditions along the Riviera in 1942 worsened. "There's nothing left in France," wrote Matisse's sister-in-law Berthe, "no thread, no nails, no materials, not to mention anything to eat."[15] Behind Nice's pastel-colored façade burned the fires of far-right hatred. For their hardships, some Niçois wanted someone to blame. The city's Jewish refugees, called by the newspapers "stateless," "dependents," "Israelites," provided an easy target. Right-wing youths shoved Jews from ration lines and joined the Service d'Ordre Légionnaire, a pro-fascist militia. On Sunday, February 21, 1942, in the Roman arena atop Cimiez, just feet from the Hôtel Régina, 2,000 men knelt on one knee, raised their right hand, and shouted in unison when asked a series of questions.

> "Are you against skepticism and for faith?"
> *OUI!*
> "Are you against democracy and for authority?"
> *OUI!*

"Are you against Jewish leprosy and for French purity?"
OUI![16]

The torchlit spectacle was followed by more alarming news. In May 1942, Louis Aragon and Elsa Triolet learned of the executions of their comrades at Fort Mount-Valérien near Paris; in June, Heinrich Himmler set a quota of 100,000 French to be deported east; that same month news that André Derain and Maurice Vlaminck had consorted with Nazis reached Matisse. In July, food rations were reduced; in late August, the Vichy Prefect of the Alpes-Maritimes Department, Marcel Ribière, ordered the first roundup of Jews in Nice, where perhaps 25,000 refugees faced official persecution and random violence. The prefect delighted in anti-Semitic ordinances, which emboldened the thugs of the Parti Populaire Français. Under the command of collaborator Joseph Darnand, the PPF attacked Jews in the streets; one young mother was brutally murdered along the Promenade des Anglais.[17] In September, the "*relève*" system was established whereby three Frenchmen were forcibly sent to German factories in exchange for the release of one French prisoner of war. Meanwhile, plans were being drawn up for the direct conscription of French workers in Germany.*

Since the Franco-German Armistice, conditions in the free zone had allowed for a measure of sovereignty, but on Wednesday, November 11, 1942, the last vestige of freedom was taken.

At noon that day, walkers on the beaches of Nice heard the roar of an aircraft engine. Despite the autumn sunshine, the anniversary of the end of World War I was a somber day as every village, town, and city in France marked Armistice Day. An hour earlier, at eleven o'clock in the morning, church bells rang as solemn crowds

---

* Russell, *Matisse: Father & Son*, 235. This moment is also the beginning of a gap in the letters in the archives between Pierre and his father (from October 1942 to July 1944 there are no letters), perhaps reflecting greater censorship or postal mismanagement.

gathered at local memorials to the "glorious fallen." Veterans in their tricolor pins and ribbons, some with canes, with scars visible and invisible, paid their respects. War widows dabbed swollen eyes with handkerchiefs.

Armistice Day was always a day of mixed emotions. National pride for the victory in the war of 1914–1918 and the memory of the cry of the valiant defenders at Verdun, *"On ne passe pas!"* ("They shall not pass!"), was tempered by a hollow feeling knowing the victory over the Kaiser's army was secured by the sacrifice of a generation of the sons of France. In 1942, the eleventh hour of the eleventh day of the eleventh month was a moment even more fraught, and not just because two-fifths of France was under a puppet administration.

Three days before in the predawn hours, 65,000 Allied troops came ashore in Vichy North Africa at three landing zones across the vast southern Mediterranean coast. The Operation Torch landings were at Casablanca in Morocco, and Oran and Algiers in Algeria. The next day, the French government severed a diplomatic relationship with the United States of America that was forged in 1778. Until that day, the United States had diplomatically recognized Vichy France hoping to steer the regime away from total subservience to Nazi Germany. After Pierre Laval, the Chief of Government of Vichy cut ties with Washington, the American government acted swiftly. Agents from the Federal Bureau of Investigation entered the French Embassy in Washington as the Treasury Department moved to freeze French assets. The U.S. Coast Guard seized Vichy vessels in American waters. "We have not broken relations with the French [people]," President Franklin D. Roosevelt was careful to say. "We never will." Still, the American president complained to the press that Laval was "still speaking the language prescribed by Hitler."

Roosevelt was right. In the hours following the Allied landings, Laval drove through sleet and snow to Munich for an audience with the Führer. The German dictator kept him waiting for several hours before dismissing him like a schoolboy. Laval's mistake? The failure of Vichy forces in North Africa to repel the Allied invaders. At 7:00 a.m. the next morning, November 11, twenty-four years to the day after the end of the First World War—German and Italian troops launched Operation Attila, crossing the Demarcation Line to occupy the whole of France.

Following the muted Armistice Day speeches by officers from the Ville de Nice and prefecture, the quiet crowds crossed the coastal road from the massive stone memorial carved into Castle Hill to stroll the Promenade des Anglais below. No one seemed worried about the noise above. In the absence of air raid sirens, it could be assumed the plane overhead was part of the day's commemoration. Yet, as they squinted into the sunlight, an Italian military aircraft flying low over the Bay of Angels came into view pouring leaflets from its open bomb bay. Countless pieces of white paper shimmered in the sun and moved together as one, hither and yon, pushed by the gentle breeze. Children grabbed them in the air and shook them loose from the palm trees. Mothers and fathers took them and read: "*CITOYENS DE LA ZONE NIÇOISE!*" it began in both French and Italian, "*because of the Allied landings, [the Italian Army is] temporarily occupying the demilitarized zone.*" The crowd murmured. "Not one of you should think of taking hostile actions against us."[18] A few young men threw their leaflets down, spitting out *sale Macaronis!* (damn Italians!). Such an invasion had been feared by the citizens of the city since the beginning of the war. From Cimiez to the pebbly beaches and from Cagnes-sur-Mer in the west to Saint-Jean-Cap-Ferrat in the east, everyone knew the contested history of Nikaia/Nizza/Nice, and what that portended in the current struggle. As early as September 1940, Henri Matisse had written Pierre to tell him of the "widespread fear that Nice may be occupied at any moment."[19]

That moment was here.

With American and British forces now just across the sea, Nice was not only going to be occupied, but risked becoming the next theater of the war.

Within hours, truckloads of helmeted troops from the *Piave* motorized division poured into the nerve center of Nice. They were followed by the infantry divisions of the Italian Fourth Army: *Legnano* and *Lupi di Toscana*, the Wolves of Tuscany. These first units were part of the 150,000 strong *Regio Esercito* (Royal Army) deployed to the zone east of the Rhône following the Allied invasion of North Africa. The inhabitants of Nice found the Italian soldiers very different from their Teutonic allies. The collars of their military shirts were unbuttoned; their trousers were dusty and stained; their belts hung loose. Many went about with their hands in their pockets—something not even the footmen at Agincourt would have dared do. Like the locals, they were "severely short of food," recalled Pierrot Matisse; they "fraternized, played music, and [sang] love songs."[20] A "pervasive immorality," complained a military chaplain, led the soldiers to forget "their more important duties." In bedrooms and bordellos, the result was *loquacità imponderata*—"careless loquaciousness."[21]

Notwithstanding their disheveled uniforms, and their reputation as *brava gente*, the good fellow as agreeable occupier, the *Regio Esercito* turned the pristine coastline of Nice into a heavily defended beachhead. They laid minefields, unfurled barbed wire, set up machine gun nests, and fortified positions with mortars and anti-tank guns. French civilians were forbidden their own coastline.[22] *Nissa La Bella* was now *Nissa la Fortezza* (*Nice the Fair* was now *Nice the Fortress*).

On December 13, 1942, a month after the German-Italian invasion, Matisse handwrote and illustrated the "Ballade au Duc de Bourbon" to send to André Rouveyre.

> *My dear cousin, with good heart I thank you*
> *For the white rabbits you gave me.*
> *And furthermore, I confirm as true to you,*
> *As for the rabbits that I loved,*
> *Several years have passed, for me they are*
> *Forgotten.*

In this short poem, copied from the medieval French ("Mon chier cousin de bon cueur"), Matisse is lamenting that as the war years dragged on he "had forgotten what freedom and hope were like," and yet the rabbit, a "recognized (Greco-Roman) symbol of fertility and regeneration," was a "coded symbol for the future."*

By working with a medieval subject, Matisse was able to evade Vichy censors, as the ancient era of monarchs and clerical power predating the Republic fit nicely into the regime's retrogressive triptyque of *famille, travaille, patrie*.[23] In doing so, the fascist nostalgia for an era of the Middle Ages' strongman and his docile peasantry was subverted to a ransomed hero, a poet who used language not as a weapon but to reflect the richness of the culture that brought him into being. As for the censors, Louis Aragon, who shared Matisse's fascination with France's medieval past, explained that the use of coded language of the *trobar clus*—the courtly poetry of the troubadours embedded with hidden clues—was a way for the French to communicate under the noses of the uncomprehending Germans.[24] Numerous letters written by Matisse during the war were stamped *"ouvert par les autorités du controle."* By coding his messages, he hoped nothing would be redacted.[25]

---

* Victor Dancette and Jacques Zimmermann. *La Bête Est Morte! La Guerre Mondiale Chez les Animaux.* Illustrations by Edmond-François Calvo. Artistic direction by William Péra. Paris: Editions de la Générale Publicité, 1944, 1945. Also published as a single album by Générale Publicité in 1946, Futuropolis in 1977, and Gallimard in 1995. A similar symbolic use of the rabbit appeared in *La Bête Est Morte! La Guerre Mondiale Chez les Animaux* (*The Beast Is Dead! World War Among the Animals*), a comic book meant for French children to process the war. The narrator is a grandfatherly rabbit with a wooden leg (a war wound). In recounting "the frightening torment which shook our poor world" to his young rabbit audience, the Germans are portrayed as wolves. In one panel, the illustrator depicts two wolves pointing rifles at a female rabbit who has been put onto a train and a third wolf who is carrying away a child-rabbit. The Russians in *La Bête Est Morte!* are shown as polar bears, and Italians are hyenas, the opportunistic scavengers of the field who mistake wounded France for "a cadaver."

In Aragon's poem cycle of Middle Age France, *Brocéliande*, the forest of the title is not a misty land of knightly adventure and rescue, but a dark and dangerous exile where the oppressed survive in order to plan the retaking of their homes. In another poem from the cycle, a prayer for a parched land, it isn't the deliverance or rain the poet wishes for, but of the long-sought Allied landings. The drought-stricken people pray for a storm with the heaviness of iron (*"génerosité du fer"*). The storm of steel would not fall until D-Day on the Norman coast; until then, like the lady for her knight, France waited.[26] Aragon, according to scholar Jennifer Stafford Brown, buried "trenchant illusions . . . in the apparently innocuous setting of medieval myth."[27] The French under the Occupation "expressed their thoughts and feelings in a coded fashion."[28] Louis Aragon, whose very life was in danger, agreed: "In 1942, it seemed wiser not to dot one's I's." A poem titled "Pour un Chant National" became "Pour un Chant." Writers used pen names or published anonymously; Matisse too well-known to hide, sought to illuminate through his illustrations.*

Whether through Matisse's appropriation of Charles d'Orléans or Aragon's medieval poems, the censors didn't have the linguistic or historic sophistication, or the time, to decipher the coded messages.

Matisse was "adamant and vehement about the absence of symbols in his work," but this was a way to get outside the parameters of the prying eyes. [29] Recalling an exhibition in Paris in May 1943, Françoise Gilot described to journalist Charlie Rose how wartime artists expressed themselves within the confines of an enemy occupation. She told him how German officers would appear at the openings to scan the art for anti-Nazi sentiment.

---

* Louis Aragon and Matisse used coded language in their correspondence. When Aragon wrote from Villeneuve to tell Matisse of the roundup of Jews there, Matisse wrote back, "There must be a harsh wind blowing through the streets of Villeneuve in a temperature that often drops to freezing."

> What we did was to do it symbolically! I had a painting . . .
> a still life, it was called '*The Hawk*' and there was a taxi-
> dermized hawk in the first plane and knife and scissors,
> you know, things that are hurting. And behind was a land-
> scape of Paris.[30]

Gilot's piece didn't ruffle German feathers; perhaps the officers were used to seeing the Teutonic eagle with a swastika in its talons.

Striking a different tone from Gilot's knife and scissors are Matisse's white rabbits in "Ballade au Duc de Bourbon" representing resilience and renewal. Rodney Swan noted that to further sharpen his symbolism, Matisse created eight rabbits, a number that connoted baptism in numerology. The octagonal baptisteries of medieval French cathedrals were where birth of life was celebrated. This image is "a powerful code calling for the rebirth and resurrection of Matisse's country, a vision of liberation."[31] As for the color, of course Matisse's choice of white was deliberate, for white is the color of animals in captivity.[32]

The heraldic lily Matisse employed on Tériade's *Verve* cover from June 1, 1940, as the Germans were racing toward Paris is another powerful symbol that Matisse not only used repeatedly throughout the Charles d'Orléans *livre d'artiste*, but also embedded in two of his paintings done in 1943.[33] In the two works, both titled *Lemons Against a Fleur-de-Lis Background*, a vase holds forget-me-nots, and a rust-rose background is decorated with the white lily. Lemons are placed around a green vase. The choice of green, too, carries meaning as the color of spring, of hope. In *La Bête Est Morte!* as Aparna Nayak-Guercio notes, "Pea-green, apple-green and reseda . . . permeates the French countryside . . . evok[ing] an atmosphere that is vernal, fresh and full of vigor."[34] In Matisse's painting, the hopeful green is countered by the bitter, acidic lemon. Above the fray of the competing symbols is the queen, the fleur-de-lys, "epitomizing the longevity of French cultural heritage."[35] These paintings and illustrations were like a riddle, said Françoise Gilot. "Cryptic allusions were a necessity at the time." Notably, the background is partly made up of red brick, an uncommon backing surface in Matisse's works, here representing the hearth.

Like his courtly subject, Matisse believed art to exist on a plane above the earthly fray of swinging maces in the muck. "As long as some painters continue to be interested in our ideas and our work," he told Picasso and Gilot, "we will not be dead . . . to remain alive in the mind of another artist" is to "ensure immortality."[36] The belief in beauty's ability to withstand and outlast was at the heart of Matisse. According to Gilot, during the Occupation the very act of painting was a way for Matisse to "uphold the value of humanism." Matisse believed that to inform artists of the future was a sort of immortality. At the same time, he was divining an artist from the fifteenth century, updating a medieval poet for the World War II generation while placing himself "in the context of a lengthy literary history."[37] The thoughtful artist existed in the continuum of not only the future but the past. "I share the greatest intimacy with Charles d'Orléans," he wrote Rouveyre, "I continue to find new satisfaction in [the poems]."[38]

When he put his name on the volume of the poems of Charles d'Orléans, Matisse was consciously connecting the war-weary people of France with a hero from a wounded nation five centuries earlier; to one scholar, this was Matisse's "symbolic call for unity and regeneration."[39] Being the proxy of the knightly poet from the mists of Agincourt let Matisse add to the cultural armory and to do his part in the Resistance.[40]

CHAPTER FOURTEEN

The War Within

*It was a time when we listened tensely to the barking
of dogs in the depths of the night; a time when ... para-
chutes, laden with weapons and cigarettes, fell from the
sky ... a time of cellars, and the desperate cries of the
torture victims, their voices like those of children ...
The great battle in the darkness had begun.*

—ANDRÉ MALRAUX AT MEMORIAL
FOR JEAN MOULIN, 1964

O N THE EVENING OF TUESDAY, February 9, 1943, a new art gallery opened at 22 rue de France in Nice. The opening soirée,
attended by no less than the departmental prefect, was hosted by the
gallery's manager, Colette Pons, twenty-seven, and recently divorced.
Galerie Romanin was named after her boss, the artist and collector
whose private collection adorned the walls. Romanin was fifteen
years Colette's senior, and under her spell. As guests mingled with
coupes of fizzy champagne in hand, the handsome couple discussed
their plans to make the gallery a mecca of art along the Côte d'Azur.
Soon its walls would hold works by Dufy, Utrillo, Renoir, Marie
Laurencin, and the great man who lived on Cimiez, Matisse. Like

its magnificent scenery, the social life of the French Riviera was mostly intact well into 1943. Figures from the art world and the intelligentsia paid visits to or kept homes on the coast. Jean-Paul Sartre and Simone de Beauvoir in Saint-Jean-Cap-Ferrat, Man Ray in Antibes, and the couturier Christian Dior nearby.[1] So no suspicions were aroused when Romanin leased the space and subsequently opened his showcase with the help of his beautiful companion.

No one that evening could have imagined that the gallery owner was at that moment the single most important figure in Occupied France. For Romanin was not in Nice for the purpose of running an art gallery, and his surname was not Mercier, and he did not teach in New York. Romanin was Jean Moulin, the chief emissary of General Charles de Gaulle who had parachuted into Provence the year before to find only an "unstructured body of courage" in the south. From the apartment above the gallery, Moulin would, over the next few months, do the impossible: unite the various clandestine forces and place them under the command of General de Gaulle. Under Moulin's leadership the men and women who were French resistance fighters became the French Resistance.[2]

Not even Colette Pons knew the true Romanin. "He took me to see big names in painting like Nicolas de Staël or Pierre Bonnard, then disappeared. We arranged to meet in the evening, but I was not to know who he was meeting or what it was."[3] Pons was entrusted with the keys to the apartment. On several occasions over the first half of 1943 unknown men came to her to leave letters and packages for her patron, whom they called "Max" or "Rex." The young woman asked no questions.

Moulin's mission was helped immeasurably by the very enemies he hoped to defeat. One week after the opening of the gallery, the Vichy government announced the *Service du travail obligatoire* (STO)—a mass exportation of French labor to German war industries. All French men over twenty now "faced the choice of taking a train to Germany or the path to the mountains."[4] Betrayed by their government, the STO immediately became a recruiting tool for local Resistance groups. Doctors wrote fraudulent medical certificates, and sympathetic town and village authorities ignored no-shows at the registration offices. Thousands of others simply fled for the hills rather than entrain for virtual slavery in Germany. Encampments sprang up in the Alps, the Massif Central, and the Pyrenees. Learning to shoot and to make Molotov cocktails were "the grocer, the truck driver, the schoolteacher, the policeman, men from this district and from the next, men from the water's edge and men from the farms lost in the plains."[5] At night, the sound of distant flak guns reverberated off the hills; dogs barked; sometimes a plane engine could be heard in the distance. They were the *maquis*. "Driven from their jobs and homes, hungry and embittered, these young people [would] be the most hardened and most dynamic part of France's 'secret-army.'"[6]

The *maquisards* eagerly joined in the anti-fascist mayhem already being conducted by established Resistance groups like *Combat, Libération*, and *Franc-tireur*. Rail lines were sabotaged at Cagnes, Cannes, Èze, Golfe-Juan, Roquebrune, and Nice. Shops and apartments owned by collaborators were attacked with improvised bombs, offices of the STO were machine gunned, military telephone lines were cut, and enemy fuel reserves were set alight. The *maquis* stole what they needed, whether it was food, cigarettes, or weapons. Over the course of a single night, April 27–28, 1943, two Italian officers were wounded in Nice, a thrown bomb killed a German soldier in Lyon, and a Wehrmacht major was found dead at 4:00 a.m. in a street in Clermont-Ferrand.[7] Along the Riviera and in the hills above, in 1943 alone, there were 204 incidents of sabotage against German, Italian, or Vichy targets.[8]

The leaflets, as disparate as the groups fighting the enemies—Communist, anti-fascist, and Gaullist—carried a common message: "Liberation from the external enemy, liberation from [Vichy's] National Revolution!"[9] To achieve this goal required sound tactics and at least some coordination among Catholics, Communists, and the *maquis.* "Strikes, sabotage, the fight against deportation for forced labor, are directed against Hitler. Unity of all the French . . . action against the enemy!"[10]

The dangerous work of uniting the heads of internal Resistance with the Free French leadership in London could not have been done by Jean Moulin alone. The British Special Operations Executive had set up networks or circuits throughout the southern zone. With code names like "Carte" and "Donkeyman," each circuit needed at least a trio of commander, radio operator, and courier.[11] The brave souls who infiltrated into France by parachute or submarine were Brits, Czechs, Danes, Poles. Whatever their nationality, they all spoke flawless French, *sans accent.* They had been trained in "parachuting, map reading, 'silent killing,' use of a variety of weapons, and/or operation of a wireless." They knew plastic explosives, timed fuses, and the weak points of the Axis infrastructure. They also knew their fate should they be discovered was a concentration camp, torture, or death. The SOE circuits, in turn, needed locals to collect the agents from the night sky or the dark waters, to shelter and arm them, and to put them in contact with others in their network.

Jean Matisse was one such *résistant.*

Rather than shiftlessly moving about France during the war, there was a method to the movements of Henri Matisse's eldest son. In the Battle of France, Jean Matisse's unit had been overrun and he had been taken prisoner.[12] Perhaps because the Germans were moving at speed, he was able to escape. After the armistice, Jean's son, Pierrot, was told his father was lying low "somewhere between Bordeaux and Toulouse."[13] In fact, Jean was at several locations. An apartment on rue de Clamart in Paris was the site of underground activity; not even Pierrot was allowed there unless prior "arrangements were made."[14] At Issy-les-Moulineaux, some five miles southwest of Cathédrale Notre-Dame, Jean stored explosives. Wherever he was, Pierrot noted Jean often slept during the day and went somewhere at night.[15] At Montauban near Toulouse, Jean could feel at ease. "There are no Germans or Gestapo in this area," he told his worried wife. Louise still fretted: she knew there were spies and informants.[16] "Others are counting on me," Jean said, concluding the discussion. As the Allied invasion neared, Jean went to Nice, where he stored dynamite in his sculptures and taught recruits how to use firearms in the basement of his villa.[17] Once, he collected and sheltered a British agent using the *nom de guerre* Charlot and safeguarded the agent's four suitcases. Excited to be at the edge of this world of false walls and secret passwords, the teenaged Pierrot could only speculate what was in the suitcases: a radio receiver, explosives, detonators, grenades? Perhaps a Sten submachine gun, or better yet, a Thompson, like those carried by American gangsters?[18]

As the infiltrations increased, Jean Matisse took quarters directly across the road from a rocky cove in Cap d'Antibes. The rhythm of the waves was like a metronome, and the salty scent of the sea mixed with the kitchen odors from the apartments above. Tired of "the usual diet of fish and beans," Jean's son, Pierrot, took to foraging for snails and crabs. One day, he spotted a crate of oranges bobbing in the surf, then another. He stuffed as many oranges as would fit in the little bag attached to his belt. The next day, he walked the beach again. This time, the incoming waves pushed by the southern winds from North Africa carried oily wreckage. Scanning the rubbish, Pierrot spotted a figure "like a big bag of rags" wearing clothing of "pale blue-gray [with a red cross] and beautiful long hair . . ."[19]

The dead nurse was proof that the Mediterranean Sea was a watery war zone, crisscrossed by British submarines, German freighters, Kriegsmarine sub-chasers, and small craft. The deep water just meters off the long and craggy shoreline made it ideal for infiltration by sea. Ideal as it was, the seaborne agents still needed local Resistance to collect them onshore. The two sides, on either side of the sea, needed to communicate. Pierrot watched as his father dialed into the forbidden BBC channel on his regular radio and listened with great concentration for the coded messages therein:

Uncle Arthur has the smallpox.
The beautiful girls are still waiting.
The strawberry jam was too sweet.

Jean Matisse wasn't just listening idly.

"My father was involved with British intelligence," Pierrot told an interviewer, "assisting British spies. On more than one occasion, we set out in a small boat . . . a solid heavy rowboat with oars, a temporary short mast with a small lanteen sail . . . [We] rendezvoused with a British submarine off Cap d' Antibes on the French Riviera."[20]

Under the light of the moon and without a word, Jean and Pierrot shoved the rowboat across the smooth stones the French call *galets.* They rowed in silence out of the cove into the Mediterranean, parallel with the tip of the cape. After some time, Jean asked Pierrot to take bearings from the few lights onshore. They stopped rowing and waited. A dead silent submarine, running on battery power, surfaced. The hatch opened, and three men in civilian clothes, each carrying a suitcase, without a word boarded Jean's small vessel.[21] The rowboat scraped to a halt at the rocky cove, the men climbed out, crossed the deserted street, and entered Jean's apartment. As the men smoked and talked in hushed voices from the living room, Pierrot made a kettle of coffee from roasted black beans and strung a clothesline in the kitchen to dry the French and German banknotes from a suitcase that had fallen into the water.[22]

"We brought British spies ashore and hid them in our home. It is a miracle that we all survived the war," he said.*

Indeed, the risks were great. Taking photographs of the coastline could lead to arrest. A camera was one thing, but a weapon or radio

---

* Newspaper interview with Pierre H. Matisse. Rest of quote is: "On D-Day, I was living in Normandy and when the Nazis began to be pushed back by the Allies, I had encounters with them that should have gotten me killed." Also note Louise stayed for a time in an apartment in l'avenue de Clamart and other times at the home in Issy.

receiver could lead to a death penalty.[23] Helping British SOE agents would be a death sentence, but one not carried out until after lengthy torture to get names of others in the network.

Like his mother and sister, Jean Matisse was disgusted by the Nazi occupation and Vichy acquiescence. He may also have been motivated to join the Resistance to salvage some military dignity after he was defeated and demobilized following the shocking events of May and June 1940. Jean likely knew his father's expressed dismay at the French soldiery, including his own son.* Matisse had written Pierre reminding him of the important role women played in the Great War.

> But in this war it was the men who puffed themselves up in the family circle compensating for the failure of their efforts in the army. They make themselves as unpleasant as possible when they get back home. I know of a similar case here (emphasis added).†

Jean, who struggled more than his siblings to connect with his father, may have sought a measure of honor, not in the official army that had collapsed around him, but in the army of shadows.

The record is mostly silent as to what exactly Henri Matisse knew of Jean's underground activities (or Pierrot's abetting those activities). Still, there are clues. Françoise Gilot seems to think he had an idea of what was going on. "Matisse's family was part of the war within the war. *It was not by chance that Matisse's son Jean belonged to the underground* . . . Jean Matisse was also involved at the house—the

---

* Henri Matisse said something similar about World War I. "In the war of '14-'18 it was the women who emerged with a new assurance because they had to take on responsibility and they didn't forget it." Spurling, *The Conquest of Color*, 189.

† Russell, *Matisse: Father & Son*, 192. Matisse made a similar comment to Dorothy Dudley in the late 1930s. "Look at the women aviators," he told her. "They are marvelous, as good as men." Dudley, "Notes on Painting."

house at Issy-les-Moulineaux was full of explosives" (emphasis added).[24] Throughout the Occupation, Matisse quietly sent money to his family, at certain times increasing the allowance. In letters to Camoin and others, he expressed anxiety over Jean's well-being. And, of course, Henri Matisse himself had joined the local branch of the American-led Emergency Rescue Committee and mentioned to one of Varian Fry's men that he'd harbored refugees in a barn.

When the fugitives from forced labor took to the hills, and the underground networks, helmed by those like Jean Matisse, began to take their toll, the ensuing disorder challenged Marshal Pétain's embrace of law and order in *Zone Nono*. As if by Newtonian physics, the slackening of Pétain's grip over Vichy was met with a tightening of repression. French police arrested 9,000 people in 1943 for "Gaullism, Marxism, or hostility to the regime"; the Germans arrested 35,000.* Just as the *maquis* improvised, so did the extreme right. In Nice, just two miles away from Galerie Romanin, boutiques, and luxury hotels, a leader of a different sort than Jean Moulin was busy unifying an army in his image.

Worried that its junior partner was losing its ability to provide security, Berlin forced Vichy to name Joseph Darnand, the Nice-based right-wing militia leader, as Secretary-General for Law Enforcement.[25] The promotion of Darnand, a dedicated fascist, "marked a turn from professionalism to vigilantism . . . the final paroxysm of a moribund dictatorship."[26] The former carpenter held full power over French police, gendarmerie, secret service, and collaborationist militia. As the top police enforcer, Darnand was handed vast control over the courts-martial and the means of punishment. He would be

---

* Paxton, *Vichy France*, 297. Gaullism might be defined in the words of Jean Moulin: "To prosecute the war; to restore freedom of expression to the French people; to re-establish republican freedoms in a state which incorporates social justice, and which possesses a sense of greatness; to work with the Allies on establishing real international collaboration, both economic and social, in a world in which France has regained her prestige."

judge, jury, and literal executioner. Should Pierre Laval be sacked by Berlin or Vichy, Darnand was next in the line of succession to be "acting Chief of Government."[27]

On the last day of February 1943, a large crowd witnessed a sinister ceremony at the Casino Municipal in Nice. Under a massive portrait of Marshal Pétain, Darnand was given his own army.[28] His foot soldiers were to be called the *Milice Française* (the French Militia). The ranks of the paramilitary were filled with toughs, fanatics, and street fighters—they were government-sanctioned shock troops. Knowing the local dialects and hiding places, the *Milice* were soon more feared that the Gestapo or the SS.

The Nazification of this French force was also revealed by its symbol: the *Milice* insignia was the lowercase Greek letter gamma [γ]. In French, the swastika is known as the *croix gammée* because it resembles a cross made of four uppercase letters gamma.[29] The semiotic link to the swastika was known to Darnand, who chose the symbol, and to all those who wore the sign on their black berets and armbands and who printed it on banners and posters. Similarities between his paramilitary and the German *Schutzstaffel* were not accidental. In August 1943, Darnand swore an oath of loyalty to Hitler and was commissioned as *Sturmbannführer* (major) in the Waffen-SS. Unlike the rebels, who slung their rifles, *sans uniform*, over short-sleeve knit shirts and marched in baggy, pleated wool trousers or shorts, the *miliciens* wore a uniform of military-cut khaki shirt, dark blue trousers, a black tie, and a dark blue "Alpine" beret.[30] Leather gloves turned back at the cuffs completed the uniform. Wanting to outsource security to Darnand's militia, Nazi officials exempted the *miliciens* from STO service. By 1943, Vichy France was increasingly a police state working in concert with Nazi Germany.

The order of battle settled, the violent fratricide commenced. *Miliciens* were assassinated as they sat at café tables and strutted down public streets. From Marseilles to Nice and everywhere in between, *miliciens* were hunted. By late November, *Combat* reported twenty-five killed and twenty-seven wounded in Resistance attacks. The most prominent victim was Philippe Henriot, the Vichy regime's Minister of Information and Propaganda. The "French [Josef] Goebbels" took to the radio twice daily to urge the French people to support the German cause. He was killed in the bedroom of his apartment in the Ministry of Information in the predawn hours by a group of fifteen *résistants* wearing the uniforms of the *Milice*.

Darnand's army retaliated by killing several well-known anti-Nazi politicians, intellectuals, and prominent Jews.[31] Georges Mandel, a critic of collaboration, was handed over to a *Milice* commando, who executed him in the Forest of Fontainebleau.* At another location, seven Jewish prisoners were shot dead.† At Grenoble, city of glovemakers and students, Darnand's men killed eighteen intellectuals in one week; on a country road, they assassinated a professor and his wife.[32] The owner of the democratic newspaper *La Dépêche* was shot dead on a Toulouse street, and elsewhere two French senators were murdered.[33]

Darnand's Nazi confederates eagerly joined in the reprisals. At Corrèze, the bodies of murdered *maquis* were ordered burned at dawn. The local women, strangers to the victims and dressed in black, marched to the site under moonlight and were there to shame the German executioners at first light.[34] In Nice, two martyrs were

---

* Fontaine Thomas. "Chronology of Repression and Persecution in Occupied France, 1940-44. *Mass Violence & Résistance* (November 19, 2007), http://bok2s.sciences-po.fr/mass-violence-war-massacre-resistance/en/document/chronology-repression-and-persecution-occupied-france-1940-44 (accessed May 17, 2021), ISSN 1961-9898. "During the days that followed, throughout France, members of the *Milice*, goaded by their leaders to strike against persons linked to the organization of the crime (even remotely)," kidnapped and killed members of the Resistance, but also Jews and prominent individuals simply associated with "Gaullism" (Marcot et al., *Dictionnaire Historique de la Résistance*, 636).

† French collaborationist Paul Touvier, who had worked with Klaus Barbie in Lyon, chose at random seven of the thirty Jewish prisoners in his custody; he then took them to a cemetery and had them shot. See Morgan, "L'Affaire Touvier."

hanged from the streetlamps at the arcade at Galeries Lafayette. Schoolchildren were forced to walk past the grisly sight, lest they harbor resistance in their hearts.[35] In Tulle, ninety-nine inhabitants were hanged by an SS detachment following a *maquis* attack on a German garrison. Seeing the large number of ladders being set up, one witness thought the authorities were "laying out or repairing telephone or electricity lines."[36]

The Gestapo and the *Milice* set up torture chambers in airless cellars, casernes, and requisitioned villas. Prisoners would wonder why they'd been given access to a bathroom only to suffer the trauma of water torture—a torment even worse than the boots, fists, rifle butts, and cigarette burns. Over one of the interrogation rooms at Villa Lynwood in Cimiez, Nice, were the words from Dante's *Inferno*: "Abandon all hope ye who enter."[37] Being herded onto a cattle car to Germany would also be reason to give up hope. By the summer of 1944, historians estimate that 80,000 Frenchmen were deported to the Third Reich. A "moat of blood" separated the Vichy collaborators from those willing to die to oust Germany from France.[38]

The Franco-French war between the *maquis* and the *Milice* in the Comté de Nice played out while that area was under the nominal control of Nazi German's other junior partner: Mussolini's Italy. The Germans had long been critical of Italian laxity in the pursuit of Jews, Communists, and rebels. As an Allied invasion threatened to bring open warfare to the Riviera, the Germans deemed the Italian-made coastal defenses insufficient. In July, they ordered the requisitioning of the iconic Hôtel Negresco for a review by German General Gerd von Rundstedt, who arrived via armored train.[39] Berlin's anxiety over its Italian ally was well founded. When news spread that Mussolini had been removed from power on July 25, 1943, the streets of Nice erupted in joy; before their officers dispersed the crowds by firing into the air, the Bersaglieri and Alpini in their floppy black berets allowed themselves to be treated to kisses (and more) by local young women.

The secret army was not all assassins and bomb throwers: others performed reconnaissance, provided safehouses, forged papers, and provided food and medicine. Some mimeographed "newspapers" in their garages or cellars to counter the Vichy-German propaganda. Still others indulged in acts of passive resistance, such as listening to the BBC, wearing black for mourning or the tricolor of the French flag. Men walked by whistling the beginning four notes of Beethoven's Fifth Symphony—"... –"—which stands for *V* in Morse code.[40] The letter *V* was also painted on walls from Marseille to Nice—along with the two imperatives: *Victoire* and *Vengeance*.[41]

Whatever their means, resistors faced denunciation from their neighbors and coworkers. Denouncers (*délateurs* and *délatrices*) would describe the act of perfidy—using the anti-German slur "*Schleu*," for instance—then say *répétez-le* (pass it on). Other times, they would threaten, *J'irai le dire à la Kommandantur* (I'll go tell the Germans). It was perhaps such treachery that led to the arrest of Jean Moulin. On the afternoon of Monday, June 21, 1943, at a villa in Caluire, Moulin was arrested. He was taken to Lyon, just a few kilometers from the clinic where Henri Matisse was patiently resuscitated in early 1941. There Jean Moulin was put slowly to death. As Klaus Barbie, the Butcher of Lyon, watched on while stroking the cat perched on his lap, Moulin suffered. "Jeered at," reported his sister later, "savagely beaten, his head bleeding, his internal organs ruptured, he attained the limits of human suffering without betraying a single secret, he who knew everything." As Malraux later said, "The fate of the whole Resistance hung on the courage of this one man."

On the day that the Gestapo agent handed him writing materials because torture had left him unable to speak, Jean Moulin sketched a caricature of his torturer.

CHAPTER FIFTEEN

Falling to Earth

And their red blood flows
Same color same burst
He who believed in the sky
He who did not believe in it.
—LOUIS ARAGON[1]

O N JUNE 1, 1943, HENRI MATISSE received his old friend Tériade at the apartment in the Hôtel Régina. As always, Tériade was impeccably dressed, his skin burnished by the sun that shone over his home, Villa Natacha in nearby Saint-Jean-Cap-Ferrat. Tériade's slicked-back hair and bushy eyebrows were still black, but time had turned his moustache gray. It was for the influential publisher that Matisse had created "the war number"—the *Verve* issue they raced to print and publish as the Nazis approached Paris. Now, four long years later, he wanted another cover design from Matisse.[2] Lydia greeted the visitor and walked him through the spacious hall supported by neoclassic columns and guarded by the six-foot-tall *kouros*.[3] The apartment was a sanctum from the noise of the city below. A marble fireplace rose from one end of the stone and wood-inlay parquet floor. Fresh-cut flowers stood in vases; a small bench sat before the fireplace along with a table and chairs, upon it the local newspaper. Through the French windows with panoramic views of the city and the bay, sunlight flowed into the space.

In the studio, the two men chitchatted over tea, while Lydia brought in the four designs and placed them on a table. For the *Verve* special edition to be titled *De la Couleur* (*On Color*), the works were certainly apropos. Tériade was struck by the new work, finding them "dazzling... brimming with clanging color."[4] The images also bore the Matissean metaphysic: like *Chromatic Symphony*, they were at once brightly colored and foreboding. But unlike the national symbolism of the white lily against the black force of invasion, the images Matisse shared that day seemed to speak to individual peril.

With the Allies preparing to invade mainland Italy, it was only a matter of time until RAF Lancasters and Halifaxes and B-17 Flying Fortresses of the U.S. Eighth Air Force zeroed in on Italian-held Nice and the surrounding areas. There was a critical railway viaduct at Anthéor, as well as other obvious targets: the Nice-Breil line, the auto bridge at the Pont du Var, and the Michel Wagon Works. The air war would be a prelude to a ground invasion, as everyone expected. The first air raid sirens and the promise of the American President Franklin D. Roosevelt—"the landing in Italy is not the only landing we have in mind"—led the region to gird itself for the blows to come. The violence that started with Hitler's invasion of Poland in 1939 now threatened those who lived along the French Riviera.

The Nice opera house was converted into an evacuation center, and the city casino into a warehouse for clothes and furniture for the soon-to-be displaced.[5] Plans were being made for moving schools to towns out of harm's way and for the evacuation of children and the elderly. In case of attack, the Hôtel Régina, which had been used on occasion by Italian occupation troops, would make a conspicuous target. The imperial edifice of white marble sat less than a mile from another target, the Nice-Saint-Roch rail depot, so the decision had already been made by Lydia and Matisse to evacuate. Tériade would be one of the last friends to visit Matisse at his luxurious flat at Cimiez, but before he bid the artist adieu, maybe for the final time, he chose his cover from the four designs.

The Fall of Icarus.

As Tériade gazed down at the artwork, he could not have known it would entrance and challenge art critics for decades to come. Dominating the center is a jagged human figure "set out in white like a corpse" in a slanted "shaft of black light." The figure's limbs are akimbo as he free-falls through an infinity of "deepest blue."[6] Perhaps it was, as Matisse had described himself, "an acrobat without a net"; perhaps it was a parachutist in the moonlit night. Either way, it was a disquieting image: on the figure's upper body was an explosion of pure red. The falling figure was like a man shot in the back, arched with pain, the exit wound on his chest.[7]

The ominous mood of the piece also matched that of its creator. For Henri Matisse the summer of 1943 was "the darkest moment of that whole period," according to Aragon.[8] The fourth summer of the Occupation saw worsening conditions across France. Food rations were reduced, and the STO was sending Frenchmen to German factories. The Allies' indirect assault on Hitler's Fortress Europe was laboring interminably from Tunis to the islands of Pantelleria and Lampedusa, and then Sicily. Meanwhile, Germans were strengthening defenses in Italy while engaged at the Battle of Kursk on the Eastern Front. "I am affected by the same things that affect the community," Matisse wrote in a letter to Tériade.[9] He later reiterated the war's impact on him in an interview with a young American journalist.

"Many painters have told me that the war for instance has in no way affected their painting."

"It is impossible," Matisse replied.

"It is impossible that an artist should not feel the after-effects of the war. That makes him take things more profoundly."[10]

Not only must he worry about his own safety, but Matisse worried about his children. Marguerite was back in Paris, and, perhaps suspecting she had joined the Resistance, he wrote, "Courage, my dear Marguerite, I often take courage myself from remembering how you have suffered all your life."[11] The last missive from his daughter, in May 1943, was an aggrieved one full of reproach over his indulgence of Lydia's ever-growing role.[12] Due to censorship and the war's impact on postal services, Matisse had not had word from Pierre since October 1942, interrupting a transatlantic correspondence that was more candid and heartfelt than their face-to-face interactions.* The son who stayed in France, Jean, "alarmed his father by his activities in the resistance."[13] The artist's outburst of creativity witnessed by Louis Aragon and Monique Bourgeois seemed to falter as the war dragged on.

At the end of June, Lydia and Matisse moved into a dodgy old Provençal villa in the hill town of Vence. Henri Matisse had cheated death once and did not want to perish due to an American or British bomb dropped from 20,000 feet. On rue St. Jeannet in Vence, his neighbors were grazing goats and Foyer Lacordaire, a convalescent nursing home run by Dominican nuns.[14] While not religious herself, Lydia was sometimes referred to by Matisse as "Saint Lydia"; she earned that nickname as she handled the lease from the owners, packed up the Nice apartment, promoted their housekeeper, Josette, to cook, and retained a night nurse. "Without her," Matisse admitted, "the house no longer exists."[15]

To provision Matisse's largely vegetarian diet would not be easy. Gardeners pulled up flowers and replaced them with vegetables during the war, but the rocky and sandy soil yielded carrots "the size of a pinkie finger . . . [n]othing grew."[16] Lydia borrowed a bicycle on

---

* For postal interruption between October 1942 and July 1944, see Russell, *Matisse: Father & Son*, 235. On several occasions, the elder Matisse told Pierre he finds it possible to express thoughts and feelings in his letters that are impossible for him to discuss in person.

which to scour Vence for zucchinis, tomatoes, carrots, radishes, and eggplants, and she bargained with the town butcher for a supply of produce from his own garden.[17] Establishing a new home was especially difficult due to Matisse's ill health, which at this point, to use Hilary Spurling's phrase, was akin to "intensive care." As he himself told Pierre, "I no longer have the muscles that normally hold the left side of the stomach in place, I am seriously incapacitated. On top of that I am subject to spasms that give me great pain."[18] In a letter to Marguerite in July, Matisse rather more graphically described himself as "like someone hit by a shell blast . . . with the wall of his stomach blown away."[19]

Lydia by this time was far removed from the unsure young family assistant. She was companion, caretaker, and the de facto chief of staff of studio Matisse. Her beauty had not diminished in the years she had spent as the artist's model and companion. "Her almond-shaped eyes," observed Françoise Gilot rather lyrically, "were as blue as mountain lakes in the snowscape of her face."[20] Before their evacuation, while illustrating the poems of Charles d'Orléans, Matisse came as close as he ever did to publicly revealing Lydia Delectorskaya's central importance in his life. This "rare public declaration" was Lydia's "demure-looking" image situated with a medieval ballade that began with the line "Beautiful, good, peerless, pleasant" and ended with "The one who can comfort me / For I take you as my sole mistress."[21] Matisse had lived as a married man at the Régina, so perhaps the memory of Madame Matisse's presence was a factor in Lydia staying in the housekeepers' quarters. But Villa Le Rêve, the modest ochre-colored villa in the mountain village, was hers, theirs, the site where they may have realized they would not part before death.

In time, the artist made the interior of Le Rêve into his own miniature kingdom, as he had always done. Upon arriving at the studio, the journalist Marguette Bouvier noted that "Congolese tapestries hang on the wall" and an interior decorated with:

his shells and Chinese porcelains, his moucharaby [Moroccan textile screens] and his marble table and all the strange objects with which he loves to surround himself. Thus, he reconstructed...this Matisse-atmosphere which he needs in order to live.[22]

Inside was a large room, the light of the relentlessly bright mornings subdued by the perforated curtains, on the table was a blue China pot with white polka dots that "looked almost alive." Oil paintings adorned the walls. A pineapple sat on a wrought-iron garden seat. Shells, wine goblets, pewter mugs, a rocaille chair, Asian porcelain, a striped bergère, and amphoras were the props that had appeared in so many of Matisse's celebrated paintings.[23] These objects took on "a dreamlike quality in the half-shadow" to Françoise Gilot. They were "like ghosts in the wings of a disused theater."[24] Her young son, Claude Picasso, put it rather more directly: "His rooms are just like his paintings."[25] To Louis Aragon, these props were to Matisse as words were to a poet.[26]

In the ground-floor bedroom, everything was in easy reach without moving. A revolving bookcase with dictionaries and books from Baudelaire to the Bible, with Kipling, Poe, Mauriac, and Pearl Buck in between. In one labeled drawer were medicines; painkillers Matisse called "happiness pills." Atop the bedside table stood an assortment of lead and graphite pencils, carefully arranged and "impeccably sharpened." The quiet was broken when a pigeon fluttered from its perch on the bed's footboard to a nearby chair. "No one," observed Marguette Bouvier on her visit to Le Rêve, "could be less bohemian than this artist who requires and studies his comforts like a *grande bourgeois*."[27]

He may have retained some of the image of the *grande bourgeois*, yet there was an earthiness at Villa Le Rêve that suited the seventy-four-year-old artist. In the Provençal town overlooking a valley of red-tiled roofs, Henri Matisse was closer to nature than he'd ever been in the rococo hotel rooms and high-ceilinged flats of Nice. One opened the iron gate of the simple villa and entered a lush courtyard garden of laurels, cypresses, and olive trees.[28] "A walk with Matisse," said Bouvier, "is a real botany lesson. He knows all sorts of things about the growth of fruit, the nature of the soil."[29] Under the palms, salamanders scampered about through the acanthus thistles. Instead of the archaic Greek statue standing sentry were palms that shaded all four corners of the square villa, their high fronds making a silky sound in the breeze. Just a few steps from his bedroom was the garden, where Matisse would sit wearing a floppy brimmed hat, a scarf round his neck, or a shawl over shoulders. He'd puff a cigarette or cigar and watch the doves and Milanese pigeons flicker above the watchful eyes of his cats, Minouche and Coussi. "I thought I was in Tahiti," he wrote to Louis Aragon, "when the fragrance of woodland or burning grass is wafted in the breeze, I can smell the wood of the islands."[30]

Guests were surprised that the artist, so physically enfeebled, maintained his artistic verve. Even sitting upright in bed, Matisse appeared "regal" and "communicated energy." He moved about not with a heaviness, but with "an élan, a sense of weightlessness," that was matched by "the youth of his light blue gaze through his glasses."[31] Like Françoise Gilot, Marguette Bouvier found Matisse a man of "surprising intelligence and a dynamism which age has not touched." While peering at his listeners with his glasses perched on the bridge of his nose, Matisse spoke "with clarity and without a single superfluous word."[32] As he listened, the intense gaze of his blue eyes was like that of an "entomologist look[ing] at a cricket or a scorpion."[33]

Another visitor in 1943 was the photographer Henri Cartier-Bresson, who had escaped a German prisoner of war camp, lived on a riverbank with other members of the Resistance, and got hold of false papers. Thus provisioned, he made his way to Vence and to Matisse's Villa Le Rêve, where he found Matisse simultaneously "present and self-absorbed."[34] Matisse didn't say much to the younger artist, allowing him to take photos while he sketched. It amazed Cartier-

Bresson to see Matisse hold his tame white Milanese pigeon in his left hand, while drawing it with a pencil in his right. It was like an interrogation, the photographer recalled, the two were eyeball-to-eyeball.*

"You can't live in a house that's too well kept," Matisse had once remarked to Tériade. "You have to head for the jungle to find simpler ways of doing things that don't stifle the spirit."[35] In this pocket jungle, Matisse was evolving. He had utilized cut paper in the past, to mock up sets and costumes for a ballet called *Rouge et Noir*; as stand-ins for the final mural of *The Dance II* for the American collector Albert Barnes; and for the fleur-de-lys "war number" issue of *Verve*.[36] Now, by marrying an old technique to create anew through *papier découpage*—paper cutouts—Matisse found a means to furnish succor to his spirit.

Just as Matisse had required assistance for his easel painting, the process was a household task. Too weak to stand for long periods at the easel, Matisse asked Lydia to brush unmixed gouaches—thick watercolors—onto sheets of heavy white paper. There was no shading; the paper was saturated with color: leafy green, lemon yellow, cobalt blue, violet, matte black. The pure color of the Linel paints recalled the Fauve works on which pigments were "squeezed directly from the tube."[37] In bed, or in his wheelchair, Matisse would take the sheet in his left hand while his right worked the razor-sharp scissors. Using large tailoring shears or the smaller embroiderer's set, Matisse wielded both with the same fluidity and sureness as his drawing pencil. "There is nothing to resist the passage of the scissors," marveled Annelies Nelck, who studied under and modeled for Matisse in Vence. "Scissors can acquire more feeling for line than pencil or charcoal," explained the artist.[38] "Since my sickness," Matisse told Tériade, "I have led a new life." Calling his works "collages," Matisse went on:

---

* Russell, *Matisse: Father & Son*, 236-237. Although Matisse allowed Cartier-Bresson to photograph him, he forbade the photos from being published during the war. "Personal celebrity is out of place. I want to be recognized only for my work."

Tuesday, I was grouchy, in a bad mood. Madame Lydia handed me a pair of scissors, and a warmth came over me; I did not know exactly where I was going, but I just let myself loose and cut everything with precision.[39]

If Matisse subconsciously returned to the jungles of the south seas to achieve the simplicity of the cutouts, while he brandished the shears, he may also have felt a kinship with the textile artists of his childhood home in Bohain-en-Vermandois.* Textiles—screens and tapestries—served a present utility, too, as they hung over windows at the villa to dampen the strong daylight, which caused Matisse discomfort. With shutters closed, and fabric over the windows, Matisse curved the paper around the snapping blades, slivers and triangles of colored paper fell to the floor, like scraps of fine cloth.

Gone was the fluid arabesque of hip and arm; instead, the shapes that preoccupied him that summer were jagged, serrated, and star-like. Examined closely, one can see the graphite where Matisse sketched the form before cutting along a different line.[40] Once cut, the colored shapes were pasted or pinned together and then pinned to the wall where Matisse could examine it, careful that the sunlight didn't fade the fugitive dyes.[41] It had been Matisse's studio practice to photograph each step of his paintings, a

---

* Matisse's enthusiasm for fashion most likely grew from an early introduction to textiles during his childhood in Picardy. The artist was born in 1869 in Le Cateau-Cambrésis (in a weaver's cottage) and grew up ten miles south in Bohain-en-Vermandois, a manufacturing and textile town. By 1879, the town had forty-three textile mills producing various fabrics, including dress materials for fashion houses in Paris. In addition, Matisse came from a long line of textile workers: his mother, grandfather, and great-grandfather had all been weavers. At age 22, Matisse left northern France to attend art school in Paris, bringing with him an awareness of fabric and design. The artist claimed that while studying at the École des Beaux-Arts between 1895 and 1899, he "built up [his] own little museum of swatches" See Jared Ledesma, Matisse's Couture Closet and "La Conversation," from Open Space, the online platform—now defunct—of the San Francisco Museum of Modern Art, Nov. 17, 2014.

task of Marguerite's, later undertaken by Lydia. In the case of the cutouts, pinholes and pencil marks evidence the movement of the shapes relative to each other until the arrangement was, in the eyes of the artist, a finished work.

Designing the cover options for *On Color* inspired Matisse to print his own art book. Rather than illustrating the work of others, as he had done for the medieval poet Charles d'Orléans, this would be an entire book of découpage, cut from sheets of prepainted paper and arranged by the artist.[42] These compositions created at Villa Le Rêve in 1943 were an independent art form; the technique was no longer a means to an end but an end in itself.[43]

Earlier Matisse had discovered that "color *was* structure," that by pairing warm yellow with cool purple, for example, the flat surface would proceed and recede as if the image danced on different planes.[44] Now, like a mathematician obsessed with solving a lifelong problem, he arrived at another breakthrough. For Matisse, the solution to the centuries-old argument over the primacy of line versus color was neither the pen nor the paintbrush: it was a pair of shears. "Cutting directly into color," he said, "reminds me of a sculptor cutting directly into stone."[45]

Matisse had always sought to eliminate that which was not essential, and now it seemed he had reached an end point. "The cut-out" he said, "is what I have now found the simplest and most direct way to express myself."[46] That Matisse had again broken free into new artistic territory was not lost on Tériade. From the moment he saw *The Fall of Icarus*, the publisher realized the import. "This was a historic moment in modern painting. Matisse had just discovered a new pictorial device."[47]

Of all the visitors that first summer in Vence, none meant more than Monique Bourgeois, his former night nurse and model who had left his employ due to a recurrence of tuberculosis. She was convalescing at the rest home across the street from Ville Le Rêve. "Fate," she told filmmaker Barbara Freed, "destiny, serendipity, call

it what you will, played an unexpected role in my friendship with
Monsieur Matisse.

> I had never been physically strong... I became seriously
> ill. My mother sent me to recuperate at a convalescent
> home run by Dominicans. *In Vence, of all places. Directly
> across the street from Matisse's villa.* In my time with him,
> I had always felt... free, lighter, able to breathe. His stu-
> dio, his home, was a haven of peace (emphasis added).[48]

Even as she herself recovered, Monique did all she could for the
man who treated her with grandfatherly affection. "I was his night
nurse, his day nurse, and his model... for his compositions of
gouache cut-outs, I helped him to paint large sheets of Canson paper,
using various colors and shades from his palette."[49] Alongside Lydia,
"the women became his hands," helping him "cut into pure color"
as he sought to unify sculpture and painting, the decorative with the
fine, and the pen and the brush.[50] "You will simplify painting," Matisse's teacher Gustave Moreau had prophesized in 1895.[51]

As Matisse contemplated the text that might appear in the book
accompanying these audacious new creations, he reached for the Old
Testament. In his looping, decorative hand he wrote out lines from
Psalm 92:

> *The righteous shall flourish like a palm tree:*
> *he shall grow like a cedar in Lebanon.*
> *Those that be planted in the house of the Lord*
> *shall flourish in the courts of our God.*
> *They shall still bring forth fruit in old age;*
> *They shall be fat and flourishing.*[52]

Despite being removed from the dangers of Nice to the seemingly peaceful interiors at Le Rêve, there was, as always, a war within

Matisse. His "adamant and vehement" desire to keep his work free of symbols weakened as the Second World War raged around him.[53] Matisse had eschewed symbolism in his art—a lemon was just a lemon, not a symbol for all acidity—but the war, from the fall of Paris in 1940 to the Allied aircraft now patrolling the Mediterranean, seemed to change that.[54] To Louis Aragon, *The Fall of Icarus* possessed an "undoubted symbolic significance."[55] Tériade, too, recognized when he first saw the spiky human figure in free fall amid the four similar designs that for all the surface simplicity of the cut-outs, Matisse's new creations held a beguiling complexity. The deep blue, charcoal black, and red splash are the only colors save six stars of yellow, their jagged and uneven points stabbing in all directions. "From Matisse's own confidential comments," reported Aragon, "the yellow splashes, suns or stars according to mythological interpretation, stood for bursting shells in 1943."[56]

One year after his *Artists in Exile* show, Pierre Matisse was interviewed in *The New York Times*. To the art reviewer, he was the "fifty-seventh street impresario," but to his father, he was a devoted son who knew the art world and the artists within it:

> It is not in direct representation that the artist gives his utmost on the subject of war . . . But into his pictures may come the madness, the pathos, the grief, the upside-downness of values; the revolt, anxiety, and fear that accompany a state of war.[57]

As if by some unspoken connection to his son across the Atlantic, with *The Fall of Icarus* Matisse had matched the madness, the pathos, the grief, and the upside-downness of France as it tumbled through history tied to its militaristic neighbor—Germany—and its ruinous ambition.

CHAPTER SIXTEEN

The Hunting Ground

"As the war raged on and I sat by the sea and saw deep into the heart of humankind."
—CHARLOTTE SALOMON

"Manhunting season is now open."
—VICHY PROPAGANDIST PHILIPPE HENRIOT

MUSSOLINI'S ITALY WAS WITHIN WEEKS of being knocked out of the war; still, it was humiliating for the citizens of the Côte d'Azur to find themselves under the supervision of Italian forces in the summer of 1943. What was a dagger-in-the-back to French sovereignty was an unexpected asylum for thousands of Jews. With the Germans in direct control of southern France since November '42, the deportations of French and foreign Jews had accelerated. In the zone east of the Rhône River, French Jews remained subject to French directives, but foreign Jews were under exclusive Italian jurisdiction. The Italians did not see the persecution of Jewish civilians as part of their mandate. Italy, claimed a fascist police prefect, "respected the elementary principles of humanity."[1]

In the hotels and apartments of Nice, thousands of desperate people were clinging on in the hopes of procuring passage to safety. Swelling their numbers were thousands more who'd heard of the Italians' protection. The Communist underground, and even Italians, cranked out false papers from covert presses in the alleyways of Nice. At the beginning of the year, the Italians began securing housing for Jewish families in small villages in the Alpes-Maritimes and Basses-Alpes to keep them together. Units of the *Regio Esercito* were dispatched to protect the refugees; one official explaining this was to "answer a standard of justice and humanity."[2] In March 1943, the Italians prevented seizures of Jews at Valence, Chambéry, and Annecy.[3] In June 1943, Mussolini's Police Inspector General Guido Lospinoso stopped the arrest of 7,000 foreign Jews at Megève.

Latin laxity toward the local Jewish population prompted the Vichy prefect of the department to complain, "The Italian authorities at the present time are putting a stop to the . . . great measures decreed by the French government against foreign Jews."[4] The Italian indifference sometimes tipped into what was seen by the Germans as fraternization. When Jews raised three million francs for Italian victims of Allied bombing, the SS was outraged. Lieutenant-Colonel Helmut Knochen bitterly complained it was "intolerable that the final solution of the Jewish question should be rendered more difficult by an ally."[5] Eventually, the Germans would vent their anger. Until then, Nice was a "safety plank surrounded by a sea rising in the Nazi flood."[6] Within an intensifying theater of war in southern Europe with the Germans on one side and the Allied forces on the other, the fate of thousands of Jewish refugees in Nice's *ghetto parfumé* and elsewhere in the Alpes-Maritimes rested on the protection by one Axis dictator against another.

EVEN STANDING ON a safety plank, life went on.

On an impossibly bright Saturday morning in June 1943 at the Nice City Hall, the young German-Jewish artist Charlotte Salomon married Alexander Nagler, a Jewish Romanian refugee. The license listed the groom as thirty-eight and living at Villa L'Ermitage in Villefranche, the ancient port just on the other side of Nice's Castle Hill, and his bride as domiciled in Nice.[7] Their witness was Dr. Georges Moridis, who made calls on his bicycle carrying his medical bag in his hand and secret Resistance missives in his head.

As the newlyweds crossed the plaza in front of the Hôtel de Ville, booksellers were arranging their goods, and newspapers carried the day's headlines: *Allies Set to Invade Sicily*; *Goebbels Declares Berlin "free of Jews."* The couple's personal celebration of marriage was followed by a public one later that summer. On Wednesday, September 8, 1943, radios in the cafés of Promenade des Anglais crackled with the shocking bulletin: "This is General Dwight D. Eisenhower. The Italian government has surrendered its armed forces unconditionally." Niçois and foreigners took to the streets to celebrate. Nice would remain French. A rabbi among the celebrating throng shouted, "She has changed sides, we are now in Allied territory!"[8] Some remained guarded amidst the joy. "Keep these safe," Charlotte Salomon quietly told Dr. Moridis as she handed him stacks of her paintings wrapped in brown paper bags. "They are my whole life."[9]

Even as the crowds cheered in Place Massena and barmen poured drafts in the taverns of Old Nice, German units were arriving by the truckload to take control of the areas being vacated by the retreating remnants of the Italian Army. The Wehrmacht's 305th Infantry Division was in possession of the Nice rail station that first night, augmented by a patrol of submachine gun–toting *miliciens*.[10] The Hôtel Suisse was requisitioned for the Kriegsmarine, the Gestapo set up its sinister shop at the Hôtel Hermitage, and a torture annex was established at the Villa Trianon in the Cimiez district.*

---

* Villa Lynwood, 103 avenue de Brancolar, in Cimiez. Villa Trianon, the main interrogation center used by the Gestapo from 1943 on was located at 8 avenue Gustave Nadaud. The villa was destroyed in 1954. The Hôtel Hermitage, 42 avenue Emile Bieckert.

In the phrase of eyewitness and historian Léon Poliakov, Nice was, to the Nazis, the scene of the crime, the place where wealthy and worldly Jews had been allowed to live in a kind of paradise within a war that was sapping German strength more each day.* On the Eastern Front, the Battle of the Dnieper was proof the Germans could no longer halt the Red Army on the flat terrain of the steppes. On the Mediterranean Front, the first Allied soldiers had reached the Italian mainland and were headed up the peninsula. An Allied landing along the French Riviera would not be far off. Yet, with the boundaries of the Third Reich shrinking by the hour, it remained bent on reprisals.

Just one week after the Italian surrender set off the impromptu celebration, a jackbooted SS captain disembarked at the Nice train station.[11] A half hour later, Hauptsturmführer Alois Brunner installed himself and his retinue of a dozen thugs at the Hôtel Excelsior, a magnificent five-story Belle Époque hotel on rue Durante, conveniently close to the rail station. Brunner, age 31, did not look the part of the Aryan SS man. He had dark hair and a slight build that had the effect of making his head appear slightly large for his body. "Poorly built [and] puny," said one contemporary. Brunner's smooth, pale face was "expressionless" save for his "wicked little eyes."[12] To one survivor of his torments, he looked "ridiculously young."[13]

What he lacked in archetypical Nazi stature, Brunner made up with merciless efficiency. Brunner's path to Nice started in Vienna, where he had been a young adjutant to Adolf Eichmann at the commencement of the transports to the east. "The resettlement to Poland is underway," Brunner wrote to his superiors on October 18, 1939.

---

* The reasons for the Italian indifference are many, according to scholar Emmanuel Sica. Vichy and Rome did not cooperate well; if Vichy promoted anti-Semitism, the Italians were happy to oppose it. Some Italian officers may have cynically assumed that benevolence toward Jewish refugees would earn them merit among the Allies. Anti-Semitism was, moreover, never as tied to Italian nationalism as it was to German nationalism. In addition, a combination of Catholic piety and residual Renaissance humanism encouraged benevolence toward the persecuted.

"Gypsies who are now in the Ostmark [Austria] are included in a separate railway car . . . further transports will be taking place every week,
Tuesday and Friday, with 1,000 Jews."[14] Eichmann, the head of Jewish affairs for the SS in Berlin, called Brunner "one of my best men."

After the Wannsee Conference, where high-ranking Nazis for-
malized the "Final Solution," Brunner was posted to Salonika,
Greece, for centuries home to a vibrant Sephardic community. In
the basement of his headquarters were the torture rooms. Brunner
himself was the "most sadistic," flogging his victims "with a horse-
whip made of thin leather thongs threaded with iron wire." In a
month's time, Brunner liquidated the Jewish outpost that had existed for five centuries.[15] "Upon completion of the last shipment,"
Brunner was told, he was on to his next assignment: Paris.[16]

Ten kilometers northeast of the center of Paris lies the dreary
suburban commune of Drancy. In 1941, German authorities took
control of a block of apartment buildings optimistically called Cité
de la Muette. Instead of housing commuters eager to live away from
the bustle of Paris in the "Silent City," the modernist complex
became the major internment camp, where French and non-French
Jews were housed prior to their "evacuation to the East," to
Auschwitz-Birkenau.[17] France lagged behind the other occupied
nations of Europe in such transports, so Brunner was sent to Paris
to accelerate the operation. He took personal charge of the interro-
gations at Drancy; within a short time, "the walls of Captain
Brunner's office were covered with bloodstains and bullet holes."[18]
By time he was turned loose on the Jews of the Alpes-Maritimes,
Brunner had sent tens of thousands of Austrian, Greek, Slovakian,
and French Jews to their deaths.

The late-summer sun cast its golden light against the façade of
the five-story Hôtel Excelsior as Hauptsturmführer Alois Brunner,
in his *Schutzstaffel* uniform, looked down from the balcony. As he
surveyed the courtyard below, Brunner made mental calculations as
to how many people would fit into the enclosed space. The yard, nor-

mally a place for hotel guests to enjoy a morning croissant or evening
aperitif, was to be a holding pen for those fated for Poland. The hotel
basement would be a torture chamber, and elsewhere in the hotel,
young Jewish women caught in the roundup were to be sterilized to
prepare them for shipment to the Eastern Front, where they would
be sex slaves for the Wehrmacht.[19]

The Final Solution had come to Nice.

"Madame Lydia."

On the first floor of Villa Le Rêve digging through her purse for
the francs to pay the night nurse, Lydia Delectorskaya didn't hear
her cook.

"Madame Lydia."

Lydia turned around, exasperated.

"Josette, *qu'est-ce que c'est!?*"

"Madame, the Germans are here."

"Here in Vence?"

"Here at the villa, Madame."

Lydia froze.

*Was it the great artist they wanted, some kind of war prize? Was it
her, a Russian, with whom to indulge their vengeance? Did they want
information on Jean Matisse? Had Jean been arrested? Did they want
to loot the artwork?*

"The officer is at the gate," said Josette.

Lydia's fears dissipated somewhat when she realized the Germans
hadn't come for her or her patron. On that strategic corner, where
rue St-Jeannet descends into the town square, the soldiers wanted
only to commandeer their cellar to use as a canteen for the troops
marching into and out of Vence.

The life of Henri Émile Benoît Matisse was bookended by an ancient rivalry. When he was born, on December 31, 1869, the French
Empire stretched from the Gulf of Gabès to the English Channel,

and from the Mekong Delta to the beaches of Senegal. Connecting it all was the newly opened Suez Canal, the engineering tour de force directed by Versailles-born Ferdinand de Lesseps. But the Second French Empire was in its final moments. Like his more famous uncle, Napoleon III sought to enlarge his empire through war. In 1860, France annexed the duchy of Savoy and the port of Nice as part of the Treaty of Turin. The Prussians countered by defeating Austria in a brief war a few years later, setting the stage for a collision of continental powers. War between France and Prussia came in July 1870. As would be the case seven decades later, the fighting on the plains of Eastern France was quick and decisive. At the Battle of Sedan, the Prussians and their allied states encircled the massive Army of Chalôns and captured Napoleon III. The Franco-Prussian War was both an ending and a beginning. Before Henri Matisse's second birthday Paris was occupied by the Germans, the Second Empire and Napoleon III were kaput, and Germany had emerged as a unified power. The war was also a prologue to the bloody fratricidal wars between Germany and France in the first half of the next century.

Just after his first birthday in 1871, Henri Matisse's hometown had been looted by German forces. During the Franco-Prussian War, his mother "buried her valuables in the back garden."[20] Matisse as a boy had had heard the stories of Parisians surviving on bits of horsemeat. In primary school, Matisse and the other children sang war-like songs: "Children of a frontier town, / Born to the smell of gunpowder."[21] He was in his midforties when the Great War erupted in 1914 and trapped his family behind enemy lines. At his first left bank dwelling at 19 Quai St-Michel, Matisse swept up shattered glass from shell bursts and spent days in the cellar as the Germans advanced thirty miles from Paris.[22] Matisse had vowed to Varian Fry in 1941 that he could never live under "the Boches," but now they had commandeered part of his property for a canteen, he had no choice. At age 73, Matisse was once again on the front line.

The quiet of the Provençal hill town was pierced by the rumble of German trucks in front of Matisse's villa and the air raid sirens ricocheting off the slope of the Col de Vence, as the British Royal Air Force bombers headed toward Nice. Roads were blocked, trains derailed, and bridges dynamited by the local Resistance—some of whom were surely trained by Jean Matisse.[23] One night the sky was lit up after the RAF bombed the gasworks in Cannes. Like a generation earlier when two shells exploded on the roof of Matisse's Issy studio, a bomb fell outside the Villa Le Rêve, battering the front door.

Just as Marcel Sembat had instructed him to do during the war of 1914–1918, Matisse did his part in late 1943 by continuing to "paint well."* In addition to donating artworks (along with Pierre Bonnard) for children uprooted by the bombing, Matisse followed the path he'd started with *The Fall of Icarus*. That piece, with its exploding antiaircraft shells, was the first in an ambitious project being conjured by the artist. With German soldiers drinking coffee and wolfing food from the trailer-hitched stove they called the "goulash cannon" parked near the Villa Le Rêve's gate, Matisse decided upon the thematic overlay for the book of cutouts: *Le Cirque*.[24] For a Frenchman of his generation, the circus was colorful, it was nostalgic. The circus, as art historian Rodney Swan notes, was a "theme that unified people, for adults and children came together to laugh and forget their hardships."[25] As a boy Matisse would have been awed by the traveling spectacle before the age of radio and electric lights.

---

* Sembat's exhortation was in World War I, but Matisse seems to have carried on the message during the Occupation. In an interview with NPR, Stephanie D'Alessandro says, "What I think Sembat means, and what Matisse takes on, is the idea of continuing with great French painting at a time when it was being threatened by the enemy." John Elderfield of the New York Museum of Modern Art also believes there's a significant message behind Matisse's wartime art. "I think that what we learn from Matisse is that if we feel that we are engaged in a war which is a *just* war, that our culture should be responding to it in an appropriate way," he says. See Edward Lifson, "A Wartime Matisse Full of Pain and Beauty," *NPR Weekend Edition Sunday* (June 13, 2010).

But his provisional title had a meaning beyond nostalgia. The circus was also counter to Aryan ideals of physical perfection and racial and ethnic purity. To its adherents, fascism was more readily identifiable as an aesthetic than a dry theory. "The sight of certain statues by Arno Breker [the Nazi sculptor] has allowed us to reach the essence of national socialism better than dozens of big tomes of doctrine," said one believer.[26] The Nazi ideal (and Breker's statues) included warriors, indulged the cult of youth, and revealed "a taste for superior individuals." What could be more different than the itinerant outcasts who lived and worked under the circus tent? "Gypsies" targeted by Eichmann and Brunner, alongside "clowns...trapeze artists, lion tamers, human cannon balls, disfigured, giants and midgets." As Swan notes, "These were the freaks and the marginalized, typical of those that Hitler condemned."[27]

Did Henri Matisse purposefully choose a theme at odds with Hitler's Übermenschen? There are clues from the previous war. According to Matisse authority Jack Flam, Matisse's friend, the composer Erik Satie, had scored the music for the ballet Parade in 1916 and 1917. Flam noticed "striking parallels" between the costumes for Parade and Matisse's images from under the circus tent.[28] During the war, the Matisse family home at Issy had been a "meeting point and shelter for friends, neighbors, refugees...stray foreigners and homeless artists...and a steady flow of conscripts on leave."[29] Matisse sent money to support the Spanish artist Juan Gris and urged other artists to do the same.[30] One thank-you letter to Madame Matisse speaks of a home "brimming with happiness and sympathy."[31]

An early National Socialist tract cited dubious "racial science" to draw the link between physical disabilities (or differences) and the images of modern artistic expression. This Nazi doctrine held that modern artists like Henri Matisse were guilty of passing negative hereditary traits and accelerating racial degeneration through their art.[32] If the fascist ideal was physical perfection and racial and ethnic homogeneity, Matisse's response was a celebration of the opposite. By shining the spotlight of modernism on the enemies of the Nazi state, Matisse was passing on the traits of anti-fascism.

Matisse portrayed the often ugly and dangerous scenes in the circus; sights that are not uncommon in pluralistic liberal-minded cities like Paris or London or New York, but the circus also means the integration of different ethnicities, races, and abilities—a state of affairs officially *verboten* in Vichy, Munich, or Berlin. The artist had "presented an environmental model of social integration," writes Jack Flam, noting the democratic nature of Matisse's circus. Matisse's work represented France's progressive values of liberty, equality, and fraternity.

In contrast to his Great War works like *Bathers by a River*, sober and drained of color, Matisse's clown, performing elephant, trapeze artists, sword swallower, cowboy, and knife thrower are a blaze of color befitting a fantasy world. Yet, "[d]espite their vivid colors and circus themes, few of the compositions are cheerful," Flam notes. "Several are among Matisse's most ominous images" full of "subtlety and innuendo, at once bold and gay and tragic."[33] Confrontations and oppositions had been a theme in Matisse's work at least as far back as *The Conversation*. A riven France, where the *Milice* hunted and betrayed other Frenchmen, may have been reflected in the pieces like *The Knife Thrower* and *The Cowboy*, double-page images, like pages of an open book, in which the "left side represents evil and the right, good." Perhaps because he was largely confined to bed or a chair, several of Matisse's plates, like *The Toboggan* and *The Fall of Icarus* convey falling, or being pulled or dragged.[34] Rebecca Rabinow, director of the Menil Collection and a Matisse scholar, said the early cutouts reveal a sense of "evil; control; unnatural things. There is a ringmaster, a whip, violence, making animals do things against their nature."[35] In the words of Pierre Schneider, the Belgian-born authority on Matisse, the cutouts "reflect...shared anxieties, responds to them; it is a nocturnal book."[36]

Yet, as he had done before with his *livre d'artiste* on Charles d'Orléans and his use of the tricolor, Matisse embedded messages in his
cutouts. "Several of Matisse's wartime works," writes Rabinow, "carry
subtle patriotic messages . . . [such as a] desire for freedom" from the
"sense of lurking danger and/or death." Jennifer Farrell of the Metropolitan Museum of Art suggests Matisse was up to something akin
to meta-coding. Not only had he elevated the decorative arts to the
plateau of fine art by equalizing the subject and the background of
certain paintings, but with the cutouts he imbued what was considered "soothing" with malaise; a joy that held a hint of danger.

To examine the plates at close range, one is struck by the modern-
ity and power of the images.[37] To borrow Tériade's perfect line, they
are "brimming with clanging color."[38] Eight decades after they were
created, the primary yellow, orange, and fuchsia are otherworldly.
One can understand why Matisse's eye doctor advised him to draw
the curtains while studying his work. Up close, the brushstrokes and
paper joints lend the works a three-dimensionality. Yet the power of
the cutouts also derives from their sense of disquiet. Like their hues,
time has done nothing to erode the profound sense of foreboding.

The first of the twenty plates sets the tone: *The Clown* is "a shattered form; a tortured body," similar in shape to the figure in *The
Fall of Icarus*.[39] The white figure, marred by red claw marks, is bordered by black and blue bars, like those of a prison cell. At the top
and bottom of *The Sword Swallower*, Matisse used the tricolor of Na-
zism—red, black, and white—to frame the upturned face, mouth
agape to accept the three saw-edged shapes in his throat. The face is
"pained" and the daggers cause "the neck to bulge."[40] *Is this a per-
former or a torture victim?* A double-sized plate, *Nightmare of the
White Elephant*, is a heartbreaking image of a performing animal balancing itself on a ball, pierced with javelin-shaped shards of red.*

---

* Standing in front of this work at the Musée Matisse in Nice, I recalled Lydia Delectorskaya's remark that white is the color of animals in captivity.

Lydia Delectorskaya remarked, "White is the color of animals in captivity," and Matisse himself made the revealing statement, "The white elephant, it is me."[41] The initial sense of gaiety evoked by the vivid yellow, spring green, fuchsia, and cobalt in the twentieth plate, *Horse, Rider, and Clown*, cools with the recognition that the horse is bowing its head before a sinuous yellow line—the ringmaster's whip.

TEN MILES AWAY and down the mountain from Vence were all-too-real scenes of degradation and captivity. The master meting out blows of the whip was Captain Brunner. On the day of his arrival in Nice, Brunner led a *Kommando* unit through the streets of Nice. With "the hangman of Drancy" in charge, there was no time for examining papers.[42] Barricades were installed at the tops of streets and detachments of SS ransacked hotels and apartment buildings, grabbing all those who looked Jewish. The elderly and infirm, adolescent and children. Men were ordered to pull down their pants to show if they were circumcised.[43] Panicked Jews raced to the Italian consulate, vainly seeking passage to Italy; they found refuge in other people's homes or attempted to leave town, but the train stations and border posts were already full of German soldiers. Some managed to flee into the hills above; still others relied on their landlords and luck. Brunner's posting to Nice was in essence a vast search operation that ripped through the ex-Italian zone from east to west during the beautiful autumn in 1943. *Nissa la Bella* and the picturesque towns nearby witnessed scenes that echoed Warsaw or Lodz as the Riviera suffered through "one of the most brutal manhunts in western Europe."[44] Day and night the SS trucks and the black Citroëns of the Gestapo were on the prowl, *chasse à juifs*, hunting Jews. Neighbors would be awoken after midnight by the screech of tires, then a searchlight would be trained on the exterior of the apartment, then the fall of heavy boots racing up the stairs, then the screams.

While hoteliers and villa owners harbored Jews, initially some Niçois turned on them. Marguerite Becker, who worked as a secretary for the Nice Gestapo, told historian Mary Felstiner, "Every day a pile of denunciations arrived. In addition to those addressed to the Hôtel Excelsior, people were coming in person and saying: 'There are Jews at such and such a place.'"[45] But by the end of Brunner's eighty days in Nice, the citizens of the ancient port had proved a "hostile population" to the Germans. As brutal scenes played out on their streets and plazas, the Niçois did all they could to thwart the German efforts to hunt down the Jews in and around their city. The Italian files on Jews had been taken back to Rome; the new prefect destroyed the French files. ID cards were issued with non-Jewish-sounding names. Families were sheltered, and others were helped across the border to Switzerland. Some citizens merely gave "the gift of silence," while others risked their lives, like the brave souls of the Réseau Marcel, who saved 500 Jewish children. According to both French historian Serge Klarsfeld and American scholar Robert Paxton, by the time Alois Brunner returned to Drancy, he had arrested and deported 1,800 Jews out of a population, between Menton and Cannes, estimated to be 25,000. To Klarsfeld, the "result [was] very mediocre"; in the words of another historian, the *résistants* had won a "special victory."[46] The Wall of Names in Nice's Jewish cemetery, dedicated in January 2020, tells a more tragic story; on it are the names of 3,485 deported.[47]

For those caught in the dragnet, little could alter their fate.

As the sun rose over the turquoise Mediterranean on the morning of September 23, 1943, trucks dispatched from the Excelsior rumbled from the city toward towns and villages like Villefranche and Saint-Jean-Cap-Ferrat, where informants gave addresses of local villas suspected of harboring Jews. One truck became lost on the winding roads to Villa l'Ermitage in Villefranche, owned by an American woman suspected of harboring a Jewish couple. Given directions at a pharmacy, the Waffen-SS men made the five-minute drive up a steep, winding road and skidded to a halt at the hiding place of Charlotte Salomon and her husband, Alexander Nagler. As Charlotte screamed, the couple were thrown into the truck; they were tossed about as the truck rounded the turn at Castle Hill and headed back to Nice. There, the newlyweds were made to register at the Excelsior Hotel before being taken to the station where they were loaded onto a transport bound for Drancy, arriving on September 27, 1943. Ten days later, they were sealed into a cattle car—convoy No. 60, with "Charlotte Nagler, draftswoman" listed as passenger No. 660.

The train arrived at Auschwitz on October 10, 1943. Alexander Nagler was ordered to leave the couple's suitcase on the huge pile of luggage stacked in front of the train car. Then he was shoved into the left-hand line of able-bodied men as they trudged toward an SS guard with a coiled whip under a gate with the words *"Arbeit Macht Frei."* Charlotte, five months pregnant, was helped from the train by other doomed passengers, and directed to stand in the right-hand line of the platform, along with the sick and the elderly, women and their children.

CHAPTER SEVENTEEN

The Stuff of Warriors

*"As for me, I am made of the stuff of warriors, fanatics,
and all those consumed by ardor."*
—MARGUERITE MATISSE-DUTHUIT

RENNES, FRANCE
APRIL 13, 1944

The elegant woman on the train looked like any other well-heeled Parisian on her way to check on a widowed older sister or to a weekend at her country house. Dark hair tucked under an expensive-looking hat, the woman had large, deep-set eyes and wore a touch of lipstick. She wore a dress with an amply pleated skirt cinched at the waist by a thick Portuguese sailor's belt, a gold pendant, and shoes with leather straps.[1] Though middle-aged, her dimpled chin and petite figure made her appear younger. Her gloved hands were folded in her lap as the train slowed on its approach into the Gare de Rennes.

Crowds on the quay appeared in her window, and as the train came to a rest, Marguerite Matisse-Duthuit cuffed her left wrist. It was there, tucked into her glove. Rolled more tightly than a Gau-

185

loises cigarette was the secret communiqué she was to deliver to her
contact in Brittany, the coastal prefecture next to Normandy, where
her father had taken the family so many times as he perfected his
gray landscapes in the years prior to the Great War.

Like all train stations in Occupied France, the one in the re-
gional capital of Brittany was crawling with French plainclothes
police and the Germans they answered to, both easily identified
by their fedoras pulled low and their ill-fitting dark suits. Marguerite kept a keen eye as she made her way to the nondescript café
near the Champ de Mars, where she was to meet her contact at the
corner table. Clutching her handbag, Marguerite ducked through
the commuters, past the fish and oyster vendors and the crêpe stalls,
toward the appointed meeting place. The swastika flew over the
city of medieval half-timbered structures, and Marguerite shared
the simmering resentment of her countrymen. "Even if I get my
wings clipped," she had written to her father earlier, she would *do
something*. Three years into the Occupation, "most things seem to
me so utterly without importance."[2] In the spring of 1944, the simmering anger was tempered by a sense that fortunes would be
changing: it was widely assumed the Allies were preparing for a
cross-channel assault.

The Resistance networks in France were counted on by the Allied
planners of Operation Overlord to do what they could prior to, and
during, the invasion. The official policy of the Supreme Headquarters
Allied Expeditionary Force (SHAEF) was detailed in December 1943.
SHAEF would:

> promote disaffection and if possible, revolt or guerilla
> warfare in all enemy occupied territories. To hamper
> the enemy's war effort by means of sabotage and sub-
> versive warfare in those areas and to combat enemy
> interests and fifth column activities by unacknowledge-
> able means.[3]

In the months leading up to the invasion of Normandy, this meant gathering intelligence in France and getting it across the channel, to General Charles de Gaulle and the Allies, in utter secrecy.

Marguerite's letter to Henri foreshadowed her intentions and the risk she was willing to take for her country. Knowing his headstrong daughter, it is possible Matisse knew what she was up to. A clue is the fact that he increased her monthly allowance, but he surely did not know the specifics of her role. Now acting as a courier for the *Francs-Tireurs Partisans* (FTP), the military arm of the underground Communist Party, under the *nom de guerre* Jeanette, Marguerite ferried intelligence from the FTP to Rennes and to Bordeaux on the Atlantic coast, both under German occupation. From those cities, the communications were taken across the English Channel to London.

The FTP was on the left flank of the several covert Resistance operations that had emerged since the Fall of France. The range reflected the breadth of French politics and adapted to different local conditions. There was the conservative *Ceux de la Libération* ("Those of the Liberation"), the Christian-Democrat *Combat*, the nonpolitical *Ceux de la Résistance*. The FTP assassinated a high-ranking German officer in Nantes, derailed a trainload of German troops near Lille, and blew up trucks and convoys throughout the region. Reprisals were swift and terrible. No one was safe from German vengeance, not vicars, curates, women, or teenage boys.

"Bonjour, Jeannette," said the blond woman at the café table, her local contact with the *Francs-Tireurs Partisans*.*

"Bonjour," said Marguerite, taking her seat across the table. She carefully removed her gloves and folded them in her lap. The scene would have been a common one in every town and city in France.

---

* *Service B* reports Marguerite's code name was Monique, but to avoid confusion with Monique Bourgeois, I use Jeannette, which another source claims was her code name.

Two rather well-dressed women, each thinner in wartime due to the food shortages, commiserating over *une tasse de café*. After their coffee, the dark-haired woman said her farewell and left. If the waiter had glanced over at that moment, he would have seen that Madame had forgotten her gloves. But his worries would have been allayed seeing her friend put them safely in her handbag. *C'est pas grave*, he might've thought to himself: "No big deal."

Marguerite ducked out of the café and was heading back to the station when two men flanked her. Marguerite stared straight ahead and quickened her pace, but the two men, in fedoras and dark trench coats, kept pace stride for stride. At the end of the commercial zone, one of the men spoke.

"*Madame, avez-vous quelques minutes pour nous parler?*"

Marguerite ignored the man and kept walking.

"*Madame, arretez s'il vous plait.*" The men squeezed her to a stop. *Certainly, you have a few minutes to talk with us.*

When she said nothing, each man linked an arm with Marguerite and steered her into an alleyway. A black Citroën sat waiting.

Jacques-Cartier Prison was built in the nineteenth century according to a functional and rational design. Used as a jail by the Germans for Resistance fighters and political prisoners during the Second World War, there was little rationality within its walls. The 238 cells housed mostly women with a series of underground passages reserved for interrogation. The food consisted of a daily half loaf of bread to be shared among cellmates. One prisoner recounted:

> Always the same soup. Sometimes very clear; on better days, it consist[ed] of water with a few leaves of cabbage, or carrots, or beans; sometimes we [received] two or three potatoes, a piece of cold meat or cheese. Sometimes the National Relief and the Red Cross manage to get us an egg...

Men were incarcerated there as well, but were interrogated off-site at KdS Rennes across the street from Stalag 221, the German Hospital for Allied Prisoners of War. Prisoner Julia Barry told a British newspaper immediately after the war of her and fellow prisoners' ordeal. "At Rennes, where I was questioned, all the men were taken in the 'Black Maria' to the Gestapo HQ, then back to the prison. They were beaten half dead."[4] Another man witnessed a fellow prisoner returning from a Nazi interrogation: "His face was swollen, with an extremely damaged eye, and his back and buttocks covered with wounds which still bore the marks several months later." Pierre Dordain, the leader of the Resistance network in Mordelles, was tortured to death in the prison in 1943.

Marguerite Matisse-Duthuit was a prized prisoner to the Gestapo: not only was she a member of the Series B network they were trying to dismantle, broken bone by broken bone, but her husband, Georges Duthuit, hosted an anti-fascist radio broadcast from the United States called *America at War Speaks with the French*.[5] Under the imposing redbrick rotunda of Jacques-Cartier Prison, the forty-nine-year-old daughter of the world-famous artist was stripped, searched, and her belongings confiscated. She was issued a prison uniform and sent to cell 23, on the second floor. The cells, five square meters with whitewashed walls and lit by a small light bulb hanging from the ceiling, were cramped and dark. Two women inmates sat on an iron bed in the corner; another sat at the stool in front of the table that folded down from the wall. The fourth woman bent over a small sink and splashed cold water on her face. At the top of the wall opposite the cell door with a peephole was a transom crisscrossed with iron bars; the only natural light came from the courtyard beyond. Two mattresses sat on the floor; three total for five women.[6] Marguerite might have wondered if she would have to sleep on the cold floor.

Women, too, were subjected to Nazi sadism at Jacques-Cartier, where the acrid odor of flesh burned by quicklime and cigarettes wafted from interrogation cells. Thérèse Pierre, who like Marguerite served the FTP and was taken to Jacques-Cartier, was beaten and flogged over a period of two days and was found hanging in her cell by her stocking. An act believed to be a staged suicide.[7]

Whether Marguerite was betrayed because of her famous last name or simply picked up on a hunch, she would have known, as all Resistance cell members knew, the Germans spared no one. "In case of arrest," she had been told by her network, "we don't know you; we cut off all ties." The Resistance cell members also knew the Gestapo "applied torture over several interrogation sessions."[8] In order to allow her compatriots time to cover their tracks, it would be imperative to hold fast—at least over the first few days.

In Paris, Amélie waited nervously for Marguerite's return. Like their shared roles in Henri Matisse's art career, resisting the Occupation was a family affair. Madame Matisse typed communications for the Communist underground, whom she chose because they seemed to her the best organized of the Resistance groups. She kept an apartment on rue de Miromesnil, in Paris, and stayed at the family home in Beauzelle, near Toulouse, but perhaps that was not the extent of her wartime movements. Jean's son, Pierrot, said of his grandmother, she'd "been traveling all over the country."[9]

At seventy-three, Amélie had long ago emerged from the "mysterious invalidism" brought about by her disintegrating marriage.[10] She wore her hair, now gray, in a chignon. Her figure was trim, and her legs well-muscled from the countless kilometers she'd walked during the Occupation. Physically and mentally, Madame Matisse was again the tough, proud, and independent Toulousaine, made more so by her "open contempt" for the Nazis and their art thievery.[11] Amélie, who "had spent much of her life searching for a cause in which she could put her faith," seemed recharged.[12] As she went about her daily errands there was a "no-nonsense energy about her"—as if she were on a mission.[13]

The army of shadows relied on women from *les jeunes filles* to *les grand-mères*. Secret messages, radio transmitters, and small arms were more easily hidden in baby carriages, grocery bags, or in the baskets of bicycles ridden by pretty girls.[14] Women rarely carried a Sten gun and were not consulted on policy, yet they were indispensable. "Like all her female comrades," wrote one woman agent, "[women] did the dirty work, typing letters, fetching this and that, bringing back the mail, connecting one person with another, arranging meetings."* It didn't matter to the Gestapo if a careless remark or a single indiscretion was made by a man or a woman; the result was all those in the network were in danger.

As she awaited her daughter's return one warm evening in April, Madame Matisse opened the French windows as she was accustomed to doing. If a black car screeched to a halt, she wanted to hear it in time to hide her clandestine work. Peeking out the window, she caught sight of Marguerite in her pleated dress, mariner's belt, hat and heels. Amélie put the tea kettle on when she heard the door unlock. Marguerite stepped in, but was looking downward, her face hidden beneath the brim of her hat. Perhaps her mission had failed? Perhaps someone had been arrested?

She looked up. *Bonsoir, Madame.*

It was not Marguerite.

IT TOOK THREE weeks for the news to reach Henri Matisse.

"Tear up my letter after reading it," Matisse warned Charles Camoin in his correspondence dated May 5, 1944, "and don't even tell your wife.[15]

"I've just had the worst shock of my life.

"My wife and daughter have been arrested separately, in different places," Matisse reported. "No further details . . . no more news . . . I don't know how they are, if they are lacking everything, and I can

---

* Olivier Wievieorka, *The French Resistance* (The Belknap Press of Harvard University Press, 2016), 407. One of Madame Matisse's tasks was to type instructions on the use of the Sten gun on her Hermes typewriter.

do nothing from here." Travel to Paris was out of the question as Matisse was too frail; all that could be done was to appeal to friends in Paris who may be able to obtain information.

Wracked by worry over his daughter, Henri Matisse suffered another blow that spring when he was abandoned by someone he saw almost as a grandchild.

"The hardest thing," Monique Bourgeois later recalled, "was to tell Monsieur Matisse of my decision to enter the convent."

On the day she went to deliver the news, she opened the gate and crossed the courtyard, where Lydia was waiting.

"Don't tell the patron," Lydia counseled. "Say that you're going away to work."

But Lydia could protect Matisse for only so long. Soon he learned of her true plans to don the Dominican veil. The young woman and the elderly artist had an "emotional farewell."

Matisse told her of his plans to put her to work drawing. He told her how he admired her illustrations in her nursing notebooks.

But her mind was made up. She thanked him for everything.

"I will never forget you; I will pray for you."*

Matisse was not a religious man, but at that moment, nearly five years after the start of the Second World War, he may have welcomed her prayers.

Matisse's anxiety over the fate of his family could only have been compounded by the Allies' heavy bombing in the south of France. Railway viaducts, military installations, and communication facilities were targets. Their destruction was in preparation for the expected Allied amphibious assault. Royal Air Force bombers and American B-25 Mitchells, B-24 Liberators, and Flying Fortresses all partook in the bombings along the Côte d'Azur. On Friday, May 26, 1944, the

---

* Goldhammer and Sister Jacques-Marie, *Henri Matisse: The Vence Chapel*, 45. Monique broke the news to Matisse in February 1944. He did not communicate with her again until July.

skies over Villa Le Rêve darkened as three waves of Allied bombers appeared on their way to strike Nice.

It was the deadliest day of the war for Nice. At dawn, the first wave of what would be ninety aircraft struck; as many as 500 high-explosive bombs fell on the ancient city that day. Electricity was knocked out; gas mains were hit, as was a principal water main and aqueduct. Water was completely cut off in nearby Villefranche, Beaulieu, and Èze. Fires, shattered glass, and black smoke rose from the wagon repair factory, a machine shop, bridges, and railways. The postcard-perfect city was a slaughterhouse: 438 Niçois were dead, another 500 were wounded, and 100 were missing.[16]

As ever, Matisse tried to cope with the personal and national crises by creating. "I suppose I shall bear it by working," he told Charles Camoin.[17] Though his liver and stomach pains meant he often worked in the prone position, he carried on. In late July, Matisse reported, "[F]or the last three months, in order to bear my anxiety, I have worked as much as possible. I have worn myself out."[18]

Matisse's exhaustion was due to his work on the album of *papiers découpés*; a project he originally entitled *Circus*, and had kept secret from everyone except Tériade. What the publisher alone had known became public at the end of April 1944 when *Comoedia* published news that the venerable artist planned to publish a new book—*Jazz*.

Jazz music was international rather than nationalistic; cosmopolitan rather than parochial; it stood for improvisation, not formality. "One takes a motif," Matisse said of his riffing cutout process, "one invents, until the sentence finishes itself... I work for hours."[19] Jazz connoted anti-fascism and was associated with *libération*.[20] During the Occupation, French right-wing periodicals decried the "mixed-race" nature of jazz and its practitioners, labeling it a *judéo-nègre-américain* mongrel. In her memoir, *Crossroads Marseille, 1940*, Mary Jayne Gold described how on clear nights her shortwave radio could receive an English jazz station: "*Le Jazz* and dancing were forbidden in the new État Français as a decadent part of the spirit of pleasure that had brought France to defeat."[21]

Henri Matisse, a friend and admirer of Roma guitarist Django Reinhardt, celebrated the sources of the music as he had the diversity of the circus.[22] As with the circus, Matisse may have been nostalgic for jazz music. As a younger man, he'd had a collection of jazz records, and of course, he had danced to the syncopated music with Marguerite at the Casino de la Jetée, the Belle Époque landmark that appeared on every postcard of Nice from the Victorian era onward. Matisse's memories endured longer than the landmark itself. When the Casino was razed by the Germans, its news agency reporting gleefully: "Thus one place of entertainment after another in Nice . . . has fallen prey to the pickaxe."[23]

Jazz or *Cirque*, the artwork therein signaled a departure for Matisse. Rather than eschewing symbolism, he embraced it. One of Matisse's new cutout pieces was a double-sided plate titled *Cowboy*, that symbol of American freedom, and a reference to the expeditionary force returning to France for the second time in the span of twenty years on a liberating mission. Like *Icarus*, whose bright colors could be interpreted as blood and shell bursts, the cowboy's lasso, a stripe of black snaking through fields of yellow and green, can be seen as a sign of captivity and release. Both compositions fit neatly into Matisse's overall effect. Like the forbidden music, both brassy and plangent, Matisse's compositions "shout [their] sorrows."[24] *Jazz* is, in the words of Jennifer Farrell, a "firmly political book [full of] melancholy, danger."*

---

* Author interview with Jennifer Farrell, Jordan Schnitzer Curator, The Metropolitan Museum of Art, April 17, 2024.

Other plates, too, carry a sense of foreboding; the sawtooth shapes in *The Toboggan*; the red splashes in *The Clown*, which could be fresh battle wounds; and *The Sword Swallower* and *The Knife Thrower* "openly evoke danger and violence," in the words of one art historian (Sooke, *Henri Matisse: A Second Life*, 25-26).

CHAPTER EIGHTEEN

Wound My Heart

Blessent mon coeur
d'une langueur
monotone
(Wound my heart
With a languorous
Monotony)
  —PAUL VERLAINE, "CHANSON D'AUTOMNE"

A MONTH AFTER THE BOMBING OF Nice and six weeks after learning of the arrest of Marguerite and Amélie, Matisse asked Camoin to check in on Jean. "He lives in the bombarded suburbs, and he leaves me without news of his family and his mother and Marguerite," Matisse complained. "He reassures me about his health and that of his family."[1] Jean had barely escaped the south before his network was discovered. Now he was quietly scouring the capital for information on his sister and mother. He kept a low profile; according to his son, Pierrot, they were "still at risk from the Antibes business."[2] Just as his father worried about him, Jean worried about *his* son. As Pierrot later recounted in his memoir, *The Missing Matisse,*

Jean sent him to live in the home of an elderly couple, neighbors in Issy-les-Moulineaux. Nearly starved from the meager food rations, the teenager augmented his diet with vitamin cookies from the Red Cross, donated by American Quakers. To earn a bit of money, Pierrot took a job as an apprentice illustrator at a Parisian print shop. It was there that trouble once again found Matisse's grandson.

The owner of the print shop had secured a batch of the heavy stock paper used by the Germans for *Ausweis*—ID cards and other official documents. The pilfered paper led to a smorgasbord of counterfeits: food coupons, extended leave passes from STO service, and "missed-connection" certificates signed by the train stationmaster allowing the holder to come back late.[3] It wasn't the counterfeiting that endangered Pierrot, but a case of being at the wrong place at the wrong time.[4]

"One day along the street where the print shop was located someone threw a Molotov cocktail at a German patrol."[5] French gendarmes and German soldiers barged into each shop along the street looking for the bomber. Pierrot barely had time to hide the counterfeits, when a German soldier collared him. He was about to break Pierrot's fingers in a doorjamb when the owner ran into the shop. Pierrot's papers were confiscated, and he was ordered to report to an address elsewhere in Paris the following day to retrieve them.

"My papers will never pass Gestapo inspection."

"You need to get out of Paris. Here's your pay," the owner said, stuffing notes into the teenager's hand, "it's best that you leave now."[6]

In search of safety and with the help of some sympathetic rail workers, Pierrot Matisse boarded a train to Normandy, where his maternal grandparents lived.

A quiet Norman farm village should have been a cocoon of safety, but not in June 1944 with the Allied invasion about to be unleashed.

At 9:15 p.m. on Monday, June 5, 1944, the BBC's *Radio Londres* crackled to life as small groups of French men and women, perhaps even Jean Matisse, clandestinely crowded around their wireless radio

sets. Four days after broadcasting the first three lines of a Paul Verlaine poem to alert the French Resistance of the impending
Normandy invasion, this cross-channel missive gave further instructions with the next three:

> *Wound my heart*
> *With a languorous*
> *monotony*

The delicate words belied the storm of steel about to break. What
the French called *Jour-J* had arrived at last, and the Resistance circuits knew what to do: cut rail lines, disrupt communications, and
harass the enemy along the roadways to prevent German reinforcements such as the Second SS Panzer Division, *Das Reich*. A German
Fifteenth Army intercept also realized the broadcast meant invasion
was imminent. *But when exactly? And where?*

At dawn the following morning, along the crest of a bluff that
overlooks the beaches between the Norman coastal towns of Vierville
and Colville, 800 soldiers of the German 916th Grenadier Regiment
were dug in. Scouts looked out over the triple belt of barbed wire,
minefields, and the six-foot-deep anti-tank trench. They may have
felt well protected by the eight concrete pillboxes, each with ten machine guns and heavier cannon. As they had their first coffee and
cigarette, one of the grenadiers peered through his binoculars. He
thought he saw large objects out in the misty, choppy sea. He looked
at his watch. It was 6:30 a.m. on Tuesday, the sixth of June.

D-Day.

The armada heading toward the Norman coastline was made up
of Americans, British, Canadian, and Free French forces. As the
916th took in the mass of ships and soldiers steaming toward the
beaches, their sense of invulnerability might have turned to disbelief.
They were directly in the path of history: the Normandy invasion,
code-named Operation Overlord, was "the largest combined land

and sea operation conducted since the invasion of Greece by King Xerxes of Persia in spring 480 B.C."[7]

By D-Day plus four, after costly fighting, the Allies held the beachheads. The Resistance, aided by special three-member liaison teams parachuted into Normandy, were tormenting the enemy, making hit-and-run attacks on German columns following the new road signs that read *Zur Normandie Front*. German General Rommel anticipated that the Second SS Panzer Division would meet the Allies on D-Day plus three, but the guerilla fighters "badly mauled" *Das Reich* as it made its way north from Toulouse, delaying it by two critical weeks. Two other panzer divisions ordered all the way from the Russian front were also held up by sabotage and bombings. "[I]t took less time . . . to travel from the eastern front to France than it did for them to proceed from eastern France to Normandy."[8]

According to SHAEF, three million French could be relied upon to actively resist.[9] Though its numbers are impossible to determine, the ranks of the Resistance swelled after D-Day with encouragement from the clandestine newspapers. The June 1944 issue of *Action* declared, "The battle of France has been undertaken, it has to be won . . . All the French want to fight.[10] *Avant-Garde*, distributed by the Communist youth, had the same urgent message: "Our Allies have finally landed! . . . General de Gaulle has proclaimed that . . . the sacred duty of all the sons of France is to combat with all means."[11] The call to arms also appeared in *L'Aurore*: "May every Frenchman, on that day, carry out an act of patriotism, an act of war against the invader."[12] In the words of the Occupation's poetic chronicler, Louis Aragon, "They have the power, but we have the numbers."[13]

With rail lines severed, the German soldiers abandoned their trains and went by road, only to discover the road signs had been deliberately falsified. With all means, the *résistants* made war against the invader. They ambushed retreating columns, picked off isolated soldiers, protected critical bridges, and provided valuable information to the English-speaking soldiers. To Supreme Allied Commander Dwight D. Eisenhower, who was not given to hyperbole, the Resistance "played a considerable part" in the battle for Normandy and were of "inestimable value."[14]

The German reprisals in the days after the Allied landings were ruthless. On June 10, 1944, elements of the frustrated *Das Reich* division, acting on reports that Resistance forces were operating in the area, shot the boys and men of the small town of Oradour-sur-Glane and burned alive the women and children in the village's six barns. In total, 642 civilians were killed in that orgy of violence; there were only seven survivors. In St-Donat, using aliases, Louis Aragon and Elsa Triolet founded the paper *La Drôme en Armes* with the help of local *résistants*, Jean and Mady Chancel. The first issue dated June 10 was handwritten by Elsa and reproduced on a roneograph. On June 14, the two couples were the recipients of a parachute drop of equipment. The next day, the Germans retaliated with a punitive expedition to St-Donat. The reprisal consisted of looting, mass rapes, and killing. Aragon and Elsa escaped, but the Chancels' thirteen-year-old daughter was raped and died due to the injuries sustained.[15] In Lyon, a German firing squad stood a young *résistant* against the corner of a stone building (so the bullets would not ricochet). As Gilbert Dru lay dead, a copy of Aragon's poem *Brocéliande*, with Matisse's portrait of Aragon as a frontispiece, was pulled from his pocket.[16]

IN THEIR NORMAN farmhouse of red brick and white stucco with oak beams, under their roof of red clay tiles, Pierrot Matisse found this set of grandparents very different from the great artist and the officious Madame who had banished him from her table. His Norman *grand-mère* served homemade apple cider, rabbit stew, and cream soups. Pierrot cut grass for the rabbits and helped his grandfather Leroy, a resourceful old man who had got hold of some pigeons even though "The Boches took my hunting rifles."[17] A grandfather clock kept time, and a Singer sewing machine kept them stocked. "I sew for the farmers," said his *grand-mère*, "which keeps us supplied with food."[18]

Tension in Normandy was brewing on the eve of the Allied landings, but it was relative calm compared to Paris. That all changed on the morning Pierrot's grandfather came back to the house and announced the Allies had landed. The liberators were forty miles away, he told Pierrot, and the Germans had declared martial law. All doors must be unlocked so Wehrmacht soldiers could enter the locals' homes at any time day or night.

"We are now on the battlefield."[19]

Life within miles of clashing armies led to privations and complications for the people of Normandy. The Germans used the power lines for their communications, so electricity for the local population was cut. That meant "no telephone, no radio, no newspaper, no mail, no public transportation, nothing." In response, locals shorted-out the power lines, forcing German soldiers to check miles of wire.

The road network in the department was washed over by a flotsam created by war: buses of German soldiers; bicyclists with wine corks glued to their rims for lack of rubber tires; and *gagozène* trucks belching woodsmoke exhaust. Germans commandeered civilian lorries, rendering the white flags flying from them meaningless. American and British wounded languished in German Red Cross trucks. Ruined trucks and half-tracks littered the sides of the dirt roads.

The drone of Allied planes was no longer confined to nighttime raids; air superiority meant the engines ran all day and night. Occasionally a parachute flare would illuminate the night sky and cast its eerie light over the countryside. As the weeks of perfect summer weather went on, the makeup and temperament of the German occupiers changed. At first, there were too young or too old German soldiers; then drunken sergeants bursting into farmhouses demanding *essen und trinken*; then German soldiers retreating and others who'd become separated from their mates looking for someone to surrender to. There were burned-out German convoys, destroyed by Allied aircraft, which left German dead rotting under the summer sun. Pierrot noticed these remnants of the once-invincible enemy had become "unpredictable" after the invasion, and they were capable of "senseless murders."

He knew he had to be careful. One misty morning, as he was crossing a farm road, Pierrot heard a shout from behind: *Stop!*

It was a soldier, but not a German.

"I'm a French civilian, and I can speak English!"

The soldier was a member of the Royal Dragoon Guards. Pierrot noticed the trooper's rifle, a bolt-action Lee-Enfield.

The British soldier wanted to know if Pierrot knew of any German defenders in the area.

"Maybe in the forest near Breteuil."[20]

At that moment the other members of the patrol crawled from the hedges and joined their comrade. Their pie-plate Tommy helmets were covered with netting and leaves to blend into the hedges. The trooper with the beret took it off and wiped sweat from his forehead with it. He knelt on the gravel and dug out an aluminum kettle and a packet of powdered milk from his pack.

Then he looked up at Pierrot.

"Fancy a cup of tea?"

CHAPTER NINETEEN

The Wolf

"It is the hardest stage, because, before he leaves, the usurper drops his mask, showing the face of a people who have let themselves be ruled by Hitler."

"Someone was awake, someone went about in the night, furtive and invisible, carrying from door to door the spirit of the Resistance . . . RESIST, YOU WHO HAVE SUFFERED!"

—ELSA TRIOLET, *A Fine of Two Hundred Francs*[*]

A S THEY LOST GROUND TO the Allies, the Gestapo saw it as imperative to redouble efforts to root out the Resistance networks providing aid to the liberators. Only after the war did the world learn what this meant. At the Nuremberg Trials in 1946, Allied pros-

---

[*] Elsa Triolet's *A Fine of Two Hundred Francs* was awarded the French literary prize, Prix Goncourt, in 1945. After the war, Triolet was named a hero of the French Resistance. These two quotes are from her lightly fictionalized account of the sacking of St-Donat. Elsa Triolet. *A Fine of Two Hundred Francs* (New York: Penguin, 1986), 282.

ecutors described the ghastly crimes committed by the Nazi secret police as they sought to obtain information:

> [A]rrests were followed by brutal treatment and tortures carried out by the most diverse methods, such as immersion in icy water, asphyxiation, torture of the limbs, and the use of instruments of torture, such as the iron helmet and electric current . . .

While such tortures were perpetrated in all the prisons of France, according to the prosecutors, the most notable torture sites were Paris, Lyon, Marseilles . . . and Jacques-Cartier Prison in Rennes.

Communication had been slow and inconsistent during the Occupation, not to mention censored. But in June 1944, with France at the epicenter of the World War, it came to a dead halt: the post, the telegraph, and the telephone all stopped. It was as if France had returned to the era of kings. "I daren't think of Marguerite," Matisse wrote, "about whom we know nothing. Nobody even knows where she is."[1] In a letter he was able to post to Charles Camoin, Matisse described his suffering "without news . . . hoping for a better situation without letting his imagination run wild."[2]

Desperate for information about Marguerite and Amélie, Matisse wrote Demetris Galanis, whose daughter-in-law was in the Resistance. Perhaps she knew something?[3] The worried father wrote the Swiss Red Cross begging for information and had his doctor in Paris scour local detention centers.[4] Marguerite's brother Jean, too, made inquiries in and around Paris without success.[5] Nothing was working, so Matisse sought help from the filmmaker Sacha Guitry, whose collaborationist tendencies, the painter hoped, would result in greater access to information from the Nazi authorities. Guitry learned nothing. "Even the high-up Germans were afraid," Matisse concluded, "because over them was the Gestapo."[6] Marguerite Matisse "had vanished into a subworld all its own."[7]

"I work a lot to keep calm," Matisse told fellow artist Camoin. "I keep myself from thinking about it, so as to make my life possible."[8] He may have tried to will himself to not think of his daughter in Nazi hands, but there is evidence her endangerment seeped into his subconscious. Of the entire Matisse catalog, perhaps the most unsettling image is plate VI of *Jazz*: *The Wolf*. Like other cutouts from the series, the colors are vibrant; in this case, a blue and magenta background, with a green and orange stripe at either end. The painted shapes of paper were arranged to create an image from negative space. A chilling image it is: a snarling, snub-nosed beast, his jaw open, and a red teardrop-shaped eye that seems too small for his head. "The wolf with a bloodstained eye," Lydia Delectorskaya wrote, taking down Matisse's comments for the portfolio, "his jaws ready to bite." In 1983, in her notes to a facsimile of *Jazz*, former chief curator of the Museum of Modern Art in New York Riva Castleman views *The Wolf* as "easily understood as a symbol for the threatening Gestapo."[9]

Discussing the plate, Jennifer Farrell made the point that there was an element of "being watched, of surveillance."[10] It is not just the Nazi enemy symbolized by the beast, but unseen enemies: lurking collaborators and covert denunciators, ready to pounce for a few francs or to settle a score. During the Occupation, there was always the question of who would be willing to go through with the threat *J'irai le dire à la Kommandatur* (I'll go tell the Germans.) Is it the cook? A fellow artist who wishes Matisse ill? One of Darnand's *miliciens* who resides in Vence? Betrayal was everywhere. Jean Moulin had been betrayed; Marguerite Matisse-Duthuit had been betrayed; Henri Matisse had been betrayed by his former mates Derain and Vlaminck; *citoyens* had been betrayed by *collabos*; the Jewish refugees of Nice, who had hoped to sail to safety in North Africa, had been betrayed by the Allies who might have saved them; France itself had been betrayed by the Pétainist collaborationist government.

In the case of the Matisse family, there was a literal wolf in sheep's clothing, a *Little Red Riding Hood* made tragically real: the woman Gestapo agent dressed in Marguerite's clothing who appeared at Amélie's apartment in Paris.[11]

IN THE BASEMENT catacomb of Jacques-Cartier Prison in Rennes, Marguerite Matisse-Duthuit was in the jaws of the wolf.

The agent in charge of her interrogation was a French-speaking German officer named Bauer. When he participated in the torture himself, he did so in mufti. On other days, Bauer would appear in his crisp Waffen-SS uniform.

"You're military today," one woman victim spat at him. "Perhaps you'll respect the uniform."

"The Allies are exploiting you to benefit the Bolsheviks," he calmly replied. *Vous irez crever dans un camp en Allemagne.* ("You will die in a camp in Germany.")[12]

The agents under Bauer beat Matisse's daughter with fists to the point of bursting her eardrum. Then, Marguerite was chained to a table by her wrists and ankles while two men beat her with a steel flail and a triple-thonged whip.[13]

Dragged from her cell for another session, Marguerite was hung from her bound wrists and punched again. Then, she was removed only to have her head shoved into a bath of ice water. The men demanded names of others in the Breton Service B network and the locations of safe houses.[14] Marguerite said nothing. They pushed her face into the tub again and again until she lost consciousness.

Marguerite awoke on the floor of a cold, dark solitary cell. For two days she suffered without treatment, without food or even water. She may have thought of that most hideous of medieval tortures— the oubliette—a cylindrical hole like a vertical coffin into which a poor soul was stuffed, without room to move. The hatch above closed, the victim was simply forgotten and left to die. Consumed by ardor, Marguerite had withstood the tortures that disfigured her face and hands. But as she wasted away in the cell, hardly able to swallow, she thought how she had been sorry during the early years

of the war that her son, Claude, was so far away. Knowing the
"fiends" of the Nazi secret police could not indulge their "demoniacal
pleasure" on him offered the only comfort.* Still, she was at the end
of her endurance. If she were dragged again to the basement rooms,
she feared she would talk. She would rather die.

Marguerite spotted a shard of broken glass on the floor of her cell;
she pinched it between her fingers and put its sharp end to her wrist.
Perhaps she was too weak or maybe the piece of glass was too small,
but Marguerite's attempt to stop her suffering via suicide was not successful. She was still in German custody and like all captives of the
Third Reich, she was subject to transport to a concentration camp.

WHEN THE AMERICAN armies broke out of the Norman hedgerows
after seven weeks of bloody fighting, they wheeled west toward Brittany's critical ports—and its capital, Rennes. By August 2, 1944, U.S.
Major General John Shirley Wood's combat groups A and B were at
the gates of the city. Due to poor communication and the absence of
available infantry, the commander nicknamed "Tiger Jack" was forced
to halt for a day, giving the Germans the gift of time. The next morning, the Germans dispatched two trains of 800 Resistance fighters,
including Matisse's daughter, and 400 Allied prisoners toward Nazi
concentration and extermination camps. By Friday, August 4, 1944,
Rennes was under the command the Provisional Government of the
French Republic, headed by General Charles de Gaulle; it was the first
major city in France to be liberated.

For Henri Matisse's daughter, the liberation came one day too late.

---

* Marguerite Matisse-Duthuit was not one to dwell on the trauma of her imprisonment. The closest she came to telling her brother the details she'd told her
father in January was to say she had been sorry during the early years of the war
that her son was so far away. "Until, that is, I was arrested. Only then did I see
the demoniacal pleasure that those fiends took in the idea that I had a son aged
13 whom they could round up and torture." Marguerite Matisse to Pierre Matisse,
Apr. 14, 1945, cited in Russell, *Matisse: Father & Son*, 240.

Rumors rippled among the forty women prisoners in the cattle car carrying Marguerite, part of a train convoy chugging east along the Loire Valley. *There were Allied POWs in the wagons of the lead train. They were headed to this camp or that camp inside the Third Reich. A band of Resistance fighters was planning to intercept the convoy before it crossed the frontier into Germany.* Facts were as scarce as food. What meager sustenance they'd been given had been provided by sympathetic mayors, curates, and Red Cross volunteers. "*Pas un mot!*" the guards shouted as they boarded at the brief station stops. "Not a word, or you'll be on this train, too!"[15] Late in the afternoon of the fourth day, as the train arrived in Langeais, a city of castles and bridges on the Loire, the roar of aircraft engines sounded overhead.

The Germans had disguised the train with camouflage, but the ruse didn't work. As several wagons, including Marguerite's, sat protected by the station building, other cars farther ahead were out on the open track. Zeroing in on them were six American P-38s, with their distinctive twin-boom design and 20mm cannon. The powerful fighter-bombers descended on the German train; their .50 caliber machine guns thudding into the cars, while the larger 20mm rounds blasted chunks of masonry from the station and serrated the unprotected wagons. The strafing lasted only minutes, but it was enough time for hundreds of prisoners to escape from the torn train while their German guards hid under the cars. In the chaos, one Resistance leader jumped into the Loire and hid for hours, the rushing river up to his mouth. Two escapee doctors broke into a wine cellar and set up a temporary infirmary.[16] The Red Cross volunteers, who only minutes before had handed out "army spread," canned cheese and ersatz coffee, set up a triage for the wounded. Marguerite's car was not hit, so she remained locked in, but the wagon with the Allied prisoners had been shredded. Another rumor charged through the train: dozens of Allied POWs had been killed by friendly fire.[17] The rumor proved true: twenty-eight prisoners were dead, and sixty were wounded.[18]

Tragedy struck Langeais that day, but the Allied air superiority was a sign that the liberators were gaining ground. On Sunday, August 13, 1944, Parisians made out the first sounds of distant gunfire.[19] This was followed by news that the long-anticipated Allied landing on France's southern coast also had commenced. The assault, code-named Operation Dragoon, hit the Mediterranean beaches on the morning of August 15. This second D-Day was far less bloody than the misty day in Normandy ten weeks earlier. Nearly 100,000 Americans, British, and Free French forces, including an Algerian infantry division, landed onshore, suffering only 395 casualties.[20] Within days, the French flag was once again flying over the ports of Toulon and Marseille. The "Champagne Campaign," as it was dubbed, then moved east toward Italy along the coast, the liberating armies racing for Fréjus, Antibes, Cannes, and toward their final prize: Nice. Events were happening quickly: on August 19, 1944, the Paris prefecture Île de la Cité was self-liberated by local Resistance, now known as the "French Forces of the Interior," or *Fifis*.[21] For the first time since June 1940, the *tricolore* flew above Paris. With their occupation of the French capital coming to an end, the Germans assembled one last train of stolen art to be sent eastward. Included in the 148 cases were works by Braques, Picasso, and Matisse. Due to Resistance efforts, including those of rail personnel, the art train made slow progress. On Sunday, August 27, 1944, American and French soldiers secured the train and its priceless cargo in the northeastern Paris suburb of Aulnay-Sous-Bois. The episode was the basis for the 1964 film, *The Train*, starring Burt Lancaster and Jeanne Moreau.

That France's northwest and southeast was liberated did not stop the train carrying Matisse's daughter and her comrades, the prisoners from Rennes, toward its terminus within Nazi Germany. Now packed into a single train, the prisoners from Rennes reached Belfort, a hill city in occupied Eastern France not far from the German frontier. There, the train was ordered to halt to allow passage of another train full of Frenchman bound for the Third Reich. This train was not headed for slavery or death in a concentration camp, but to a fortress of safety within Hitler's Germany. And this train did not hold weakened prisoners, but the symbolic and literal strongmen of Vichy France: Marshal Philippe Pétain and Joseph Darnand.* The Vichy government and its assorted courtesans were headed to exile in Sigmaringen, a castle stronghold on the Danube. Following Pétain's train was the prisoner train carrying Henri Matisse's beloved daughter, bound for the Third Reich.

---

* After the war, Joseph Darnand was captured in Italy, tried for high treason, and sentenced to death by the French High Court of Justice. Upon hearing the verdict, Darnand collapsed. He was executed by firing squad on October 10, 1945. The same fate befell the *grand collabo* writer Robert Brasillach, the editor of the pro-Nazi newspaper *Je Suis Partout* (*I Am Everywhere*). As France was liberated and collaborationists scattered, Brasillach's weekly was jokingly renamed *Je Suis Parti* (*I'm Gone!*). Brasillach, who was thirty-five, begged for a reprieve from Charles de Gaulle, who expressly denied it, in part because of de Gaulle's admiration for Georges Mandel, the Jewish politician who was a frequent target of the pugnaciously anti-Semitic Brasillach. Mandel was murdered by the *miliciens* in the last days of the Occupation. Brasillach was executed by the French state on February 6, 1945.

——————➤——————

CHAPTER TWENTY

La Libération!

"*Is Paris burning?*"
—ADOLF HITLER

"*Welcome to France, gentlemen. If I might offer a slight criticism, you are a few years later than we would have preferred.*"
—A FRENCHMAN OFFERING CHAMPAGNE TO A
BRITISH LANDING PARTY NEAR ST. TROPEZ

WITH THE CITY OF LIGHT a literal powder keg, the Supreme Allied Commander Dwight D. Eisenhower ordered General Omar Bradley and his Fourth Division to make for Paris, supported by the French Second Armored Division. The question turned to whether the Allies could reach the French capital before its *Kommandant*, General Dietrich von Choltitz, and the SS detonated the naval torpedoes wired to the Luxembourg Palace, the Opéra, and the bridges across the Seine? Eisenhower had promised General de Gaulle that Free French forces would liberate the city, but General Philippe Leclerc, not wanting to ascend the stage of history in a supporting role, deviated from the line of march so his tanks could enter Paris from the south.[1] At midday on Thursday, August 24, 1944, von Choltitz received a two-word command—*"Demolitions started?"*—just as leading elements of Leclerc's division rumbled through the Porte d'Orléans, the entrance used by Napoleon. Thousands of delirious Parisians waded into the streets to get a look at the liberators. Upon hearing the cheers and the peals of the entire city's church bells, von Choltitz ignored his order and calmly told his aide-de-camp to pack his kit for a prisoner of war camp.[2]

The next day, General Charles de Gaulle, the leader of the Free French who had been taken prisoner by the Kaiser's army at Verdun in 1916, defeated by the blitzkrieg in 1940, and exiled in England during the course of the war under a Vichy death sentence, strode triumphantly down the Champs-Elysées. In his brigadier general's uniform and trademark képi, lean-faced with a commanding bearing, de Gaulle arrived at the Parvis de Notre-Dame, where the sun-drenched Parisians buzzed with pent-up emotion. Among the throng were Colette Chauvelot, the brave teenager who broke curfew to fetch bread for her family, and her mother. As they eagerly awaited a glimpse of the heroes de Gaulle and Leclerc, gun shots were fired from an elegant apartment building opposite. *"French fascists!"* shouted someone in the panicked crowd, as the French Forces of the Interior, known as *Fifis*, took aim at the rooftop snipers. Colette and her mother fell to the ground to take cover, but in the melee, both were hurt. Fortunately, their injuries were superficial: Colette's mother took a piece of shrapnel in the wrist, and Colette suffered a wound to the back.[3] The snipers were immediately caught and dragged through the jeering crowd; Red Cross volunteers tended to the wounded; and General de Gaulle calmly smoked a cigarette. When order was restored, Colette saw General Leclerc standing in the turret of a tank as it crossed the bridge over the Seine. From there, de Gaulle was driven in an open-air sedan to Hôtel de Ville, where the tricolor was hoisted for the first time since 1940, to address his fellow citizens. Emotions were feverish. Cries of *"Vive La France! Vive de Gaulle!"* were chanted as the *bleu, blanc, et rouge* fluttered overhead. Many wept with joy and relief as their new leader spoke of "fighting France, the only France, the true France, eternal France."[4]

Six hundred miles south, Nice braced for its battle of liberation. As it prepared itself, the city of Henri Matisse's studio seasons past was unrecognizable. Where there had been flower beds, there were sand-bags. Sumptuous hotels were draped in camouflage netting. The Promenade des Anglais was deserted, the buildings lining it empty and barricaded. Tank traps like giant ugly sculptures of the letter *X* sat in the streets and squares.[5] The beaches were densely seeded with German mines, and the coastline was scarred with "fortified positions . . . barbed wire . . . machine guns, mortars and anti-tank weapons."[6] An American major general called Nice "the most heavily defended site he had seen in the entire theater."[7] The spikes and traps and guns marred the cosmopolitan jewel, but there were invisible scars, too: Ni-çois who looked toward the sea to catch a glimpse of their beloved Casino de la Jetée saw only its ghostly absence.

The Franco-American army was just a few days away; its immi-nent arrival giving the local Resistance license to act. As the fighters counted the hours until battle, "the air was like a stiff drink," in Aragon's poetic phrase.* The Germans, too, were abandoning their inhibitions to violence. At the execution grounds of Ariane, a rural quarter on the outskirts of Nice, the Gestapo shot twenty-three young *résistants* and a prominent anti-fascist couple from Monaco.[8] Allied forces were still on the other side of the Var valley, but for the soldiers without uniforms, the killing of their mates was the signal. Just before dawn on August 28, 1944, their guerrilla operation began

---

* The line is from "Les Roses de Noël": *"L'air est alcool et le malheur courage."* See Adereth, *Aragon: The Resistance Poems*, 65. A more literal translation might be "the air is alcohol and unhappiness courage."

with simultaneous attacks all over Nice. Every available explosive was detonated, even Molotov cocktails and firecrackers, to give the impression of a much larger force. At 6:00 a.m., three teenaged boys were posted with a machine gun at the corner of Boulevard Auguste Raynaud. The resistors seized a German munitions storehouse that restocked arms for the veterans and provided fresh weapons for so-called eleventh-hour resistors. At 10:00 A.M., the German commander of the 239th Regiment telephoned the prefect and ordered the insurrection to stop. The prefect refused. As the day of reckoning progressed, the Nice liberating force grew to 1,500 against 2,000 of Hitler's men. The fighting intensified at Place Garibaldi, Riquier, and Gambetta; the Germans responded by firing down into *Vieux Nice* from the heights of Colline du Château. With the liberators running low on ammunition, it seemed possible that the city would remain occupied by the enemy.

The first American units started to arrive from the hills behind the city, rather than the heavily defended coast. The Germans knew their occupation was coming to an end. At four o'clock, the first tricolor appeared atop a conspicuous hillside villa. At 7 P.M., the Wehrmacht evacuated their fortifications on Castle Hill, blowing up the Port of Nice on their way out. As the sun set on the Mediterranean Sea, the guns on Allied ships pounded the German fortifications on the beaches.* Just before midnight, the Germans executed four *résistants* in the garden of a villa on the city's edge.[9]

For the American soldiers, the next few days were a surreal atmosphere of pleasure and danger. American tanks were in Place Massena in the center of Nice even as the last German soldiers retreated and their snipers took their last aim. "We could go out on patrol during the day . . . getting into a little firefight," recalled a

---

* The battle that day cost the lives of thirty-one insurgents with 280 injured; the Germans lost twenty-five of their men and 105 were taken prisoner. (In a side note, some of those prisoners were later made to clear the beaches of mines, and several were killed by exploding mines that they themselves had placed.)

sergeant major, "then five hours later be sitting in one of the biggest nightclubs in the world with a babe and a bottle of champagne." A young combat engineer, Sergeant Norm Krug from Bellville, Illinois, was taken with the beauty of the city. He wrote his parents, describing the colorfully dressed women on bicycles, and the taverns bedecked with signs that read: "Welcome, Soldier." Like Paris, France's Mediterranean jewel had helped liberate itself and emerged with a minimum of damage. Sergeant Krug even remarked on the "art shops" and "very fine paintings displayed in some of the windows." Nice, he said, was "a showplace if ever there was one . . . in spite of all attempts of the Nazis to [do] their dirty work."

He signed off, "See you in Berlin!"

When the retreating Germans marched past Villa Le Rêve in Vence, Henri Matisse, of course, continued working. "Never let it be said that I stopped work to watch the Germans depart."[10] In the chaos, three shells landed near the property. At the start of the war Matisse and his daughter, Marguerite, had to take cover in an air raid shelter in Paris, and now he found himself four years older and 600 miles south sheltering from the shrapnel with Lydia and Josette, their cook.

Marguerite, Matisse's beloved daughter, had been with him cataloging his artwork that day in Paris in the spring of 1940, and now he still had no idea where she was. During this period, rather than allow the evidence of their atrocities to be examined by American or British forces, scores of prisoners of the Reich were summarily executed in the haste of the German retreat. Matisse's anguish is revealed in a letter to Tériade, telling him it was difficult to work and complaining of terrible nightmares. "I know he scarcely sleeps anymore," wrote the young Dutch painter Annelies Nelck, who spent time at the villa that summer. "Anguish for his wife and daughter gnaws at him ceaselessly, but he allows nothing to show."[11]

WHILE THE VICHY and Nazi flags flying over the villages, towns, and cities of eternal France were replaced with the *bleu, blanc, et rouge* in the late summer and fall of 1944, Henri Matisse was in the process of completing the *Jazz* cutouts. Matisse and Tériade intended to publish twenty plates of the intensely colored *découpage* as a portfolio, of which there would be hundreds printed. Matisse's large rectangles of bright, often primary, color indeed call to mind flags.[12] On earlier trips to Siena, Tuscany, Matisse would have seen the colorful banners of the Sienese *contrade*, the seventeen districts that administered and defended the Italian hilltop city-state in the Middle Ages. Examining the Matisse *Jazz* plates at the Musée Matisse Nice and the banners in Siena, one is struck by the similarity of vibrant colors and bold imagery, often depicting animals—*Aquila, Civetta, Giraffa*. Matisse's *Le Loup* (*The Wolf*) with its stripe of orange on the right side has a cognate from six centuries earlier: the *contrada Lupa*, a she-wolf in white and black, and at the left, a stripe of orange.

Scholar Frederic Spotts notes that "[f]lags are the most primitive of tribal totems, proclaiming the unity of the group against outsiders."[13] Especially primeval is the swastika. Rather than the national colors or a design with universal historic import, the Nazis used the ancient swastika as the symbol of a single political party meant to reinforce *us versus them*; a tricolor of emotive xenophobia, symbolizing nationalism rather than patriotism and a mythical, reactionary past instead of future progress.

The red-black-white swastika is also a militaristic flag. Once its enemies are named, the foaming fascist public demands territorial conquest. Its background the color of blood and combat, its diagrammatic figure of four black hammerheads in rotary rightward movement on the white disc are like the wheel of a tank; the swastika is a battle flag. Hung from a Roman pike or painted on a *panzer*, the flag as psychological weapon is as old as history. Gibbon, the chronicler of ancient Rome, describes how "Lincinius...dreaded the power of this consecrated banner [which in battle] animated the soldiers...with an invincible enthusiasm, and scattered terror and dismay though the ranks of adverse legions."[14] Exclusionary, overtly political, and psychologically offensive, the swastika was a fitting symbol for National Socialism. It is hardly surprising that the Third Reich was, in Spotts's phrase, "festooned with flags."

Matisse inverted the swastika. With gouache, push pins, and scissors, his cutouts of circus actors, which comprised a number of the images included in *Jazz*, are standards of inclusion and banners of human solidarity. Flags for and of outsiders. The *Jazz* plates are not banners of a nation or a political party, but symbols of shared human emotions: fear and powerlessness, joy and sadness, courage and hope. There is a "public element" to the *découpage*, according to curator Jennifer Farrell.[15] Matisse never intended these pieces to hang on the wall of a Russian collector or an American industrialist. The work was an "amalgam of visual allusions, it was at once a book, an album, and a series of plates, each one of which could lead a life of its own."[16] As a book, it could only be examined by one person at a time. But taken out of the book, the plates have a "concision, a vivacity, and a compelling strangeness" that "can still startle."[17] The twenty plates were to be a portfolio, of which there would be hundreds printed. The plates were unfolded and removable to be more readily shared. For those so inclined, they could be framed or pinned to a wall. "Collectors of limited means," notes Matisse expert Rebecca Rabinow, "could pool their resources and divide the plates among themselves."[18] It was not enough to gaze at them on a gallery wall, said one reviewer: "One must turn the pages of the book and caress the vibrant colors ... the book is a living object that does not like being stared at on a wall."[19] Like the musical art form that had given the project its name, *Jazz* was democratic.

Color choice was also symbolic. Red is what gives passion and intensity to Matisse's groundbreaking *The Red Studio*; a certain red, the artist said, affects "blood pressure." But the common denominator of *Jazz* is not the color of fire, danger, and blood—it is blue. In eighteen out of twenty of his plates, Matisse used blue, the color of the sky-god Zeus, the Blue Mosque of Cairo, the color of the

heavens; a color, he said, that "enters the soul."[20] In Biblical He-
brew the color was *teleketh*, from the rare snail who provided the
expensive pigment. "*Teleketh* resembles the sea," so it is written in
the Book of Numbers, "and the sea resembles the firmament." To
more modern observers, blue is "the color of truth because blue always appears after the clouds."[21]

The azure of Biblical snails and heraldic crests was, for Henri Matisse, just outside his French doors. When at Place Félix or the Hôtel
Régina, Matisse's view from the terrace encompassed the Côte
d'Azur—the azure coast and the inimitable blue of the Mediterranean sky. Blue was "his favorite color," says Françoise Gilot; it was
a lifelong affair.[22] "Light was blue, and Matisse allowed that color
to suffuse his universe."[23]

The moment he stood in the Arena Chapel in Padua and took
in the cobalt of Giotto, Matisse set off on a lifelong quest. "When I
see Giotto's frescoes . . . I immediately perceive the feeling that
emerges, because it is in the lines, the composition, the color." To
replicate the blue of the early fourteenth-century Florentine, he said,
was "the height of my desires."[24] The miniatures of the fifteenth-
century Jean Fouquet, with their robin-egg and cobalt blues, appeared at the Bibliothèque Nationale in Paris just before the
outbreak of the war; the color signifying the enduring France as
much as the fleur-de-lys.[25] Matisse said the color scheme of both
The Dance and its companion *Music* were "made with a beautiful
blue for the sky, the bluest of blues (the surface was colored to sat-
uration, that is to say up to a point where the blue, the idea of absolute blue, appeared conclusively)."[26]

In Matisse's hands, blue was "essential" and "noble," the life-
giving water and sky, but it was also a moodier substance. The blue
between the pajama-wearing Matisse and the seated Amélie in *The
Conversation*, for instance, "doesn't even seem like an attempt to
capture light"; it is "an emotion," a "membrane stretched between
the man and the woman and humming with rage and love."[27]

Through the alchemy of Matisse, even Tangiers, the "White City," is transformed:

> [It] is not white at all. It is a city ruled by blues. The gleaming domes, the minarets, the garden paths...and the shadows of 'The Casbah Gate' are all washed with cooled-down...blues. If Matisse had a blue period, it was his period in Tangier.[28]

In her interview with Charlie Rose, Françoise Gilot explained, "You know, like when you compose music in a major key. If you use the blues, it's, like, a minor key, you know, so it's melancholy. The blues are melancholy."[29] Of all the paintings Matisse owned in his life, none was more important than Cézanne's *Three Bathers*, which he acquired by pawning Amélie's engagement ring, and which was tinged in blue.

Finally, after five months without news, in September, Henri Matisse learned Marguerite had been held at Jacques-Cartier Prison in Rennes but little else.[30] Adding to his anxiety was the news of Amélie's imprisonment in the massive Fresnes complex south of Paris.[31] With Eastern France still occupied and half his family imprisoned, Matisse labored on one of the most remarkable images of his planned book.

Monsieur Loyal.

Monsieur Loyal was the French name for "ringmaster," an apt image central to the circus-themed portfolio that symbolized something greater. This ringmaster's profile is defiant, his chin tilted upward, lips pursed. The "brilliant blue background...accentuates the figure's prominent nose."[32] The head is cropped at a certain angle, as if M. Loyal is wearing a cap—or a képi. Indeed, the profile appears "strikingly similar" to the distinctive profile of General Charles de Gaulle.[33] Even the "decorative details" of the plate—the blue background with four white dots horizontally on the left and five gold ones on the right—"recall the general's dark uniform and round gold buttons, familiar to anyone who read the daily newspapers."[34] To Jack Flam, the image was meant to convey hope. France indeed had a new ringmaster, but instead of holding a whip, he wore the symbol of the Resistance—the Cross of Lorraine—and the colors of a free France.

The circus was over; the Republic was back.

The Miracle of Marguerite

Il faut libérer ce qu'on aime
Soi-même soi même soi-même
(You must free what you love
Yourself yourself yourself)
—LOUIS ARAGON[1]

MARGUERITE WAS ALIVE.

On January 16, 1945, after a nightmarish nine months, Marguerite Matisse-Duthuit arrived in her father's Provençal hill town, Vence. For Matisse, who spent months during this time forced to wonder if she was even alive, her appearance at the door of Villa Le Rêve was like a dream.

Every afternoon over the next two weeks, while Lydia was away running the household errands, Matisse sat with Marguerite as she struggled to share her ordeal.

She recounted her April arrest and initial interrogation at KdS Rennes, Gestapo headquarters.[2] She described her time in cell 23 at Jacques-Cartier Prison, and how she and the other women pris-

oners had been loaded onto the last train out of Brittany, just before the Americans liberated the city of Rennes. Matisse listened,
his blue eyes fixed on his daughter, as she told him of the deadly
attack at Langeais. "I was as if hypnotized—really hypnotized,"
Matisse reported to Pierre in New York, "by the memories that
came flooding back within her, and by the power with which she
put them into words."[3]

Facing his daughter for hours each day had once been a foundation of their relationship. As painter and model, an emotionally taut
and silent energy ricocheted between them. Matisse had a ready subject in his lovely child, drawing her in profile, pen-and-ink sketches
and innumerable paintings. By adolescence he'd transformed her
into the celebrated Fauvist painting: *Marguerite Reading*.[4] During
the war years of 1914–1918, having grown up at "sharp-end of the
artistic avant-garde," the "studio kid" had grown into "a stylish
young woman."[5] There she is "on a balcony, wearing an exuberant
hat and a smart plaid coat . . . often in close-up, full-face, asleep, in
bed, in different moods and clothing."[6] In a charcoal drawing made
just before Marguerite's marriage to Georges Duthuit, Matisse depicts her as "solemn and withdrawn . . . [a] compelling emblem of
fragility and introspection." That she would appear withdrawn to
her father on the cusp of her marriage was most likely Matisse's response to his imminent loss. Louis Aragon thought Marguerite was
the real love of Matisse's life, "his little girl."[7] Marguerite, however,
couldn't play that role forever; she had to chart her own course, and
that meant no more posing for her father.

Two decades later, at age 51, Marguerite was a woman of steely
substance, one among a minority of French citizens who dared to
risk her life in the cause of freedom. When she emerged from her
months-long recuperation in the winter of 1944–1945, she appeared
notably transformed. André Rouveyre described her as "ringed with
light."[8] Christian Zervos also used saintly terms:

Her outward appearance was astonishing. Not only did
she look younger than . . . before the war, but there was
a light in her face that made her beautiful—a supernat-
ural beauty . . . Looking at her, I realized what suffering
in the service of a great cause can do for a human
being.[9]

Matisse, of course, also recognized his daughter's transformation.
"She has never looked so young," he told her brother Pierre. "For
years I have seen her absent herself from the present moment (poi-
soned, as that moment was, by something or other). And now I
have watched her in front of me, her eyes in mine, completely identified with her true self."[10] The extreme trials Marguerite withstood
for her role in the Resistance had seemingly liberated her. She unburdened herself from the horrors, she explained, like stepping out
of a coat she no longer wished to wear. "I always wanted to master
my body and the suffering it imposed on me," she told her father.
From earliest childhood, having withstood several surgeries, Marguerite knew physical pain; as a middle-aged woman in a Gestapo
dungeon, it was her body that bore the blows, while her spirit
stayed strong. "You have to show yourself in face of everything,
against everything, tough enough to stay upright."[11]

Matisse took out his sketch pad while he listened intently to
his beloved daughter as she told him how she came to escape the
cattle car traveling eastward across the whole of France toward the
border of Nazi Germany. Marguerite recounted that she and the
other prisoners, including Yvonne Kervarec, an agent for British
intelligence who was rounded up in the dismantling of the network "Turquoise," had been on the train for three weeks, when
it suddenly halted at Belfort, less than fifty miles from Germany;
it stopped there to make way for the Vichy government going into
exile in the Third Reich. A rumor spread that the women political

prisoners on the train would be released. This act of clemency in the chaotic last days of the Occupation turned out to be true, but the actual release, requiring identities to be checked and re-checked, was excruciatingly slow. Starting at last names beginning with the letter *A*, the authorities had only reached the last names beginning with the letter *D* when the train was to resume its trek to the concentration camps. Marguerite Matisse-*Duthuit* would be one of the lucky ones, but not her friend and fellow prisoner Yvonne Kervarec.

Marguerite owed her life to the younger woman.

Following one torture session at Jacques-Cartier Prison, Marguerite, too weak to walk, was dragged back to her cell and thrown to the ground. Her arms were swollen and black; her face was bruised.[12] It was at this point, beaten and hopeless, that Marguerite tried to kill herself. "Due to the extent of her injuries, she could not make her own bed," Kervarec later said. "I took care of her." When the German military doctor visited the room to examine Marguerite's wounds, Yvonne could not help herself: "Strange times," she said to the doctor, "where they treat you one day only to hurt you worse the next."[13] Whether it was Yvonne's remark or the ghastly condition of Marguerite, the Nazi doctor seemed moved.

Marguerite hastily said au revoir to Kervarec and clambered off the cattle car into the streets of Belfort. She and the other freed prisoners found only drawn curtains and locked doors. The French citizens of Belfort, still firmly under Nazi control, apparently weren't prepared to risk harboring an enemy of the Reich.[14] Marguerite headed for the nearby Vosges Mountains, where she and the other refugees came across the camp of a pro-German Russian regiment hiding in the woods. The remnants of the infamous Vlasov Division were cowering from the Soviets, who wanted to shoot them for treason, and the Americans, who wanted to turn them over to the

Soviets. From the camp, Marguerite hiked the last few miles to a poorly guarded border post and into Switzerland.*

Two days later, on August 29, convoy no. 453 departed Belfort with the remaining 702 prisoners, including Yvonne Kervarec.† Shortly thereafter, the train arrived at the notorious women's camp near Berlin—KL Ravensbrück. From there, the journey of Kervarec improbably worsened; she was sent to the Bendorff mines, where she was a slave laborer in a hellish subterranean aircraft factory, 500 meters underground.‡ The horrific camp and the mine could have been Marguerite's fate, too, but for her hyphenated surname: Matisse-Duthuit.

When she was strong enough—and likely provided new identity papers—Marguerite returned to Belfort, where this time local Resistance sheltered her while awaiting the liberation.[15] In late November 1944, the French Army successfully took the heights overlooking the city, freeing Belfort. Marguerite then spent the next two months recuperating in Paris, before being flown to Nice to see her father.§

Despite the claims of postwar critics who viewed Matisse's wartime life in Nice and Vence as a deliberate escape from the war, the ailing artist was deeply affected by the loss and suffering. His friend and dealer Paul Rosenberg had been hounded and his galleries

---

* *Service B* by Faligot and Kauffer is the most detailed account of the journey of the Rennes train convoy. While many sources recount how Marguerite hid in the Vosges Mountains (see, e.g., Russell, *Matisse: Father & Son*, 238; Schneider et al., *Matisse*, 739), *Service B* includes the detail that a group of prisoners crossed into Switzerland.

† Kervarec spent eight months in a concentration camp. *Service B.*

‡ Yvonne Kervarec survived the mines and in early May 1945 boarded a train for Sweden, where she recuperated. She was repatriated to France in the summer of 1945 and was recognized by the French government with the Legion of Honor, the Resistance Medal and the *Croix de Guerre avec Palme*. She died in 2007.

§ In a letter to Albert Marquet, dated November 6, 1944, Matisse gave news of his daughter: "I suppose she is only very tired, because I have not been told anything else to spare myself. The doctor said it was a miracle she came out that way.

looted. Gaston and Josse Bernheim suffered the same fate. Friends died prematurely, alone, or far from home. Matisse's former student Rudolf Levy was murdered at Auschwitz, as was the son of Georges Bernheim. Matisse was powerless to prevent German soldiers from using his property. Five of his paintings, looted from one of Rosenberg's galleries, including one in which Lydia was the model, had the ignominious fate of being commandeered by Reichsmarschall Hermann Göring for his private collection. Matisse's son Jean was in constant danger for his sabotage efforts; his companion, Lydia, risked questioning by the authorities as an alien, and his ex-wife, Amélie, was arrested as an accessory and imprisoned for six months at the infamous Fresnes Prison. His whole family was separated by war.

None of these terrible events prepared Matisse to hear what the Nazis did to his Marguerite. "I could see and experience every one of the abominable scenes that she described to me with word and look and gesture," he told Pierre. "They are still vivid to me [. . .] When I was with her I often thought that I was a witness to the most terrible of human dramas."[16] Matisse seems almost disoriented by what he learned from Marguerite after her escape: "I was so stupefied," he told Pierre. "I couldn't have said if I still belonged to myself."[17]

Reeling from his daughter's experiences, Matisse posted two letters of uncommon detail to Pierre in New York. In the first, he reports how fortunate she was to survive:

> She was lucky enough to fall in with a doctor who was not a sadist and managed to stop her from being tortured. But for that, she would have died, like so many others whose faces had been burned with quicklime, inch by inch, or been tortured from head to foot with burning cigarettes. These tortures had been inflicted with the sadistic frenzy that is beyond all imagination.[18]

On February 12, 1945, the same date as the second letter to Pierre, Matisse described his daughter's travails in a letter posted to "Sister Monique Bourgeois," whose brother was held in Germany, and to whom he paid a fatherly attention. "I wish that you were easy in your mind about your family," he began:

> I have just spent two weeks with my daughter, who was a prisoner of the Germans for six months. She came out of it alive, although suffered torture. She got over this thanks to strength of character, which is particularly strong in her . . . She never talked in spite of the horrors which she underwent . . .[19]

Once Marguerite had described her searing experiences, the silence in the room was broken only by the soft sound of the charcoal scratching on paper. This was the first time he'd drawn his daughter in twenty years. "It is only very rarely," he told Pierre, "that one can participate so intensely in the experience of another human being."[20] The drawings were not the result of "emotion recollected in tranquility"—there wasn't time for that. This was emotion in real time. The first of the "miracle" portraits depicts a "frail, ghostly woman," its spectral quality the result of the sketch being rubbed off on another sheet of paper to transfer the image. The second work is a more abstract rendering of a "strong and spirited" Marguerite; a woman who had experienced much. "It's such an important pair, in terms of showing his process and how he moved from one work to the next," according to the late Jay Fisher, curator and inaugural director of the Ruth R. Marder Center for Matisse Studies of the Baltimore Museum of Art. "The first view is carefully observed in nature and is deeply felt. He gradually moves to the second, [sketching her] more abstractly to communicate a totally different emotional result. She moves from suffering to strong, as though she's looking ahead to the future."[21] As they sat face-to-face for what would be the last portraits of her by her famous father, a half century of shared life swirled: marriages and separations, wars and occupation, the tribulations of a family bound to France's monumental creator of modern art.

"What has happened to Marguerite," Matisse reported to Pierre, "is a miracle."[22]

Only for the Light

"One looked at the walls and saw the future."
—A VISITOR SEEING MATISSE'S WORKS IN
ETTA CONE'S BALTIMORE APARTMENT

S HAKEN BY MARGUERITE'S ORDEAL AND unable to work after she
left, Matisse received an unwelcome response from Monique
Bourgeois, his former nurse and model. In the months since she told
Matisse of her plan to enter the convent, Monique had taken the
vow. Now known as Sister (*Soeur*) Jacques-Marie, and finally allowed to communicate with the outside world, she wrote Matisse a
letter "with the fervor of youth" in which she spoke not of what they
shared, but what divided them: "Outside the Church there is no sal-
vation."[1] As she composed the letter, the Dominican sister "felt
ungrateful" and worried her decision to separate from Matisse might
result in another creative valley for the great artist. But in the end
her decision was an easy one: she had but to weigh "God's call"
against "the fragility of a true artist's creative temperament."[2]

Matisse's response was "ten overflowing pages filled with crossed-
out words" and "apparently written in a rage."[3] In his curvy script

Matisse attacked what he saw as a self-righteous lecture from the sister. "You are living your spiritual life in the light. And I? I live only for the light . . . The need to answer you forced me to look deep inside myself for things that I never formulate in words."

Matisse prayed at the altar of nature, he said. Pencil in hand, in front of a pomegranate covered with flowers. Was that so different?

"Our paths converge in the same spiritual realm."[4]

They had been friends since 1942, but when he signed off his long defense in "comradeship in our respective yet different routes," Matisse likely knew that this chapter of his "second life" was at its end.[5] While stewing over the critical letter from Sister Jacques-Marie, Matisse made a state-of-the-family report to Pierre. "Despite the misfortunes . . . and after two terrible wars [and] the terrible ordeals" of Marguerite and Amélie, "we are all alive and well."[6] Matisse reported, "I have not seen your mother, but I hear she goes [everywhere] on foot . . . she walks from the Miromesnil to the [Place Saint-Germain des-Prés] and back again. She, too, has made a miraculous recovery. This, if ever, is a case in which good has come from evil."[7]

On April 14, 1945, Marguerite provided Pierre with a further update. Their mother was monitoring French radio every day for news of prisoners who had been released. When comrades from the Resistance were released, Amélie Matisse walked about spreading the good news to members of the network. With Paris finally liberated, the war, now in the heart of Germany, was in its agonizing final days. On the day she penned that letter, the Red Army entered the eastern suburbs of Berlin, where the Russians began to repay the Nazis for their savagery along the Eastern Front. In Washington, DC, a memorial for Franklin D. Roosevelt was held in the East Room of the White House. America was in a state of mourning for the president who had given his last years to fighting fascism. It would be the responsibility of the new commander-in-chief, Harry Truman, to finish that fight.

At 4:00 p.m. on April 25 on a damaged bridge that once spanned the Elbe River in Torgau, Germany, Second Lieutenant William Robertson of the U.S. Sixty-Ninth Infantry Division tentatively extended his hand to a soldier from the Fifty-Eighth Soviet Guards. "Put it there," said Robertson. With the handshake, Nazi Germany was conquered; Hitler's thousand-year Reich had lasted a dozen years.[8] Days later, with the Red Army closing in, the Führer committed suicide in his command bunker. On May 7, 1945, German Chief of Staff General Alfred Jodl was flown from northern Germany to Reims, France, in an American C-47 transport plane with a pinup model painted on its fuselage. The nominal leader of Nazi Germany at that moment was escorted into a redbrick secondary school where General Eisenhower had established Allied HQ. There, at a scarred old table in a French high school, the armed forces of Nazi Germany surrendered. "*L'Allemagne est Capitulé*," cried the next morning's headlines, "*La Guerre est Finie!*" Germany had surrendered; the war was over.

As the war was ending, Matisse's first *Jazz* images were nearing publication. Tériade foresaw "a much bigger splash that we could have predicted," and told Matisse he "would like [*Jazz*] to be a monument of modern publishing."[9] The two friends waited for the publication of the *Verve* issue with *The Fall of Icarus* on the cover and for the critical verdict on that cutout as well as the others within the issue. In the meantime, Henri Matisse seemed on an end-of-the-war victory tour. In May 1945, he was made an "Honorary Member of the Mark Twain Society," whose members that year included Franklin D. Roosevelt and Winston Churchill.[10] In June, his works appeared in an exhibition at the Baltimore Museum of Art attended by the French ambassador to the United States. On July 1, 1945, Matisse made his first return to Paris.[11] In October 1945, he was back in the French capital to be honored at the very place he first gained fame—and derision—as the leader of the Fauves. In an article entitled "Brighter Days in Paris," *London Daily Post* correspondent

Marcelle Poirier described the long-awaited reopening of the Salon d'Automne. "Matisse, more than seventy-five years old, is the star of the exhibition . . . a great number of his works [. . .] show his great influence on the artists of the past fifty years, down to the younger contemporary painters."[12]

As 1945 came to an end, Tériade's prediction for *Jazz* was coming true. The *de la Couleur* issue appeared at the end of the year to "rave reviews." It was, in the words of one critic, full of "splendid color," a "magnificent edition—dedicated to, and written [with] Henri Matisse."[13] The unveiling of the cutouts, as Rebecca Rabinow notes, was timely: in December, Matisse was featured in the inaugural exhibition at Galerie Maeght in Paris, where the French government bought a painting, and the novelist François Mauriac a drawing.[14] That same month his works were shown at London's Victoria and Albert Museum. Pierre reported from across the Atlantic that the *Verve* issue in the United States was a "crazy success" (a *succès fou*) and a "personal triumph" for his father. Edward Alden Jewell, the art critic for *The New York Times*, agreed. Matisse's new palette, he wrote, "is keyed higher than ever. The designs are free, bold, economical, and plangently decorative."[15] The finished book was some ways away from publication, but these first published images signaled that *Jazz* was on its way to being regarded as "not only [Matisse's] greatest *wartime* work, but among his greatest works" (emphasis added).[16] With pride of place in Paris, London, and New York that first fall and winter after the end of World War II, the critics called it the "season of Matisse."

According to one early review, the images that would later appear in *Jazz* were "Expressing life, beauty, the gravity of life, the fullness of life, evoking movement and space haunted by man."[17] As France was regaining its national independence, its most eminent artistic son was completing his profound war work. "Despite age and failing health," concluded one review, Matisse had sought new paths of creation with "élan, brilliance, and the audacity of youth."[18]

At the beginning of 1941, Matisse had asked his surgeons to give him three or four more years to "finish his work." He was given years of war and occupation, when the military and political situations were in violent flux. When Matisse finished *Jazz*, there was a sense of resolution, a "valedictory flourish," in the words of one art historian.[19] Reflecting the "tragic ambiance of the time," Matisse had pioneered a new technique that allowed him to transcribe his emotions with the acuity of a scissor blade. *Jazz* was, in the words of Jack Flam, "the closest thing to an autobiography that Matisse has left us."[20]

The war was over, but the bitter divisions of the Occupation tempered the celebration within France and within *la famille* Matisse. This was the time of trials of those who aided the enemy, when *collabos horizontals* were paraded in shame, the women's heads shaved, swastikas drawn on their faces. Vichy leaders and notable collaborators stood in the docks, tried for their conduct during France's darkest years. Artists like André Derain, whose goodwill tour of Nazi museums and galleries revealed him to be "anesthetized to right and wrong," faced a dubious future.* For his part, Henri Matisse had no interest in recriminations, and Marguerite Matisse-Duthuit spoke no more of her ordeal. A simple gesture from father and daughter was enough: a set of lithographs, showing a poised Marguerite, to be auctioned for the benefit of her fellow Resistance fighters and their families.

---

* Russell, John. "Was Derain a Collaborationist?" Art Mailbag, *The New York Times*, Nov. 29, 1981. It is worth noting Henri Matisse had as a young man passed a "capacity at law" exam and clerked at an attorney's office; it was an experience that perhaps further insulated him from the moral variability of his former colleagues.

The Language of Dreams

From a country turned to sand
they shall bring your noble dust,
bright birds, flying. This they cast
on the living, breathing skies.
—RESISTANCE POET AND WRITER, JEAN CASSOU

"Color, what a deep and mysterious language, the language of dreams."
—PAUL GAUGUIN

VENCE, FRANCE

After the war, Matisse and Lydia remained in Vence for a time, where they hosted acquaintances and old friends, including Pablo Picasso and Françoise Gilot. "Picasso came to see me with a very pretty young woman," Matisse reported to Pierre. "He could not have been more friendly."[1] Inside Villa Le Rêve, Gilot found a world that was at once balanced and magical. Sitting in the dimly lit rooms, one might brush an elbow on an object recognizable from a Matisse masterwork. "The ordinary was enmeshed with the extraordinary," she recalled. "Things were both tangible and intangible, in and out of space, in and out of time."[2] Matisse's world had become one where "great beauty" was counterbalanced by melancholy; where serenity co-existed with the "vibration of a future farewell." Matisse was seventy-six; he spent much of each day in bed; he wore dark sunglasses for his eyes, even indoors. Having survived grave illness and enemy oc-cupation, Gilot saw how Matisse "now greeted each new day as a day of respite, and thus his work during the latter part of his life was a per-manent miracle."[3] One such piece of work was a portrait of Gilot, her hair green and her face pale blue, like an updated *Woman with a Hat*, which caused such a furor at the Salon d'Automne in 1905. In this case, the only unhappy critic was a jealous Pablo Picasso. "What nerve he has, to want to do your portrait. What about me?"

Despite his occasional ill temper, Picasso, too, knew Matisse would someday be gone. "There are a number of things," he ad-mitted, "I shall no longer be able to talk about with anyone after Matisse's death."[4]

On that and subsequent fortnightly visits to Villa Le Rêve, Fran-çoise Gilot, an acclaimed artist herself, watched the two greatest modernists of their age converse and debate about art. They evaluated the "angular intricacies" of German Gothic style and examined the "flowing clarity" of the Italian School.[5] They did so in the rarest of human languages, known only to the two of them. "All things consid-ered," said Picasso, "there is only Matisse."[6] For the older artist, "Only one person has the right to criticize me... It's Picasso."[7] Both men were aware of the singularity of their dialogue. "We must talk to each other as much as we can," begins a quote credited at different times to Matisse and Picasso. "When one of us dies, there will be some things that the other will never be able to talk of with anyone else."[8]

Picasso was friendly on that visit to Vence, but their cordiality had always been weighted down by their competitiveness. "He saw what he wanted to see..." Matisse told Pierre, "my works in cut paper... He will put it all to good use in time. Picasso is not straightforward.

Everyone has known that for the last forty years."[9] For four decades, the two artists, perched on a "seesaw of esteem," had waged their polite war of artistic ideas.[10] As Gilot put it: "In their meetings, the active side was Pablo; the passive, Matisse. Pablo always sought to charm Matisse, like a dancer, but in the end, it was Matisse who conquered Pablo."[11]

A point of common peace was what Matisse and Picasso called "the chain." The two saw themselves as successors in "the great chain of artists."[12] They talked of "how an earlier artist might remain 'alive in the mind of another artist' to maintain the continuity of the chain."[13] They were proud to be the latest links in a connection that went back to the prehistoric hunt scenes in the caves of Western Europe. From the unknowable ancestors at Lascaux, the chain continued into recorded history: the Greeks and Romans, Giotto, Raphael and Leonardo, Vermeer and Velázquez, Ingres and Turner, Delacroix, Renoir, and Manet, who "disengaged pure painting from subject matter."[14]

And, of course, Paul Cézanne.

The artist Max Weber remembers Matisse showing his painting students Cézanne's *Bathers*: "His silence before it was more evocative and eloquent than words."[15] As Matisse himself later told the Irish-American writer Frank Harris, "My masters were Cézanne and Renoir. I never met Cézanne, I regret to say; but four years ago, I got to know Renoir, and he made a profound impression on me." Renoir's lesson was as much on aging and creation as it was about art. By the time Matisse met the great artist, Renoir's fingers were horribly swollen from rheumatism.*

"And he still did beautiful things?" asked Harris.

"All his best work," said Matisse. Renoir's was a noble end, continued Matisse. "Dying in agony, yet determined to put all the

---

* Frank Harris, *Contemporary Portraits*, 140-142. Renoir gave Matisse another lesson: "When I have arranged a bouquet for the purpose of painting it," Auguste Renoir once told Matisse, "I always turn to the side I did not plan." "An artist," he went on, "should never be a prisoner of himself, prisoner of a style, prisoner of a reputation, prisoner of success." Sooke, *Henri Matisse: A Second Life*, 18-19.

loveliness of desire and all the beauty of nature, all the sweet joy of living into one deathless scene as a possession of men forever, a blessing without alloy."[16]

The question of whether he would leave his own unalloyed legacy was on Henri Matisse's mind more and more. The meaning of an art career to Matisse was not the contents of a bank vault or even the works hung on a gallery wall; true meaning was to nourish future artists. Even before the war ended, he had fretted to Pierre about being "haunted by my inability to pass on to others the best of what I felt."[17] Matisse explained, "Every artist has to stand on his own feet and learn his own lessons, and that I, too, *must for the future concentrate on my work* and leave others to their own inspiration . . . Now, from time to time, I have the joy to believe that this or that piece of my work has real stuff in it and *may endure*. That's heaven for the artist" (emphasis added).[18] Or, as he put it to Picasso more succinctly, "As long as some painters continue to be interested in our ideas or our works, we will not be dead."[19]

The great chain of artists went into the future as well as the past; it was a continuum of creation, a dialogue between the present and the past. "Who among the painters will still carry a part of us in his heart," Matisse wondered aloud to Picasso, "as we do Manet and Cézanne?" Matisse had been to New York, and his son was an art dealer there. He certainly sensed that the city would become the postwar capital of modern art, the new debate stage on which contemporaries sparred with the dead. Matisse showed one of the Pierre Matisse Gallery catalogs to Françoise Gilot and Picasso. There in black and white were the new names of the great chain: Arshile Gorky, Robert Motherwell, Jackson Pollock. There would be others: Ellsworth Kelly, Mark Rothko, Richard Diebenkorn, Shirley Jaffe.* Perhaps, too,

---

* A friend once asked Andy Warhol what he really wanted out of life, and he replied, "I want to be Matisse." Quoted from Calvin Tomkins, "Raggedy Andy," in John Coplans's *Andy Warhol*, (New York, New York Graphic, 1971.)

Matisse and Picasso were aware of the unknowable number of artists they had inspired, as anonymous as the hands that scratched deer, horse, and oxen into the stone by firelight, names like Charlotte Salomon, who, in a life cut tragically short, saw the fullness of life resonant in Matisse's lines and color.

HENRI MATISSE HAD asked his surgeons at the clinic in Lyon in 1941 for three or four more years; despite their worries that he would not live through 1942, the surgery and subsequent care gave him nearly a decade and a half. By the spring of 1947, Matisse's second life— what he called *le sursis*—the grace period—was nearing its midpoint. In April of that year, Henri Matisse received a surprise visitor at Villa Le Rêve: Sister Jacques-Marie. They hadn't spoken since Matisse sent his former nurse his fitful ten-page defense of his artistic spirituality. By her second visit, the artist and the nun had fallen into their old habits. "He asked me to turn so he could see me from every angle," she said. "He said he could still make out my figure . . . but that my headdress really bothered him."[20] Lydia sensed "a certain tenderness" in Matisse's conversations with Sister Jacques-Marie.[21] Matisse confirmed these sentiments in a letter to André Rouveyre: "She is always a magnificent person, we talk of others and things—a little soft teasing." To another friend, he wrote, "When my Dominican sister goes by on her bicycle . . . one can think of nothing better than to watch her."[22]

But there was something else Sister Jacques-Marie wanted Matisse to see. On her second visit she brought with her a sketch she'd made for a new oratory window—a bit of literal window dressing for the dilapidated and leaky garage the Dominican nuns were using as a chapel across rue St. Jeannet. "To my surprise, he really liked it," she recalled. That peace offering under the shade of olive trees was just the beginning. "I'm going to build your chapel," Matisse said, and over the next four years he designed everything from the building itself, to the crucifix for the altar, to the very vestments to be worn by the priests.* The sisters had dreamed of a new chapel, but when Matisse agreed to design it and finance it, the dream became a reality.[23] Once the plan was in motion, the young nun asked the Mother Superior if she had informed the church leadership that Henri Matisse, known for his agnosticism and progressive values, planned to build a chapel. "Absolutely not!" she replied.[24]

Remove that which is not essential, Matisse said. Throughout his career Matisse sought to carve away the superfluous to reveal only what was vital to the transcription of his feelings onto a creation. *"Rouge, bleu, jaune, et blanc,"* he had said as his grandson sat down with his set of paints. "Red, blue, yellow, and white. That's all!" Along the chapel's south wall are six slender columns of stained-glass windows, each fifteen feet high with rounded tops, in lemon yellow, lapis blue, and emerald green. His four-color edict to Pierrot had been halved: yellow, for the Mediterranean sun; blue, the summit of Matisse's desires; and green, the combination of the two.

In the vestibule, Matisse painted the scenes of the stations of the cross using rough black brushstrokes onto white tiles, which were then glazed and installed on a huge 10' by 18' field. "I am not doing it as compartmentalized scenes," he wrote of the mural he'd waited a lifetime to paint, "but as a great unfolding drama."† The chapel is at once stark and sublime, "breathtaking in its simplicity."[25] The white marble floor, white walls, and white tiles let Matisse use the Midi light "almost as an element of the building."[26] To modulate the strong light and soften the stark whiteness, Matisse applied his *Jazz*-like cutout technique to create leaf-shaped patterns of brightly

---

* Matisse designed the vestments, copies of which were acquired by the Museum of Modern Art. For her own funeral, Sister Jacques-Marie asked a brother to wear Matisse's black chasuble, with white wings sewn onto the back. Like his paintings, there was light even in the darkest moods. "A chasuble of resurrection," Matisse said (Soeur Jacques-Marie, *The Vence Chapel*, 12, 64).

† Soeur Jacques-Marie, *The Vence Chapel*, 83. The two other murals are Saint Dominic and Virgin and Child—each bearing Matisse's oval featureless face similar to *Bathers by a River*.

colored glass. "They will be made of pure color shapes," he said, describing the windows to Rosamund Bernier,

> very brilliant. No figures, just... the shapes. Imagine
> when the sun pours through the glass, it will throw col-
> ored reflections on the white floor and walls, a whole
> orchestra of color.[27]

The result echoes the remarks of Dorothy Dudley years earlier when she saw Matisse's mural *The Dance II*. Like a "physicist," she said, Matisse had caused "light to yield secrets not known before."[28]

Painting, sculpture, textiles, ceramics, glasswork, and cutouts: all of the instruments of Matisse's life as an artist went into the Chapelle du Rosaire. That it was the culmination of Henri Matisse's genius in three dimensions was apparent to its first visitors. "Through the strength of the colors and the lines themselves," said Father Marie-Alain Couturier, "the narrow [space] was carried to the infinite."[29] *A wonderland*, said Sister Jacques-Marie, who described it with uncharacteristic lyricism: "The windows sparkle with reflections of a rare beauty on the ceramic tiles. In the course of a day the reflections change color, moving from mauve to rose, enhanced by the blues and the greens. No day is the same throughout the year." There on a hillside looking down toward the sea, the earth rotates, and with each passing hour, the white tiles reflect vibrant light, an ever-changing light, a harmony of yellow, green, and, of course, blue.

"Blue-blue-blue," he'd written in a letter to Amélie on his first stay in Nice, the color never ceased to express his emotions.[30] From the *Blue Nude* of 1907 to the tense midnight membrane of *The Conversation*, blue was human, desirous, and moody. Horizon blue was the color of French Army uniforms, and royal blue one-third of its flag. There was blue paired with black, as in *Interior with a Violin Case* a moody work from the Great War, and the infinity of *The Fall of Icarus* in the next war. Blue was as life giving as it was life draining; its shades encompassing the edge of the void of space, and the sky blue of limitless

optimism. *The Blue Eyes* were Lydia Delectorskaya's, and she was the model for *Woman in Blue*. For her essay on Lydia in *Matisse: In Search of True Painting*, Rebecca Rabinow chose the title, "The Woman in Blue."[31] "I come from the North," Matisse said. "You can't imagine how I hated those dark churches." The Vence Chapel windows were a blue the intensity of which he'd been searching for since he was a child: the blue flame of burning sulfur flame, the glint of a butterfly's wing, the cobalt blue bottles in a window of the local hardware store.

The lapis blue of the chapel windows was the penultimate step to the thin-aired summit Matisse finally reached with the series of blue nudes in 1952. As much as any of his works, *Blue Nude IV* is what we think of today when we think of Matisse. Nearly abstract, these cut paper forms in simple blue on white achieved the "timeless intangibility of celestial bodies," in Françoise Gilot's exquisite words, "released to swim in ethereal space and to dance in the Milky Way."[32] Perhaps Matisse himself realized he'd conquered his last and tallest peak. Years before, in a note to Louis Aragon, Matisse stated his goal to go "beyond any motif [to] a cosmic space."[33]

Commencing the design of an entire chapel at such an advanced age was "an improbable, grueling commission."[34] Matisse's undertaking came as no surprise to Tériade, who called it "the supreme endeavor by a painter who has always been involved with the problems of radiant color and light."[35] Even near the end of his life Matisse was adhering to the dictum he'd told his painting students at the beginning of his career. "It was better," he told them, "to strive for things [you] are not yet able to do than to go on repeating [your] successes."[36] The eminent artist, as ever, set out to reach new artistic heights, but Matisse's former nurse asked herself, "How could this eighty-year-old handicapped man [manage] to get up and down from the scaffolding."[37] Never shy of hard work, even in the winter of his life, Henri Matisse toiled willingly, enduring dizzy spells, piercing stomach cramps, asthma, insomnia, and spasms of the optic nerve.[38] "There are no secrets," he once remarked to his grandson Pierrot, "one has to pay his dues with work and sweat."[39] When Sister Jacques-Marie admitted her worry over Matisse's health, as well as her own, a senior nun reminded, "A church or a chapel destined for the offering of a sacrifice cannot be built without requiring considerable self-sacrifice on the part of those who have undertaken it . . . the price will be high."[40] Or, as the young nun herself put it succinctly: "A chapel can't be built without pain." In fact, it was Sister Jacques-Marie who was hospitalized during construction when she required an operation for appendicitis. She was surprised one day when Matisse visited her, short of breath even after taking the elevator, with an armful of flowers, candy, a book, and a bag of oranges.

"I know," said Sister Jacques-Marie, "that he expended his remaining health in completing the chapel." Yet like Renoir before him, Matisse continued to create, without complaint. He worked around his infirmaries. Unable to climb a ladder, and sometimes from his wheelchair, Matisse used a nine-foot-long bamboo pole with a small rag or charcoal at the tip to draw the models for the murals. When his eyes bothered him, he made light of it. "I see better at night than by day, not easy for a painter."[41] He was never agnostic about the centrality of his art; creating remained his raison d'être. "Matisse was dedicated to his art in the way that others are dedicated to religion."[42] In a way Matisse was proving to Sister Jacques-Marie what he'd argued in his long letter to her, a position succinctly summed up by Peter Schjeldahl: "Matisse served [art], as a monk serves God."[43] Or, as Matisse explained in a letter to Pierre: "I live through moments of spiritual fulfillment that make all my sufferings worthwhile."[44]

When Rosamund Bernier, an old friend, paid a visit to him in Vence for a piece in *Vogue*, she found him "a figure of Edwardian elegance," sitting up in bed in a faded turquoise sweater and tie, but "completely absorbed" in his project. As with his paintings, he obsessed. A cigarette dangling from his lips, he studied the problems that had to be solved. "A masterpiece is never finished!" Even as his handwriting became almost illegible, he jotted notes.

I have to reduce the leadwork in the floweret...
I have to choose a special shade of yellow...
The chapel will be useless if it isn't perfect.[45]

Did acting as draftsman, decorator, and architectural designer keep him from the easel, Rosamund Bernier wanted to know? "I have time for painting," he replied cheerfully, "I am only eighty!"* For Matisse, the labor was worth it. "For me this chapel represents the result of an entire lifetime of work and the flowering of an enormous effort, sincere and difficult."[46] In addition to being the subject of magazine articles, Matisse's new church was celebrated by the Museum of Modern Art, which acquired copies of the "butterfly-like" vestments and full-scale designs for the stained-glass windows. Exhibitions in Philadelphia, Lucerne, Switzerland, and Tokyo also celebrated the artist's latest project.[47] While others were impressed by the artist's ambitious project, his rival, who by this stage was a Communist, was not. When Pablo Picasso learned of Matisse's work on the chapel, he went on the offensive.

"Do you pray," he wanted to know.

"No, not really," said Matisse, "I meditate."[48]

"You're crazy to make a chapel for those people. Do you believe in that stuff or not?" Instead of a chapel, Picasso told Matisse, he should have designed a fruit and vegetable market.

"For me, doing this is essentially a work of art... it is essential to work in a state of mind that is close to prayer," Matisse said.

---

* Rosamund Bernier. "Matisse Designs a New Church." *Vogue*, Feb. 15, 1949. Matisse was assisted on the architectural side by Father M.A. Couturier and Brother Louis-Bertrand Rayssiguier, who asked a sister how he could meet Matisse. "Just say you're an architect," she replied (*A Model for Matisse* film). Matisse wanted the cornerstone plaque to mention the contributions of Sister Jacques-Marie and Lydia Delectorskaya—"two excellent assistants without whose help I could never have done this chapel," but both women declined. See Sister Jacques-Marie, *The Vence Chapel*, 98-99. Nevertheless, Matisse appreciated that Sister Jacques-Marie was the (often reluctant) liaison for the religious community, the artisans, and the press.

Moreover, "My greens are greener and my oranges more orange than any actual fruit," he added, his smiling blue eyes peering over his glasses.[49]

The older artist had once again danced around Picasso, pulling the cape away from the charging bull.

In time, too, other critics came around. There had been a Christian church in Vence since 419 CE, so there was a question of whether his modern place of worship would be accepted by the conservative authorities. When the Chapelle du Rosaire was consecrated in 1951, led by the Archbishop of Nice, a young monk remarked, "I feel less and less Gothic, and more and more Matisse." After overcoming their initial skepticism, the Dominican sisters came to appreciate the simplicity of the space and the shifting colors within.[50] *What does it all mean?* sightseers demanded to know when they entered the simple chapel and stood before its semi-abstract stations of the cross. The nun in charge had a ready reply:

"It means modern."[51]

THE FIRST FALL and winter after the end of the Second World War had been called "the season of Matisse." It was more than a season. In the first half of the twentieth century Europe had suffered a murderous internecine war in the trenches, economic depression, the rise of dictators, blitzkrieg, and death camps. After four decades of tumult, a new, brightly colored world beckoned. On the centenary of Henri Matisse's birth in December 1969, critic James R. Mellow could write in *The New York Times* of the painter's "still ripening art." More than half a century after *those* words, Matisse's works remain evergreen. "When you look at this painting," said Tériade, "you are not afraid of old age anymore, since the spirit is thus shown to be forever young."[52]

"The painter of the future," Vincent van Gogh once said, "will be such a colorist as has never yet been seen." The painter of the future died in Nice on November 3, 1954, the day after finishing a sketch of Lydia and declaring it "good enough." Lydia and Marguerite were by his side.

On the day of Matisse's requiem mass, held at the Cimiez Monastery, Amélie, who had lived apart from Matisse since 1939, was accompanied by their children, Marguerite, Jean, and Pierre. Lydia Delectorskaya did not attend the funeral. Whether in deference to Amélie or as an acknowledgment that the family had never accepted her role as their father's companion, immediately following Matisse's death, Lydia departed. She left Matisse's home just as she had arrived two decades earlier: carrying a single suitcase.

To conclude Matisse's funeral mass, the Archbishop of Nice read an excerpt from a letter Matisse had written to the Dominicans in Vence: "I offer you, with greatest humility, this chapel which I consider the masterpiece of my life, despite its imperfections. I hope that those who visit it will be purified and solaced."

Henri Matisse left behind his life's work—his life *was* his work—which he created in a Europe we know only through photographs and newsreels, jerky and violent, in black and white. In our own time, autocracy is again in season, part of the cycle of history. Matisse's bravura outlasted his era of invasions and occupations just as his palette had outdistanced "the grayness of newspapers and pipe smoke" of northern France.[53] "His art spoke of joy and happiness almost beyond human reach," wrote Françoise Gilot, "it carried the dream of an ever-present golden age and a promise of beauty for tomorrow."[54] Matisse endures because the joy in his works is finely counterbalanced with beguiling energies; his paintings are at once simple and complex, overt yet unknowable, celestial and terrestrial. Standing before the "gorgeous tragedy" of *Bathers by a River* in Chicago, or the spontaneous fireworks of *Creole Dancer* in Nice, or moved by the power of the chapel on that sunlit hillside in Vence, it is possible to believe that with grace and equilibrium, the art of Henri Matisse has transcended history itself, in fullest color.

Epilogue

AMÉLIE MATISSE DIED IN NOVEMBER 1958 and was buried next to her husband.

The three children of Henri Matisse remained fiercely dedicated to his legacy. Jean, who had been "famously difficult," immediately went to work cataloging his father's sculptures, becoming at last "the archetypical good son."[1] Marguerite tended the Matisse archive, and when she died at age 87 in Paris, she and her son, Claude, were in the midst of indexing his engravings. Her last words were "My work! My work! My work!"[2] The massive two-volume catalog was published in 1983. Pierre died in 1989 as an internationally renowned art dealer and champion of modern art (and artists) in the United States.*

Among the Matisse children, only Pierre remained in contact with Lydia Delectorskaya after Henri Matisse's death (and he did so for the next thirty-five years). Though he once referred to her as a "green-eyed dragon," Pierre fully acknowledged that Madame Lydia was vital to understanding the evolution of Matisse's cutouts in the last two decades of his life and to learning the full story of the war-

---

* Pierre Matisse obituary, *New York Times*, Aug. 11, 1989. Pierre died at his home in Saint-Jean-Cap-Ferrat, just a few kilometers from Nice, but his attachment to New York remained after his death. The archive of his gallery was left to the Morgan Museum, and the contents of his gallery, valued at nearly $150 million, to the Metropolitan Museum of Art.

time icons that became *Jazz*. She had been in the studio, often more a partner than mere assistant. She knew how the colors and shapes came to be so intimately that when the fragile cutouts needed to be restored or repaired, Pierre turned to Lydia. Having lived far from his father for so long, Pierre was "engrossed" by Lydia's memories of Matisse in his studio in Vence and her recall of his pronouncements. When an inspiring moment passed, he'd say, "There goes my champagne!" "Make some blue," he'd command, or "bring me any sheets of blue." With her typical precision, Lydia could recall the contemporaneous remarks of Matisse during the Occupation as he shaped the cutouts like *The Wolf*, with its "bloodstained eye, his jaws ready to bite."

For lending her expertise over these four decades, Lydia Delectorskaya sought nothing. Quietly, even anonymously, she served the legacy of Henri Matisse, adding critical detail to Louis Aragon's *Henri Matisse: A Novel* (1971) and Sister Jacques-Marie's *Henri Matisse: The Vence Chapel* (1993). In 1986, Lydia's book *With Apparent Ease* was published, covering the years 1935 to the outbreak of World War II, and in 1996, its companion, *Contre Vents et Marées*, was published, revealing Matisse's work during his "second life" in the years of war and occupation.

Lydia Delectorskaya died in Paris in 1998 at the age of 87; in her will she asked that a shirt of Matisse's be placed in her casket next to her.

Acknowledgments

AH! NICE IS A BEAUTIFUL PLACE!

So said Henri Matisse to Charles Camoin the first spring he spent in the city. Those were my sentiments, and those of my wife, Elizabeth, when we, having just been married, walked hand in hand out of the simple pastel-colored church into an almost unreal beauty: blue sky, piney mountains, and the sea, bobbing with ships' masts in the port of the picturesque village just a few miles from the center of Nice.

Nice and the villages around it became part of our lives that day. On our many return visits over the past twenty-five years, we've never tired of the place so layered with history, art, and beauty. We've trod the dusty paths among the Roman ruins, stood before somber Great War memorials, and seen Henri Matisse's haunts in Cimiez, Cours Saleya, and nearby Vence. While researching this book, I was grateful to have the opportunity to again spend time in the places where the great artist still casts his shadow under the abundant Mediterranean sun.

I am also grateful for those who shared with me their expertise. I would especially like to thank Rebecca Rabinow, a Matisse expert who directs the Menil Collection in Houston, Texas. I was also fortunate to be welcomed to the Metropolitan Museum of Art by curator Jennifer Farrell. During a gray and misty day in New York,

we examined the startlingly fresh colors of the Museum's copy of
Jazz. The skies were a crystalline blue a few months later as I sat
at a café table in Saint-Jean-Cap-Ferrat. Speaking with Madame
Colette Chauvelot, who lived under both Italian administration in
Nice and Nazi occupation in Paris, was riveting. Over an afternoon, she described in sharp detail how she worked around the
thousand little indignities of authoritarianism—a truer example of
le système D cannot be found. I would also like to thank her son,
Gérard Francès, who helped facilitate that conversation. Dr. Elizabeth Vihlen McGregor was good enough to discuss with me her
doctoral thesis on how jazz music became woven into French society in part due to the American soldiers in France during the two
world wars.

As was the case with my previous book, *The Confidante*, I owe a
tremendous debt of gratitude to the archivists, curators, and staff at
several fine institutions and museums in the United States and in
Europe: Ruth R. Marder Center for Matisse Studies at the Baltimore
Museum of Art, Barnes Foundation, Philadelphia Museum of Art,
Chicago Institute of Art, Morgan Library and Museum in New York,
National World War II Museum in New Orleans, Fogg Museum
at Harvard University, Tisch Library at Tufts University, and Boston Public Library. European institutions include the Archives
Matisse Paris (with gratitude to Georges Matisse); the Courtauld In-
stitute of Art, London; Fondation Maeght in St-Paul de Vence; the
Musèe de la Resistance and Musée Matisse in Nice (special thanks
to Delphine Ménage); Musée Henri Matisse in the north, at Le
Cateau; the Picasso Museum in Antibes; and, of course, the Chapelle
du Rosaire in Vence, France.

I am also indebted to the scholars of Henri Matisse and his art. The
late John Russell and his wife, Rosamund Bernier, Jack Flam, Rebecca
Rabinow, Catherine Bock-Weiss, and, of course, Hilary Spurling,
whose marvelous two-volume biography illuminated the private life
of the artist so long misunderstood. Françoise Gilot, in interviews and

in her writing, conveys, often with lyricism, a deep connection to Matisse the man and the artist. I found her a vital source.

Heartfelt thanks are also due to my literary agent, John Rudolph, of Dystel, Goderich & Bourret, and to the team at Citadel/Kensington Publishing, including publisher Jackie Dinas, senior editor Liz May, senior communications manager (and artist!) Ann Pryor, production editor Rebecca Cremonese, and Sarah Selim.

At numerous book events around the country, I am proud to be the author with the best video book trailers. For that, I thank my longtime friend, the award-winning John MacGibbon.

My family supported me throughout the research and writing. My godfather Randy Baidas's appreciation of art and literature translated to helpful guidance on the manuscript. My appreciation also to Will Reeves, Judy Fox Gorham, Hilary Gorham, Courtney Hayes-Sturgeon, Chloe and Theo Sturgeon, and my father, Gregory Louis Gorham, a lifelong artist whose dedication to his art is positively Matissean.

No one's support meant more than that of my wife, Elizabeth Hayes, my first and best reader. Since we stepped into the Mediterranean sun together that day long ago, she has been a source of limitless encouragement. It is impossible to convey how much she meant to this book. There is hardly a page that did not benefit from her keen input. She helped make my ideas about a story of war and occupation, art and family, cohere into what I hope is a worthy narrative of a critical period of Henri Matisse's operatic life.

This book is dedicated to you, Elizabeth. *Je t'aime.*

Bibliography

Adereth, M. *Aragon, the Resistance Poems: (Le Crève-coeur, Les Yeux D'Elsa and La Diane Française)*. London: Grant & Cutler, 1985.

Alexander, Sidney. *Marc Chagall: A Biography*. London: Cassell, 1978: 440.

Ambrose, Stephen E. "Eisenhower, the Intelligence Community, and the D-Day Invasion." *The Wisconsin Magazine of History* 64, no. 4 (1981).

Aragon, Louis. *Henri Matisse; A Novel [by] Aragon*. Translated by Jean Stewart. New York: Harcourt Brace Jovanovich, 1972.

Auster, Paul. *The Random House Book of Twentieth-Century French Poetry: With Translations by American and British Poets*. New York: Vintage Books, 1984.

Baldwin, Thomas, J. E. Fowler, and Ana Maria Sousa Aguiar de Medeiros. *Questions of Influence in Modern French Literature*. Houndmills, Basingstoke, UK: Palgrave Macmillan, 2013.

Barbier, Mary K. *D-Day Deception: Operation Fortitude and the Normandy Invasion*.Bloomsbury Publishing, , 2007.

Barr, Alfred H. *Matisse: His Art and His Public*. New York: Museum of Modern Art, 1951.

———. "Picasso 1940-1944: A Digest with Notes." *The Bulletin of the Museum of Modern Art* 12, no. 3 (1945).

Barritt, D. P. "Modern Church Design: Matisse's Dominican Chapel at Vence." *The Irish Monthly* 80, no. 949 (1952).

Bell, Clive. "Matisse and Picasso." *Europa* 1, no. 1 (1933).

Bell, Quentin. *Elders and Betters*. London: John Murray, 1995.

Bentley, Toni. "The Obsessive Art and Great Confession of Charlotte Salomon." *The New Yorker*, July 15, 2017.

Bernauer, Germaine, and George Bernauer, eds. *Defeat and Beyond: An Anthology of The French Wartime Writing 1940-1945*. N.p.: Pantheon, 1970.

Bernier, Rosamund. "Matisse Designs a New Church." *Vogue*, February 15, 1949.

Birmingham, Stephen. "Reckless: The Artistic Love Life of Peggy Guggenheim." *Vanity Fair*, February 1986.

Bishop, Janet C., Cécile Debray, and Rebecca A. Rabinow. *The Steins Collect: Matisse, Picasso, and the Parisian Avant-garde*. San Francisco: San Francisco Museum of Modern Art; in association with Yale University Press, 2011.

Bock, Catherine C. "Henri Matisse's 'Bathers by a River.'" *The Art Institute of Chicago Museum Studies* 16, no. 1 (1990).

———. "'Woman Before an Aquarium' and 'Woman on a Rose Divan': Matisse in the Helen Birch Bartlett Memorial Collection." *The Art Institute of Chicago Museum Studies* 12, no. 2 (1986).

Bock-Weiss, Catherine, and Henri Matisse. *Henri Matisse: Modernist against the Grain*. University Park, PA: Pennsylvania State University Press, 2009.

Bonnard, Pierre, and Henri Matisse. *Bonnard/Matisse: Letters Between Friends, 1925-1946*. New York: H.N. Abrams, 1992.

Boyer, Marie-France, Hélène Adant, and Henri Matisse. *Matisse at Villa Le Rêve*. London: Thames & Hudson, 2004.

Brée, Germaine, and George Bernauer. *Defeat and Beyond: An Anthology of the French Wartime Writing 1940-1945*. N.p.: Pantheon, 1970.

Brereton, Geoffrey. *A Short History of French Literature*. 2nd ed. Harmondsworth, UK: Penguin, 1976.

Brown, Jennifer Stafford. "'Au feu de ce qui fut brule ce qui sera': Louis Aragon and the Subversion of the Medieval." *Romantic Review*, 2010.

Brown, Kathryn. *Henri Matisse*. Enhanced Credo edition. London, Boston: Reaktion Books, Credo Reference, 2023.

Bussy, Jane Simone. "A Great Man." *The Burlington Magazine* 128, no. 995 (1986).

Calvo, Edmond-François, and Victor Dancette. *La Bête Est Morte!* Paris: Éditions Gallimard, 2011.

Camoin, Charles, Claudine Grammont, and Henri Matisse. *Correspondance entre Charles Camoin et Henri Matisse: Lettres Présentées et Annotées*. Lausanne: Bibliothèque des Arts, 1997.

Carco, Francis. *L'Ami des Peintres*. N.p.: Éditions de Milieu du Monde, 1944.

Carrier, David. "The Beauty of Henri Matisse." *Journal of Aesthetic Education* 38, no. 2 (2004).

Cassarini, Jean, ed. *Matisse à Nice*. Nice, France: Imprimerie Ciais, 1984.

Cassou, Jean. *Henri Matisse Exposition Retrospective 1956*. N.p.: Editions des Musees Nationaux, 1956.

Cassou, Jean, and Timothy Adès. *33 Sonnets of the Resistance and Other Poems = 33 Sonnets Composés Au Secret Et Autres Poèmes*. Todmorden, UK: Arc Publications, 2004.

Caws, Mary Ann. *The Yale Anthology of Twentieth-Century French Poetry*. New Haven: Yale University Press, 2004.

Chauvelot, Colette, and Gérard Francès. Interview by Christopher C. Gorham. Nice, France. June 25, 2024.

Cone, Michèle C. *Artists under Vichy: A Case of Prejudice and Persecution*. Princeton, NJ: Princeton University Press, 1992.

Couturier, Rev. Father. "Church Full of Joy." *Vogue*, December 1951.

Cowart, Jack. *Henri Matisse: Paper Cut-outs*. St. Louis, MO: St. Louis Art Museum, 1977.

Cowart, Jack, and Dominique Fourcade. *Henri Matisse: The Early Years in Nice, 1916-1930*. Washington, NY: National Gallery of Art; H.N. Abrams, 1986.

Cross, Robin. *Operation Dragoon: The Allied Liberation of the South of France: 1944*. New York: Pegasus Books, 2019.

Cullen, Stephen M., and Mark Stacey. *World War II Vichy French Security Troops*. London: Bloomsbury Publishing Plc, 2018.

Curtis, Michael. *Verdict on Vichy: Power and Prejudice in the Vichy France Regime*. New York: Arcade Pub., 2003.

Dagen, Philippe. "Que faisiez-vous pendant la geurre? Je peignais." *Le Monde* (Paris), October 15, 2012.

D'Alessandro, Stephanie, John Elderfield, Art Institute of Chicago, and Museum of Modern Art (New York, N.Y.). 2010. *Matisse : Radical Intervention 1913–1917 [Published on the Occasion of the Exhibition Held at the Art Institute of Chicago, 20 March–20 June 2010 ; the Museum of Modern Art, New York, 18 July–11 October 2010]*. Chicago: Art Institute of Chicago.

Delectorskaya, Lydia. *With Apparent Ease—Henri Matisse: Paintings from 1935-1939*. Paris: Adrien Maeght Editeur, 1988.

Delectorskaya, Lydia, and Isabelle Monod-Fontaine. *Henri Matisse: Contre Vents et Marées: Peinture et Livres Illustrés de 1939 à 1943*. Paris: Editions Irus et Vincent Hansma, 1996.

DiCrescenzo, Casimiro. *Tériade and Matisse: A Friendship*. N.p.: Yoshii Gallery, 1997.

Dixon, Kenneth L. "Nice's Defenses Intricate but Fail to Serve Purpose." *The San Bernardino County Sun*, September 10, 1944.

Dorléac, Laurence Bertrand. *L'Art de la Défaite: (1940-1944)*. N.p.: Seuil, 2010.

Dudley, Dorothy. "Notes on Painting: The Matisse Fresco in Merion, Pennsylvania." *Hound & Horn* 7 (March 1934).

Elderfield, John, and Henri Matisse. *Henri Matisse: A Retrospective*. New York: Museum of Modern Art; Distributed by H.N. Abrams, 1992.

Engel, Gerhard, and Hildegard von Kotze. *Heeresadjutant Bei Hitler, 1938-1943*. Stuttgart: Deutsche Verlags-Anstalt, 1974.

Escholier, Raymond. *Matisse: From the Life*. N.p.: Faber and Faber, 1960.

Farrell, Jennifer. Jordan Schnitzer Curator, The Metropolitan Museum of Art, Interview by Christopher C. Gorham. New York, NY. April 17, 2024.

Feliciano, Hector, and Timothy Bent. *The Lost Museum: The Nazi Conspiracy to Steal the World's Greatest Works of Art*. New York: Basic Books, a member of the Perseus Books Group, 2006.

Felstiner, Mary. "Commandant of Drancy: Alois Brunner and the Jews of France." *Holocaust and Genocide Studies* 2, no. 1 (1987).

Felstiner, Mary Lowenthal. *To Paint Her Life: Charlotte Salomon in the Nazi Era*. New York, NY: HarperPerennial, 1995.

Flanner, Janet. "How War Changed the Way We See Matisse," *The New Yorker*, December 21, 1951.

"Foreign News: New Bully." *TIME*, February 7, 1944.

Fraser, Kennedy. "Matisse and His Women." *Vogue*, September 1992.

———. *Ornament and Silence: Essays on Women's Lives from Edith Wharton to Germaine Greer*. New York: Vintage, 1998.

Freed, Barbara, director. *A Model for Matisse: The Story of Henri Matisse, Sister Jacques-Marie and the Vence Chapel.* First Run Features, 2003.

Freedman, Ariela. "Charlotte Salomon, Degenerate Art, and Modernism as Resistance." *Journal of Modern Literature* 41, no. 1 (2017).

Frost, Rosamund. "First Fruits of Exile." *Art News* 15, no. 31 (1942).

Gabriel, Mary. *The Art of Acquiring: A Portrait of Etta and Claribel Cone*. Baltimore, MD: Bancroft Press, 2002.

Gilbert, Martin. *The Righteous: The Unsung Heroes of the Holocaust*. New York: Henry Holt & Sons, 2003.

Gilot, Françoise. *Matisse and Picasso: A Friendship in Art*. New York: Doubleday, 1990.

Gilot, Françoise, and Carlton Lake. *Life with Picasso*. New York: New York Review Books, 2019.

Gold, Mary Jayne. *Crossroads Marseilles, 1940*. Garden City, NY: Doubleday, 1980.

Gowing, Lawrence. *Matisse*. New York: Oxford University Press, 1979.

Griswold, William, Jennifer Tonkovich, Alessandra Carnielli, and Margaret Loudon. *Pierre Matisse and His Artists*. New York: Pierpont Morgan Library, 2002.

Grubbs, Henry A. "Nazi Domination of the Press: Publishers in France Conform to New Order." *Princeton University Library Chronicle* 2, no. 3 (1941).

Hall, Anthony. *D-Day Day by Day: The Planning, the Landings, the Battles*. New York: Chartwell Books, 2012.

Hanna, Martha. *The Mobilization of Intellect: French Scholars and Writers During the Great War*. Cambridge, Mass.: Harvard University Press, 1996.

Hanotaux, Gabriel. *L'Aisne Pendant la Grande Geurre*. Paris, F. Alcan, 1919.

Hanson, Victor Davis. *The Second World Wars: How the First Global Conflict Was Fought and Won.* New York: Basic Books, 2017.

Harris, Frank. *Contemporary Portraits.* New York: Brentano's, 1923.

Herrera, Hayden. *Matisse: A Portrait.* New York: Harcourt Brace, 1993.

Hilary Spurling. Hosted by Charlie Rose. Aired January 3, 2006.

Horne, Alistair. *La Belle France: A Short History.* New York: Knopf, 2005.

———. *Seven Ages of Paris.* New York: Vintage Books, 2004.

Isenberg, Sheila. *A Hero of Our Own: How One American in Marseille Saved Marc Chagall, Max Ernst, Andre Breton, Hannah Arendt, and More than 1000 Others from the Nazis.* New York: Random House, 2001.

Jackman, Jarrell C., and Carla M. Borden. *The Muses Flee Hitler: Cultural Transfer and Adaptation, 1930-1945.* Washington, DC: Smithsonian Institution Press, 1983.

Jacobs, Vivian, and Wilhemina Jacobs. "The Color Blue: Its Use as Metaphor and Symbol." *American Speech* 33, no. 1 (1958).

Jewell, Edward Alden. "'Accent on Modernism.'" *The New York Times*, March 24, 1946.

Kauffer, Rémi. *Les Femmes De L'ombre: L'Histoire Occultée Des Espionnes.* Paris: Perrin, 2019.

Klarsfeld, Serge. *Vichy-Auschwitz: la rôle de Vichy dans la solution finale de la question juive en France, 1942.* Paris: Fayard, 1983.

Kleff, Patrice. *Ceux De Verdun: Les Écrivains Et La Grande Guerre.* Ed. rev ed. Paris: Flammarion, 2006.

Klein, John, and Henri Matisse. *Matisse and Decoration.* New Haven, CT: Yale University Press, 2018.

Kundahl, George G. *The Riviera at War: World War II on the Côte D'Azur.* London: I. B. Tauris & Co., 2019.

Langdon, Gabrielle. "A Spiritual Space: Matisse's Chapel of the Dominicans at Vence." *Zeitschrift Für Kunstgeschichte* 51, no. 4 (1988).

Larew, Karl G. "From Pigeons to Crystals: The Development of Radio Communication in U.S. Army Tanks in World War II." *The Historian* 67, no. 4 (2005).

Laudon, Paule, and Henri Matisse. *Matisse in Tahiti.* Paris: Adam Biro, 2001.

Levitov, Karen, and Melissa Klein. *Collecting Matisse and Modern Masters: The Cone Sisters of Baltimore.* New York, New Haven, CT: Jewish Museum, under the auspices of the Jewish Theological Seminary of America; Distributed by Yale University Press, 2011.

Lieberman, William S., ed. *Modern Masters, Manet to Matisse.* N.p.: Museum of Modern Art, 1975.

Luxe, Gene. "What Is Wrong with Modern Art?" *Current History (1916-1940)* 38, no. 3 (1933).

MacChesn, Clara T. "A Talk with Matisse, Leader of the Post-Impressionists." *The New York Times*, March 9, 1913.

Manzoni, Delphine. "Maintenir l'ordre à Lyon 1940-1943." Master's thesis, Université Lyon 2, 2007.

Marcot, François, Bruno Leroux, and Christine Levisse-Touzé. *Dictionnaire Historique De La Résistance: Résistance Intérieure et France Libre*. Paris: Laffont, 2006.

Marnham, Patrick. *Resistance and Betrayal: The Death and Life of the Greatest Hero of the French Resistance*. New York: Random House, 2002.

———. *War in the Shadows: Resistance, Deception and Betrayal in Occupied France*. London: Oneworld Publications, 2021.

Marshall, George C., Larry I. Bland, and Sharon R. Ritenour. *The Papers of George Catlett Marshall. Vol. 3, 'The Right Man for the Job,' December 7, 1941–May 31, 1943*. Baltimore, MD: Johns Hopkins University Press, 1991.

Matisse, Henri, Pierre Courthion, and Serge Guilbaut. *Chatting with Henri Matisse: The Lost 1941 Interview*. Los Angeles, CA: Getty Research Institute, 2013.

Matisse, Henri, and Jack D. Flam. *Matisse on Art*. New York: E.P. Dutton, 1978.

Henri Matisse, Jean Leymarie, Herbert Read, and William S. Lieberman. *Henri Matisse*, Berkeley, CA: University of California Press, 1966, 26.

Matisse, Henri, Pablo Picasso, and Elizabeth Cowling. *Matisse Picasso*. Ed. to accompany the exhibition ed. London, [France]: Tate Pub.; Réunion des Musées Nationaux; Museum of Modern Art, 2002.

Matisse, Henri, André Rouveyre, and Hanne Finsen. *Matisse, Rouveyre: Correspondence*. Paris: Flammarion, 2001.

Matisse, Henri, Colette Taylor-Jones, Jean-Benoit Ormal-Grenon, Thomas Bari Garnier, Elizabeth G. Heard, and John Lee. *Matisse in the 1930s*. Philadelphia, PA: Philadelphia Museum of Art; Musée de l'Orangerie: RMN-Grand Palais; in association with Yale University Press, 2022.

Matisse, Pierre H. *The Missing Matisse [a Memoir]*. Carol Stream, IL: Tyndale Momentum, an imprint of Tyndale House Publishers, 2016.

Matisse: Une Seconde Vie: 1941-1954. Paris: Société française de promotion artistique, 2005.

May, Ernest R. *Strange Victory: Hitler's Conquest of France*. New paperback ed. London: I.B. Tauris, 2009.

McGregor, Elizabeth Vihlen. Interview by Christopher C. Gorham. Boston, MA. April 3, 2024.

———. *Jazz and Postwar French Identity: Improvising the Nation*. Lanham, MD: Lexington Books, an imprint of The Rowman & Littlefield Publishing Group, 2016.

Mellow, James R. "Matisse: A Celebration of Pleasure." *The New York Times Magazine*, December 1969.

The Montreal Star. "Henri Matisse Found in Lyons Hospital." March 5, 1941.

Morgan, Ted. "L'Affaire Touvier: Opening Old Wounds." *New York Times*, October 1, 1989.

Morris, George L. K. "A Brief Encounter with Matisse." *LIFE*, August 28, 1970.

Mosier, John. *The Blitzkrieg Myth: How Hitler and the Allies Misread the Strategic Realities of World War II*. New York: HarperCollins, 2004.

Moynahan, Brian. *The French Century: An Illustrated History of Modern France.* Paris: Flammarion: Distributed in North America by Rizzoli International, 2007.

Muel-Dreyfus, Francine, and Kathleen A. Johnson. *Vichy and the Eternal Feminine: A Contribution to a Political Sociology of Gender*. Durham, NC: Duke University Press, 2001.

Murphy, Robert. "Françoise Gilot Reminisces about Henri Matisse." *The Wall Street Journal*, 2014.

Nayak-Guercio, Aparna. "The Project of Liberation and the Projection of National Identity: Calvo, Aragon, Jouhandeau, 1944-45." PhD dissertation, University of Pittsburgh, 2006.

Nelck, Annelies. *L'Olivier Du Rêve: Matisse à Vence: Témoignage*. Nice: Achevé d'imprimer sur les presses d'Imprimix, 1999.

Nelson, Michael. *The French Riviera: A History*. Leicestershire: Matador, 2017.

Nettelbeck, Colin W. *War and Identity: The French and the Second World War: An Anthology of Texts*. London: Routledge, 2023.

Nicholas, Lynn H. *The Rape of Europa: The Fate of Europe's Treasures in the Third Reich and the Second World War*. New York: Knopf Doubleday Publishing Group, 2009.

Nivet, Philippe. *La France Occupée: 1914-1918*. Paris: A. Colin, 2013.

Panicacci, Jean-Louis. *L'Occupation Italienne*. Rennes, France: Presses Universitaires de Rennes, 2010.

Panicacci, Jean-Louis, ed. *La Résistance Azuréene*. Nice, France: Editions Serre, 1994.

———. *Les Lieux De Mémoire De La Deuxième Guerre Mondiale Dans Les Alpes-Maritimes*. Nice: Serre, 1997.

Panicacci, Jean-Louis, and Jean Combes. *Les Alpes-Maritimes Dans La Guerre: 1939-1945*. Paris: De Borée, 2013.

Paxton, Robert O. *The Anatomy of Fascism*. New York: Vintage Books, 2007.

———. *Vichy France: Old Guard and New Order, 1940-1944*. New York: Columbia University Press, 2001.

"Pierre Matisse Gallery." *The Brooklyn Daily Eagle*, February 14, 1943.

Pleynet, Marcelin. *Henri Matisse*. Paris: Gallimard, 1993.

Pollard, Miranda. "A Question of Silence? Odette Rosenstock, Moussa Abadi, and the Réseau Marcel." *French Politics, Culture and Society* 30, no. 2 (2012).

Poznanski, Renée. *Les Juifs En France Pendant La Seconde Guerre Mondiale.* Nouv. ed., mise à jour et corr ed. Paris: Hachette, 1997.

Rabinow, Dr. Rebecca, Director, The Menil Collection Interview by Christopher C. Gorham. Houston, TX. April 2, 2024.

Rabinow, Rebecca. "The Legacy of la Rue Férou: Livres d'Artiste Created for Tériade by Rouault, Bonnard, Matisse, Léger, Le Corbusier, Chagall, Giacometti, and Miró." PhD dissertation, New York University, 1995.

Rabinow, Rebecca A., Dorthe Aagesen, and Henri Matisse. *Matisse: In Search of True Painting.* New York: Metropolitan Museum of Art, 2012.

Reverdy, Pierre, Pablo Picasso, and François Chapon. *Le Chant des Morts.* Paris: Gallimard, 2016.

Rewald, Sabine, and Magdalena Dabrowski. *The American Matisse: The Dealer, His Artists, His Collection: The Pierre and Maria-Gaetana Matisse Collection.* New York: Metropolitan Museum of Art and New Haven, CT: Yale University Press, 2009.

Richard, Paul. "'Matisse in Morocco': Dreaming in Color." *The Washington Post*, March 18, 1990.

Roe, Sue. *In Montmartre: Picasso, Matisse and the Birth of Modernist Art.* New York, NY: Penguin Books, 2016.

Russell, John. "Art: Henri Matisse in Nice, 1916-1930, An Exhibition at the National Gallery." *The New York Times*, November 2, 1986.

———. *Matisse: Father & Son.* New York: Harry N. Abrams, 1999.

———. "New Exhibition Illuminates the Greatness That Was Matisse." *The New York Times*, October 26, 1986.

———. "'Was Derain a Collaborationist?'" *The New York Times*, Art Mailbag, November 29, 1981.

Sapiro, Gisèle. *The French Writers' War, 1940-1953.* Durham, NC: Duke University Press, 2014.

Scarry, Elaine. "On Beauty and Being Just." Lecture, Yale University, New Haven, CT. March 25, 1998.

Schjeldahl, Peter. "Art as Life: The Matisse We Never Knew." *The New Yorker*, August 29, 2005.

Schneider, Pierre, Michael Taylor, and Bridget Marzo. *Matisse.* New York: Rizzoli, 1984.

Semerjian, Victor. "Artists in Exile: The Great Flight of Culture." Master's thesis, University of British Columbia, Sept. 1990.

Serge, Victor, and Peter Sedgwick. *Memoirs of a Revolutionary, 1901-1941.* Reprinted with corrections and additions ed. Oxford: Oxford University Press, 1980.

Sica, Emanuele. *Mussolini's Army in the French Riviera: Italy's Occupation of France*. Urbana: University of Illinois Press, 2017.

Silver, Kenneth E. "Matisse at Vence: An Epilogue to 'Van Gogh and Gauguin: The Search for Sacred Art." *French Politics, Culture and Society* 24, no. 2 (2006).

———. *Esprit De Corps: The Art of the Parisian Avant-garde and the First World War, 1914-1925*. Princeton, NJ: Princeton University Press, 1989.

Simpson, Louis. *Modern Poets of France: A Bilingual Anthology*. Brownsville, OR: Story Line Press, 1998.

Soby, James Thrall, comp. *Artists in Exile Exhibition Catalog*. New York: Pierre Matisse Gallery, 1942.

Soeur Jacques-Marie, Arthur Goldhammer, and Henri Matisse. "Henri Matisse." *Grand Street* 50 (1994).

Soeur Jacques-Marie, Henri Matisse, and Barbara F. Freed. *Henri Matisse: The Vence Chapel*, new edition. Paris: Bernard Chauveau Éditeur, 2014.

Sooke, Alastair. *Henri Matisse: A Second Life*. London: Penguin Books, 2014.

Spotts, Frederic. *Hitler and the Power of Aesthetics*. Woodstock, NY: Overlook Press, 2009.

———. *The Shameful Peace: How French Artists and Intellectuals Survived the Nazi Occupation*. New Haven, CT: Yale University Press, 2010.

Spurling, Hilary. *The Unknown Matisse: A Life of Henri Matisse, the Early Years, 1869-1908*. 3rd ed. New York: Alfred A. Knopf, 2008.

Spurling, Hilary, *Matisse the Master: A Life of Henri Matisse: The Conquest of Color, 1909-1954*. New York: Alfred A. Knopf, 2005 (hereinafter "*The Conquest of Color*")

Stirling, Monica. "Elsa Triolet." *The Atlantic*, September 1949.

———. "A Touch of Magnificence." *Vogue*, 1945.

Swan, Rodney T. "Cultural Resistance in Henri Matisse's Poèmes de Charles d'Orléans." *Visual Resources* 36, no. 1 (2018).

———. "Resistance and Resurgence: The Cultural and Political Dynamic of the Livre d' Artiste and the German Occupation of France." PhD dissertation, University of New South Wales, 2016.

———. "Symbolism and Allusion in Matisse's Jazz." *RIHA Journal* 0209 (May 15, 2019).

Thériault, Mark J. "Art as Propaganda in Vichy France, 1940-1944." PhD dissertation, McGill University, 2007.

Thomas, Georges-Michel. *Le Finistère Dans La Guerre: II, La Libération*. Brest: Editions de la Cité, 1981.

Triolet, Elsa. *A Fine of Two Hundred Francs*. New York, NY: Penguin Books-Virago Press, 1986.

Tuchman, Phyllis. "I Shall Always Love Painting More." *The Washington Post*, September 25, 2005.

Venturi, Lionelli. *Marc Chagall.* New York: Pierre Matisse Editions, Inc., Feb. 1945.

Vinen, Richard. *The Unfree French: Life under the Occupation.* New Haven: Yale University Press, 2006.

Weld, Jacqueline Bograd. *Peggy: The Wayward Guggenheim.* Paperback ed. New York: Dutton, 1988.

Welsh, Alfred Hix. *Development of English Literature and Language.* N.p.: S.C. Griggs, 1886.

Werth, Alexander. *France, 1940-1955.* Boston: Beacon Press, 1966.

Whittick, Arnold. *Symbols: Signs and Their Meaning and Uses in Design.* 2nd ed. London: Leonard Hill, 1971.

Wieviorka, Olivier. *The French Resistance.* Cambridge, MA: Belknap Press of Harvard University Press, 2016.

Wilkin, Karen. "Through Her Father's Eyes." *The Wall Street Journal,* November 5, 2013.

Wilson, Sarah, and Henri Matisse. *Matisse.* New York: Rizzoli, 1992.

Wullschlager, Jackie. *Chagall: A Biography.* New York: Alfred A. Knopf, 2008: 395.

Matisse Works Referenced

Anemones in a Terracotta Pot
Bathers by a River
La Blouse Roumaine
The Blue Eyes
Blue Nude (Memory of Biskra)
Blue Nude IV
Blue Still Life
Blue Window
Bonheur de Vivre
The Breton Serving Girl
The Casbah Gate
Le Chant
The Checkerboard and Music
Chromatic Symphony (Verve cover)
The Clown
The Conversation
The Cowboy
Creole Dancer
Daisies
The Dance (1909)
The Dance I
The Dance II
The Dream
The Fall of Icarus
French Window at Nice
Girl in Yellow and Blue with Guitar
Girl with a Black Cat

The Girl with Green Eyes
The Green Line
The Guitarist
Horse, Rider, and Clown
The Idol (the 1942 painting of Monique Bourgeois)
Interior with a Violin Case
Interior with Bars of Sunlight
The Italian Woman
Jazz (collection of cutouts)
The Knife Thrower
Large Reclining Nude
Marguerite
Marguerite Reading
Marguerite with Black Velvet Ribbon (in photo insert)
Monique in a Grey Robe
Monique in Green Dress and Oranges
Monsieur Loyal
Moorish Screen
The Moroccans
Music
The Music Lesson
Nightmare of the White Elephant
Odalisque with Tambourine
The Painter's Family
The Piano Lesson

Pink Nude
Portrait of Madame Matisse
Portrait of Marguerite
Quai Saint-Michel with Lorette
The Red Studio
Self-Portrait
The Sword Swallower
Tabac Royal
Tea in the Garden
The Toboggan
The Wolf

Woman in Blue
Woman in Blue in Front of a Fire-
    place
Woman on a High Stool
Woman Reading at a Yellow Table
Woman Seated in an Armchair
Woman with a Branch of Ivy
Woman with a Hat
The Yellow Dress
The Young Sailor
Young Woman Sitting

Endnotes

PROLOGUE

1. Hilary Spurling, *The Conquest of Color*, 253. Henri Matisse said this to his wife, Amélie.
2. John Russell, *Matisse: Father & Son* (New York: Harry N. Abrams, 1999), 19.
3. Frank Harris, *Contemporary Portraits* (New York: Bretano's, 1923), 134-135.
4. Bell, Quentin, *Elders and Betters* (London: John Murray, 1995), 157. Bell was the son of the critic Clive Bell and the interior designer Vanessa Bell; he was the nephew of the writer Virginia Woolf.
5. Jane Simone Bussy, "A Great Man." *The Burlington Magazine* 128, no. 995 (1986).
6. "Devoured": *Hilary Spurling*. Hosted by Charlie Rose. Aired January 3, 2006. "Vortex": Kennedy Fraser, "Matisse and His Women." *Vogue*, September 1992.
7. Alfred Barr, *Matisse: His Art and His Public* (New York: Museum of Modern Art, 1951) 55-56, citing contemporary newspaper critiques. Author's
8. Claude Duthuit, Matisse's grandson, recalls this quote in his interview in *Collecting Matisse and the Modern Masters: The Cone Sisters of Baltimore*, by Karen Levitov (Yale Univ. Press, 2011), 13.
9. Matisse, Henri, Pierre Courthion, and Serge Guilbaut. *Chatting with Henri Matisse: The Lost 1941 Interview*. Los Angeles, CA: Getty Research Institute, 2013, 105.
10. Spurling and Matisse, *The Conquest of Color*, 330.
11. Spurling and Matisse, *The Conquest of Color*, 255.
12. "Interview with Léon Degand" (1945) in Henri Matisse and Jack D. Flam, *Matisse on Art*. New York: E.P. Dutton, 1978.

13. Henri Matisse to Marguerite Matisse, June 20, 1926, Archives Matisse, Paris (hereinafter "AMP"; Spurling, *The Conquest of Color*, 284.

14. Bell, *Elders and Betters*, 157.

15. Georges Duthuit to Henri Matisse, n.d. AMP; Spurling, *The Conquest of Color*, 331.

16. Françoise Gilot, *Matisse and Picasso: A Friendship in Art* (New York: Doubleday, 1990).

17. *World's Fair* magazine, Volume VIII, Number 1, 1988.

18. Peter Schjeldahl was a longtime *New Yorker* art critic and the father of author Ada Calhoun. Schjeldahl, Peter. "Art as Life: The Matisse We Never Knew." *The New Yorker*, August 29, 2005.

19. Casimiro DiCrescenzo. *Tériade and Matisse: A Friendship* (N.p.: Yoshii Gallery, 1997) 58.

20. Kennedy Fraser, *Ornament and Silence: Essays on Women's Lives* (New York: Alfred A. Knopf, 1996), 85-98.

21. The National Gallery of Art in Washington, DC, mounted three exhibitions of Matisse's work in a 13-year span. In 1977 (late collages and cutouts); 1986 (the early years in Nice, 1916-1930); and 1990 (the paintings inspired by his trips to Morocco). Jane Bussy, "A Great Man," 1947. First published in 1986 by *Burlington Magazine*.

22. Paul Richard, "Matisse in Morocco': Dreaming in Color." *The Washington Post*, March 18, 1990.

CHAPTER ONE: *LA FAMILLE*

1. Fraser, *Ornament and Silence*, 85-98.

2. Richard Cavendish, *History Today* 55, no. 10, October 2005.

3. Janet Hobhouse, *Everybody Who Was Anybody: A Biography of Gertrude Stein* (London: Weidenfeld and Nicholson, 1975), 46.

4. Bussy, "A Great Man."

5. For gilding cornices, see George L. K. Morris, "A Brief Encounter with Matisse." *LIFE*, August 28, 1970.

6. Escholier, *Matisse: From the Life*, 100.

7. Peter Schjeldahl, "Art as Life: The Matisse We Never Knew." *The New Yorker*, August 29, 2005.

8. Barr, *Matisse: His Art and His Public*, 37-41.

9. Ibid., 37-41.

10. Francis Carco, *L'Ami des Peintres*. N.p.: Éditions de Milieu du Monde, 1944.

11. Hilary Spurling, *The Unknown Matisse: A Life of Henri Matisse, the Early Years, 1869-1908*. 3rd ed. (New York: Alfred A. Knopf, 2008), 335.

12. Barr notes that in Matisse's work, *The Conversation* is one of the only works in which figures are shown face-to-face.

13. Fraser, *Ornament and Silence*, 85-98.

14. Spurling, *The Conquest of Color*, 252.

15. Pierre Matisse to Henri Matisse, August 2, 1927; Spurling, *The Conquest of Color*, 176.

16. Schjeldahl, "The Matisse We Never Knew."

17. Ibid.

18. Henri Matisse to Amélie Matisse, Nov. 25, 1923; Spurling, *The Conquest of Color*, 256.

19. Schjeldahl, "The Matisse We Never Knew."

20. Ibid.

21. Ibid.

22. At 25, Marguerite required lifesaving reconstruction surgery on her throat, made possible by medical advancements learned in World War I.

23. Barr, *Matisse: His Art and His Public*, 42.

24. Ibid., 42.

25. Ibid., 131.

26. Marguerite Matisse-Duthuit's obituary, *New York Times*, Apr. 3, 1982. She died in Paris at 87 and was buried in Nice.

27. "Extraordinary": Barr, *Matisse: His Art and His Public*, 206; Fraser, *Ornament and Silence*, 85-98.

28. Spurling, *The Conquest of Color*, 238.

29. Marguerite Matisse to Henri Matisse, 1933; Spurling, *The Conquest of Color*, 303.

30. Spurling, *The Conquest of Color*, 178.

31. Ibid., 178.

32. Karen Levitov, *Collecting Matisse and Modern Masters: The Cone Sisters of Baltimore* (New Haven, CT: Yale Univ. Press, 2011), 12-13.

33. Ibid., 12-13.

34. Barr, *Matisse: His Art and His Public*, 198.

35. Russell, *Matisse: Father & Son*, 380.

36. Ibid., 16.

37. Pierre Matisse to Amélie Matisse, June 25, 1925, PMP.

38. Spurling, *The Conquest of Color*, 268, citing letter from Henri Matisse to Amélie Matisse, Dec. 1924, AMP.

39. Spurling, *The Conquest of Color*, 268.

40. Marguerite Matisse to Henri Matisse, June 9, 1934; Spurling, *The Conquest of Color*, 347.

41. Spurling, *The Conquest of Color*, 276, citing letter from Amélie Matisse to Marguerite Matisse, Sept. 1925.

CHAPTER TWO: THE LUMINOSITY OF DAYS

1. The character Slavsky is based on Henri Matisse.
2. Schjehdahl, "The Matisse We Never Knew."
3. *Gauche* and *Droite* = Left and Right.
4. Fourcade, 123 and note also Spurling, *The Conquest of Color*, 205.
5. Ibid., 123. It is a tradition among the Niçois to take a dip in the bay on New Year's Day.
6. At the end of the season, the artworks and materials would be shipped up to Issy, and Matisse would return to his family.
7. Matisse and Flam, *Matisse on Art*, 85.
8. Henri Matisse to Charles Camoin, May 23, 1918; see also Cowart essay from Jack Cowart and Dominique Fourcade. *Henri Matisse: The Early Years in Nice, 1916-1930* (Washington, NY: National Gallery of Art; H.N. Abrams, 1986).
9. Spurling, *The Conquest of Color*, 221.
10. Dorothy Dudley, "Notes on Painting: The Matisse Fresco in Merion, Pennsylvania." *Hound & Horn* 7 (March 1934).
11. Matisse and Flam, *Matisse on Art*, 104.
12. Spurling, *The Conquest of Color*, 250.
13. Phrase is from Schjehdahl, "The Matisse We Never Knew."
14. Catherine C. Bock, "'Woman Before an Aquarium' and 'Woman on a Rose Divan': Matisse in the Helen Birch Bartlett Memorial Collection." *The Art Institute of Chicago Museum Studies*, Vol. 12, no. 2 (1986).
15. Spurling, *The Conquest of Color*, 206.
16. Henri Matisse in Nice to Pierre Bonnard, Feb. 5, 1942. Pierre Bonnard and Henri Matisse. *Bonnard/Matisse: Letters between Friends, 1925-1946* (New York: H.N. Abrams, 1992), 103.
17. Spurling, *The Conquest of Color*, 221.
18. "Hermit": Henri Matisse to Amélie Matisse, July 1, 1919, AMP; Spurling, *The Conquest of Color*, 226.
19. Bock, "'Woman Before an Aquarium.'"
20. John Mosier, *The Blitzkrieg Myth: How Hitler and the Allies Misread the Strategic Realities of World War II* (New York: HarperCollins, 2004), 34.
21. Marguerite Matisse to Amélie Matisse, Jan. 1923, AMP; Spurling, *The Conquest of Color*, 269. 1923 was the year of putsch in Munich. *Mein Kampf* was published the next year, 1924.
22. Matisse and Flam, *Matisse on Art*, 93, citing 1942 radio interview #1.
23. For a discussion of Matisse's living arrangements in Nice, see Jack Cowart's essay in Cowart and Matisse, *Henri Matisse: The Early Years in Nice*, 15-45.

24. Henri Matisse to Marguerite Matisse, n.d. (1927), AMP; and Spurling, *The Conquest of Color*, 292.

25. Amélie Matisse to Marguerite Matisse, n.d. (winter 1927-1928), AMP; Spurling, *The Conquest of Color*, 294.

26. Spurling, *The Conquest of Color*, 274.

27. Spurling, *The Conquest of Color*, 269.

28. Clive Bell, "Matisse and Picasso," *Europa* 1, no. 1, May-July 1933, pp. 30-31.

29. Frederic Spotts, *The Shameful Peace: How French Artists and Intellectuals Survived the Nazi Occupation* (New Haven, CT: Yale University Press, 2010), 138.

30. Ibid., 138; When the French government hosted the 1937 International Exposition, Matisse was the only major artist not asked to contribute.

31. DiCrescenzo, *Tériade and Matisse*.

32. Schjehdahl, "The Matisse We Never Knew."

33. Henri Matisse to Amélie Matisse Jan. 13, 1919; Spurling, *The Conquest of Color*, 223, 238.

34. Henri Matisse to Pierre Matisse, (n.d.), early 1927, Pierre Matisse Papers at the Pierpont Morgan Library in New York (hereinafter "PMP").

35. Spurling, *The Conquest of Color*, 237.

CHAPTER THREE: LYDIA

1. Dudley, "Notes on Painting."

2. Russell, *Matisse: Father & Son*, 62.

3. Dudley, "Notes on Painting."

4. André Masson, "Conversations avec Henri Matisse" in *André Masson: Le rebelle du surréalisme. Ecrits.* Ed Françoise Levaillant, Paris 1976,93.

5. *The Dance* was the painting of the five orange-red figures dancing around for Serghei Shchukin; *The Dance I* was a similar painting in pale blues and greens that now hangs in the collection of the Hermitage Museum in St. Petersburg. *The Dance II* is the Barnes mural. Dudley saw Matisse's *The Dance II* in May 1934.

6. Dudley, "Notes on Painting."

7. André Masson, "Conversations avec Henri Matisse" in *André Masson: Le rebelle du surréalisme. Ecrits.* Ed Françoise Levaillant, Paris 1976, 89 & 93.

8. Dudley, "Notes on Painting."

9. Bussy, "A Great Man"; for "synthesis": see Morris, "A Brief Encounter with Matisse."

10. Dudley, "Notes on Painting."

11. Gilot, *Matisse and Picasso*, 85.

12. Pierre Schneider, Michael Taylor, and Bridget Marzo, *Matisse* (New York: Rizzoli, 1984), 618.

13. Ibid., 618.

14. Spurling, *The Conquest of Color*, 338.

15. Spurling, *The Conquest of Color*, 345-377.

16. Ibid.

17. Marguerite Matisse to Henri Matisse, July 16, 1935.

18. Gilot, *Matisse and Picasso*, 84.

19. Ibid.

20. *Luxe, Calme, et Volupté* is the title of a 1904 painting by Matisse, in which he first used the subject of women, mostly nude, relaxing on a beach. The title is taken from the refrain of Baudelaire's poem *L'Invitation au Voyage*.

21. Gilot, *Matisse and Picasso*, 182.

22. Delectorskaya, *Contre Vents et Marées: Peintures et Livres Illustrés de 1939 à 1943*; and Russell, *Matisse: Father & Son*, 193-194.

23. Gilot, *Matisse and Picasso*, 180.

24. In her book *With Apparent Ease . . . Henri Matisse: Paintings from 1935–1939*, Delectorskaya describes how and when Matisse first noticed her as his next model . . . with the exception of his daughter. Delectorskaya, Lydia. *With Apparent Ease—Henri Matisse: Paintings from 1935-1939*. Paris: Adrien Maeght Editeur, 1988.

25. Graham Watt, "Lydia Delectorskaya," British Journal of General Practice, Aug. 2010 1;60 (577): 626–627.

26. Rosamund Bernier, "Matisse Designs a New Church." *Vogue* (Feb. 15, 1949).

27. Spurling, *The Conquest of Color*, 355-357.

28. Mary Jayne Gold, *Crossroads Marseille, 1940* (Doubleday & Company, Inc., 1980), 181; here Gold is describing Alma Werfel, who had been married to composer Gustav Mahler and the founder of the Bauhaus school, Walter Gropius, before marrying playwright Franz Werfel.

29. Bonnard and Matisse, *Bonnard/Matisse*, 23.

30. Schjeldahl, "The Matisse We Never Knew."

31. The full name is the Hôtel Excelsior, Régina Palace. To avoid confusion with another hotel in Nice called the Excelsior, I will use Hôtel Régina.

32. Spurling, *The Conquest of Color*, 379.

33. Louis Aragon, *Henri Matisse: A Novel*, Vol. 1, United Kingdom: Harcourt Brace Jovanovich, 1972, 23.

34. Gilot, *Matisse and Picasso*, 134-135.

35. Bussy, "A Great Man."

36. André Gide, Dorothy Bussy, *Correspondence André Gide-Dorothy Bussy*, vol. 3, 1937-1951 (Paris: Gallimard1982), 126; Bussy, "A Great Man."

37. Graham Watt, "Lydia Delectorskaya," British Journal of General Practice, Aug. 2010 1; 60 (577): 626–627.
38. Gilot, *Matisse and Picasso*, 178-182.
39. Russell, *Matisse: Father & Son*, 106.
40. Spurling, *The Conquest of Color*, 384. The attempt was "to remarkably slight effect": Schjeldahl, "The Matisse We Never Knew."

CHAPTER FOUR: THE PIANO LESSON

1. HM to PM March 16, 1938, PMP.
2. D'Alessandro, Stephanie, John Elderfield, Art Institute of Chicago, and Museum of Modern Art (New York, N.Y.). 2010. *Matisse: Radical Intervention 1913–1917 [Published on the Occasion of the Exhibition Held at the Art Institute of Chicago, 20 March–20 June 2010 ; the Museum of Modern Art, New York, 18 July–11 October 2010]*. Chicago: Art Institute of Chicago, 249.
3. Martha Hanna, *The Mobilization of Intellect: French Scholars and Writers during the Great War* (Cambridge, MA: Harvard University Press, 1996), 1.
4. Giraud, Pro Patria, 3-4, cited in Hanna, *The Mobilization of Intellect*, 77.
5. Escholier, *Matisse: From the Life*, 181; Spurling, *The Conquest of Color*, 184n.26.
6. Philippe Nivet, *La France occupée*. 1914–1918 (2011) (in French).
7. Charles Camoin, Claudine Grammont, and Henri Matisse, *Correspondance Entre Charles Camoin Et Henri Matisse: Lettres Présentées Et Annotées* (Lausanne: Bibliothèque des Arts, 1997), 67. Spurling, *The Conquest of Color*, 166, 169, 189-90.
8. Museum of Modern Art. "Matisse: Radical Invention, 1913–1917," July 18–October 11, 2010.
9. Curator Stephanie D'Allesandro says: "It's amazing to think of him painting *Bathers by a River*, *The Moroccans*, and *The Piano Lesson* in 1916, alone in his studio while he could hear the bombs, taking everything he had learned up until that point, thinking of his obligation to be a good painter, and setting a new challenge for himself." https://www.artnews.com/artnews/news/uncovering-matisse-281/amp/; Museum of Modern Art in New York explains, "While these works make no direct reference to the war in style or subject, they were physical and mental challenges for the artist, pushing his art to levels of extremity and difficulty that may be considered his responses to the conflict."
10. Barr, see Spurling, *The Conquest of Color*, 184-185.

11. Spurling, *The Conquest of Color*, 185.

12. Catherine C. Bock, "Henri Matisse's 'Bathers by a River,'" *Art Institute of Chicago Museum Studies* 16, no. 1, Aspects of Modern Art at the Art Institute: The Artist, The Patron, The Public (1990), pp. 44-55.

13. Ibid., 44-55.

14. Ibid., 44-55.

15. Painted in 1915-1916.

16. Spurling, *The Conquest of Color*, 174.

17. *Woman in a High Stool* was a 1914 painting of Germaine Raynal, wife of the Cubist critic Maurice Raynal.

18. Elizabeth Cowling, et al. eds. Matisse Picasso. The Museum of Modern Art, 2003, p. 341.

19. Spurling, *The Conquest of Color*, 196. In *The Italian Woman* painted in 1916, Matisse eliminates altogether the right shoulder of his subject.

20. Gene Lux, "What Is Wrong with Modern Art?" *Current History (1916-1940)* 38, no. 3 (1933), 316-320. http://www.jstor.org/stable/45337206

21. Spurling, *The Conquest of Color*, 264.

22. Dudley, "Notes on Painting."

23. Matisse and Flam, *Matisse on Art*, 84.

24. Gilot, *Matisse and Picasso*, 234.

25. Spurling, *The Conquest of Color*, 349.

26. Henri Matisse to Rouveyre, 1917; Hanne Finsen (ed.), *Matisse Rouveyre correspondance*, Paris: Flammarion 2001, 29; Spurling, *The Conquest of Color*, 202.

27. Hanne Finsen (ed.), *Matisse Rouveyre correspondance*, Paris: Flammarion 2001.

28. Spurling, *The Conquest of Color*, 209-214.

29. Ibid., 214.

30. Gabriel Hanotaux, *L'Aisne pendant la grande geurre* (Paris, 1919), 32.

CHAPTER FIVE: FLANKING MANEUVERS

1. Russell, *Matisse: Father & Son*, 172.

2. Ibid., 172-175. Letter Henri Matisse to Pierre Matisse, Jan. 2, 1939.

3. Henri Matisse to Pierre Matisse, March 7, 1939; Russell, *Matisse: Father & Son*, 176-177.

4. Ibid.

5. Henri Matisse to Pierre Matisse, Jan. 11, 1940; Russell, *Matisse: Father & Son*, 184.

6. Completed in 1909, the painting was later officially donated by Nelson Rockefeller to Museum of Modern Art in honor of Alfred H. Barr, Jr., Matisse's champion and first biographer.

7. Pierre Matisse to Henri Matisse, March 7, 1939; Russell, *Matisse: Father & Son*, 178.

8. For rent, see Russell, *Matisse: Father & Son*, 72-73. In fact, Pierre quietly sent Jean money (p. 197).

9. Russell, *Matisse: Father & Son*, 227-228.

10. Jean Matisse to Marguerite Matisse, n.d. 1927; AMP.

11. Pierre Matisse to Henri Matisse, Jan. 26, 1928; PMP.

12. Pierre H. Matisse, *The Missing Matisse [a Memoir]* (Carol Stream, IL: Tyndale Momentum, an imprint of Tyndale House Publishers, 2016), 122.

13. Matisse, *The Missing Matisse*, 87. After the incident, Amélie called Pierre a "barefoot, Spanish bastard."

14. Matisse, *The Missing Matisse*, 98.

15. DiCrescenzo, *Tériade and Matisse*, 46.

16. Gilot, *Matisse and Picasso*, 62.

17. Henri Matisse to Pierre Matisse, Oct. 21, 1940; PMP; Spurling, *The Conquest of Color*, 389.

18. Gold, *Crossroads Marseille*, 40.

19. See interview with Catherine Velle, whose grandmother was an archivist who worked under Jacques Jaujard. https://www.louvre.fr/louvreplus/video-les-memoires-de-guerre-du-louvre-par-catherine-velle?autoplay

20. Spurling says the Rosenbergs did not allow them to stay with them.

21. Spurling, *The Conquest of Color*, 389.

22. Spurling, *The Conquest of Color*, 388.

23. Spurling, *The Conquest of Color*, 388-389.

24. Spurling, *The Conquest of Color*, 390.

25. Russell, *Matisse: Father & Son*, 179.

26. Socialist minister Albert Sarraut; Spurling, *The Conquest of Color*, 389.

27. Russell, *Matisse: Father & Son*, 179.

28. Henri Matisse to Pierre Matisse, Oct. 10, 1939; PMP; Spurling, *The Conquest of Color*, 391-392.

29. Russell, *Matisse: Father & Son*, 180-181.

30. Spurling, *The Conquest of Color*, 390.

31. Henri Matisse to S. Bussy, April 28, 1935; Spurling, *The Conquest of Color*, 355.

32. Bonnard and Matisse, *Bonnard/Matisse*, 53.

33. Henri Matisse to Albert Marquet, Aug. 8, 1941; Spurling, *The Conquest of Color*, 391.

34. Spurling, *The Conquest of Color*, 391-392.

CHAPTER SIX: FLIGHT FROM PARIS

1. Brian Moynahan, *The French Century: An Illustrated History of Modern France* (Paris: Flammarion: Distributed in North America by Rizzoli International, 2007), 278.
2. Ernest R. May, *Strange Victory: Hitler's Conquest of France* (Hill and Wang, 2000), 434.
3. Ibid.
4. Jean Matisse, nearly 40 years old, was part of the B series reinforcements.
5. The French defensive mindset resulted in tanks being shared up and down the line. The Germans by contrast massed armor for offensive thrusts at the enemy's weak spots. For radio communications, see Karl G. Larew, "From Pigeons to Crystals: The Development of Radio Communication in U.S. Army Tanks in World War II," *The Historian* 67, no. 4, 664-677 (2005), p. 666.
6. Alexander Werth, *France, 1940-1955* (Beacon Press, 1966), 3.
7. Arthur Koestler, recounted in Moynahan, *The French Century*, 271.
8. Saint-Exupéry was a writer, poet, and journalist, as well as a pilot. He is the author of *The Little Prince*. See, e.g., Moynahan, *The French Century*, 232.
9. Moynahan, *The French Century*, 271.
10. Louis Aragon, *Henri Matisse; A Novel [by] Aragon*, trans. Jean Stewart (New York: Harcourt Brace Jovanovich, 1972), 24. Henri Matisse had stayed at Hôtel Lutétia in 1939.
11. In John Russell's account, the vault was at Banque de France on rue Rivoli. In Gilot's account, it was at Banque Nationale pour le Commerce et l'Industrie. It is possible Matisse had vaults at two locations.
12. Russell, *Matisse: Father & Son*, 187. Picasso said, "It's the Ecole de Beaux-Arts all over again!" which meant the French Army and leaders were no better at war than they were at fostering progress in art.
13. Henri Matisse to Pierre Matisse, May 22, 1940; Russell, *Matisse: Father & Son*, 186-187.
14. Russell, *Matisse: Father & Son*, 187-189.
15. "Peace and tenderness": Russell, *Matisse: Father & Son*, 188.
16. Russell, *Matisse: Father & Son*, 188.
17. Henri Matisse to Pierre Matisse long letter from Ciboure, May 1940; Russell, *Matisse: Father & Son*, 187-188.
18. I am indebted to scholars of Charlotte Salomon, including David Foenkinos, whose novel *Charlotte* was published in 2014; Griselda Pollack; Toni Bentley; and most of all, Mary Lowenthal Felstiner, author of *To Paint Her Life: Charlotte Salomon in the Nazi Era (Harper Collins, 1994)*. The

Gurs camp information is from page 92 of that book and Salomon's internment at Gurs is described at pp. 116-126. Hannah Arendt was another inmate at Gurs; she would later emigrate to the United States helped by the efforts of Varian Fry and the ERC.

19. Rebecca Rabinow, "The Legacy of la Rue Férou: Livres d'Artiste Created for Tériade by Rouault, Bonnard, Matisse, Léger, Le Corbusier, Chagall, Giacometti, and Miró" (PhD dissertation, New York University, 1995), 86.

20. Rodney T. Swan, "Symbolism and Allusion in Matisse's Jazz." *RIHA Journal* 0209 (May 15, 2019). The *Verve* journal was volume 2, number 8.

21. Rabinow, "The Legacy of la Rue Férou," 86.

22. George G. Kundahl, *The Riviera at War: World War II on the Côte D'Azur* (London: I. B. Tauris & Co., 2019), 45.

23. Emanuele Sica, *Mussolini's Army in the French Riviera: Italy's Occupation of France* (Urbana, IL: University of Illinois Press, 2017), 22-24.

24. The public papers and addresses of Franklin D. Roosevelt, 1940 (1941), p. 263.

25. Julian Jackson, *The Fall of France: The Nazi Invasion of 1940*, Oxford Univ. Press, 2003, 10.

26. Roger Faligot and Rémi Kauffer, *Service B* (Paris: Fayard, 1985)228.

27. Gold, *Crossroads Marseille*, 73.

28. Alistair Horne, *La Belle France: A Short History* (New York: Alfred A. Knopf, 2005), 353.

29. Bonnard and Matisse, *Bonnard/Matisse*, 64.

30. Spurling, *The Conquest of Color*, 394.

31. Gold, *Crossroads Marseille*, 82-83.

32. Russell, *Matisse: Father & Son*, 190-191.

33. International press thought he was missing.

34. Henri Matisse to Pierre Matisse, Sept. 1, 1940; Russell, *Matisse: Father & Son*, 190-195.

CHAPTER SEVEN: SCOUNDRELS AND MARTYRS

1. Alfred Hix Welsh, *Development of English Literature and Language* (S.C. Griggs, 1886), 464.

2. Henri Matisse to Amélie Matisse, 1917; Spurling, *The Conquest of Color*, 221.

3. Gold, *Crossroads Marseille*, 165.

4. Mary Lowenthal Felstiner, *To Paint Her Life: Charlotte Salomon in the Nazi Era* (New York, NY: HarperPerennial, 1995), 65.

5. Frederic Spotts, *Hitler and the Power of Aesthetics* (Woodstock, NY: The Overlook Press, 2003), 163.

6. This comes from the Degenerate Art catalog, but also in Felstiner, *To Paint Her Life*, 65.

7. Felstiner, *To Paint Her Life*, 65. Salomon's friend Barbara was interviewed by Felstiner, and said she'd seen the show and "I certainly assume Lotte saw it too."

8. Felstiner, *To Paint Her Life*, 66-67.

9. Felstiner, *To Paint Her Life*, 92.

10. Felstiner, *To Paint Her Life*, 134-135. As a German national, Salomon was housed at the Gurs camp in the Pyrenees from late May to July 1940; Felstiner, *To Paint Her Life*, 118-124.

11. *Poilu* is French slang for World War I soldier; it means "hairy one."

12. Denied a promotion as Othello's lieutenant, Shakespeare's Iago is responsible for four deaths.

13. CIA dossier on Darnand.

14. "Foreign News: New Bully," *TIME*, Feb. 7, 1944.

15. Sica, *Mussolini's Army*, 58-66. The Mentonese who collaborated saw their apartments defaced with graffiti *Vendu* ("Sellout") and *Traitre*.

16. Sica, *Mussolini's Army*, 44-45.

17. Pierre Bonnard to Henri Matisse, Sept. 8, 1940; Bonnard and Matisse, *Bonnard/Matisse*, 68.

18. Bonnard and Matisse, *Bonnard/Matisse*, 70.

19. Bonnard and Matisse, *Bonnard/Matisse*, 58 (Jan. 13, 1940).

20. "Professorial paterfamilias": John Russell, "New Exhibition Illuminates the Greatness That Was Matisse." *The New York Times* (October 26, 1986).

21. Russell, *Matisse: Father & Son*, 195-200.

22. Henri Matisse to Pierre Bonnard, Oct. 17, 1940; Bonnard and Matisse, *Bonnard/Matisse*, 70.

23. Henri Matisse to Pierre Bonnard, June 17, 1940; Henri Matisse to Pierre, late 1940; Russell, *Matisse: Father & Son*, 200.

24. Bonnard and Matisse, *Bonnard/Matisse*, 73.

25. Henri Matisse to Pierre Bonnard, Nov. 7, 1940.

26. *Maquis* refers to the scrublands where Corsican bandits would hide.

CHAPTER EIGHT: BRUSH WITH DEATH

1. Bonnard and Matisse, *Bonnard/Matisse*, 76.

2. Bonnard and Matisse, Bonnard/Matisse, 77.

3. Henri Matisse to Pierre Matisse, Jan 15, 1941; Russell, *Matisse: Father & Son*, 220-221.

4. Russell, *Matisse: Father & Son*, 217-224

5.   Henri Matisse to Pierre Matisse, May 2, 1941; Russell, Matisse: Father & Son, 217-224

6.   Henri Matisse to André Rouveyre, Apr. 2, 1941; Hanne Finsen (ed.), *Matisse Rouveyre correspondance*, Paris: Flammarion 2001, 35.

7.   Henri Matisse to André Rouveyre, Apr. 22, 1941; Hanne Finsen (ed.), *Matisse Rouveyre correspondance*, Paris: Flammarion 2001, 40.

8.   Bonnard and Matisse, *Bonnard/Matisse*, 84; for Montherlant, Henri Matisse to Henry de Montherlant, Jan. 13, 1941. https://www.bonhams.com/auction/25418/lot/142/matisse-henri-1869-1954-autograph-letter-signed-h-matisse-to-henry-de-montherlant-describing-his-improved-surroundings-at-the-clinique-du-parc-in-lyon/#!

9.   Soeur Jacques-Marie, Henri Matisse, and Arthur Goldhammer, "Henri Matisse." *Grand Street* 50 (1994), 78-89. https://doi.org/10.2307/25007785. Published by Jean Stein. This is Monique's 12-page account of her time with Henri Matisse, 1942 to 1945.

10. Paul Richard, "'Matisse in Morocco: Dreaming in Color." *The Washington Post* (March 18, 1990).

11. Barr, *Matisse: His Art and His Public*, 38.

12. Matisse once described models as "the burning center of my energy."

13. Matisse and Flam, *Matisse on Art*, 92, citing 1942 radio interview #1.

14. Ibid., 60.

15. Phyllis Tuchman, "I Shall Always Love Painting More." *The Washington Post* (September 25, 2005).

16. Richard, "Matisse in Morocco."

17. Gilot, *Matisse and Picasso*, 60.

18. Ibid.

19. Jack D. Flam, ed. *Matisse on Art*, revised edition, University of California Press, 1995, 232.

20. William S. Lieberman, ed. *Modern Masters, Manet to Matisse* (N.p.: Museum of Modern Art, 1975), 100, this quote from Alfred Barr.

21. Spurling, Hilary, Dumas, Ann. *Matisse, His Art and His Textiles*. United Kingdom: Harry N. Abrams, 2004.

22. Michael Woodson, "Objects of Inspiration: Here's What Fueled Matisse in the Studio," Artists Network, https://www.artistsnetwork.com/magazine/objects-inspire-henri-matisse-art/

23. Henri Matisse to Amélie Matisse, May 22, 1930, AMP; Spurling, *The Conquest of Color*, 319.

24. Bonnard and Matisse, *Bonnard/Matisse*, 38-41

25. Spurling, *The Conquest of Color*, 322.

26. Bonnard and Matisse, *Bonnard/Matisse*, 86.

CHAPTER NINE: PARIS UNDER THE SWASTIKA

1. Gerhard Engel, *Heeresadjutant bei Hitler, 1938-1943* (Deutsche Verlags-Anstelt, 1974). Diary entry June 26, 1940, pp. 83-84.
2. Author interview with Mme. Colette Chauvelot, who recalled the curfew being in German.
3. Alistair Horne, *Seven Ages of Paris* (New York: Vintage Books, 2004).
4. Gold, *Crossroads Marseille*, 70.
5. Spotts, *The Shameful Peace*, 3.
6. *Liste Otto: ouvrages retirés de la vente par les éditeurs ou interdits par les autorités allemandes* (Paris: Messageries Hachette, 1940). Henry A. Grubbs. "Nazi Domination of the Press: Publishers in France Conform to New Order," *Princeton University Library Chronicle* 2, no. 3, 97-104 (April 1941).
7. Horne, *La Belle France*, 359-360.
8. Cone, *Artists Under Vichy*, 12.
9. This document was used as evidence at the International Military Tribunal at Nuremberg and was registered as PS-1015. It is reproduced in Joseph Wulf, *Die bildenden Künste im Dritten Reich: Eine Dokumentation* (Berlin: Gebrüder Mann, 1983), 415-419. The translation presented here is based on that of the U.S. Office of Strategic Services, on file at the National Archives, Washington, DC.
10. See interview with Catherine Velle: https://www.louvre.fr/louvreplus/video-les-memoires-de-guerre-du-louvre-par-catherine-velle?autoplay
11. For the provenance of *Woman Seated in an Armchair*, see the National Gallery of Art, Washington, DC: https://www.nga.gov/collection/art-object-page.71071.html#provenance. For provenance of *Girl in Yellow and Blue with Guitar*, now at the Art Institute of Chicago, see https://www.artic.edu/artworks/191565/girl-in-yellow-and-blue-with-guitar. The fifth stolen Matisse was the painting *Woman in Blue in Front of a Fireplace*, circa 1937. The painting had been the centerpiece of the Henie Onstad Art Center near Oslo since the museum was established in 1968 by shipping magnate Niels Onstad and his wife, Olympic figure-skating champion Sonja Henie. The sixth stolen Matisse painting had Lydia as the model: https://www.nytimes.com/1997/10/21/arts/a-matisse-looted-in-41-turns-up.html. Matisse's *Seated Woman* was looted from Paul Rosenberg: https://www.npr.org/sections/thetwo-way/2015/05/15/406999313/looted-by-the-nazis-matisses-seated-woman-finally-finds-her-way-home.
12. See Lynn H. Nicholas, *The Rape of Europa, The Fate of Europe's Treasures in the Third Reich and the Second World War* (New York: Alfred A. Knopf, 1994), 166-167, and German documentation captured by the Allies.
13. Spotts, *The Shameful Peace*, 160.

14. Russell, *Matisse: Father & Son*, 237.
15. Gilot, *Matisse and Picasso*.
16. Nussbaum was gassed in 1944.
17. Gilot, *Matisse and Picasso*.
18. Ibid., 52.
19. Ibid., 53.
20. Ibid., 51.
21. Ibid., 110.
22. Ibid., 89.
23. Gilot, *Matisse and Picasso*, 60. "as complimentary": 21-22, 92.
24. Françoise Gilot and Carlton Lake, *Life with Picasso* (New York: New York Review Books, 2019), 36-37.
25. 8,000 francs = US $178.40, or US $15,500 in 2025.
26. Black doors, beams, ceiling—also windows boarded up during war—Gilot, *Matisse and Picasso*, 92.
27. Referring to the sculptor Jacques Lipchitz, who was Jewish.
28. Cone, *Artists under Vichy*, 134; Theft of bed linens from Spotts, *The Shameful Peace*, 148.
29. Alfred H. Barr, "Picasso 1940-1944: A Digest with Notes." *The Bulletin of the Museum of Modern Art* 12, no. 3 (1945): 2-9. https://doi.org/10.2307/4058086
30. Author interview with Colette Chauvelot, June 25, 2024.
31. Henri Matisse to Pierre Matisse, June 6, 1942. Also, Matisse refused to exhibit alongside Vlaminck after Vlaminck attacked Picasso in the press. See Henri Matisse, Pablo Picasso, and Elizabeth Cowling, *Matisse Picasso*. Ed. to accompany the exhibition ed. (London, [France]: Tate Pub.; Réunion des Musées Nationaux; Museum of Modern Art, 2002) and Barr, "Picasso 1940-1944."
32. James R Mellow, "Matisse: A Celebration of Pleasure," *The New York Times Magazine* (Dec. 1969).
33. Cone, *Artists Under Vichy*, 161, 237n.27.
34. Frederic Spotts, *Hitler and the Power of Aesthetics*, 183-186.
35. Spotts, *The Shameful Peace*, 44-45.
36. Cone, *Artists Under Vichy*, 155-157.
37. Matisse et al., *Matisse Picasso*, 382
38. Russell, *Matisse: Father & Son*, 228-231.

CHAPTER TEN: ZONE NONO

1. Moynahan, *The French Century*, 290.

2. Louis Aragon, *Henri Matisse: A Novel*, Vol. 1, (United Kingdom: Harcourt Brace Jovanovich, 1972), 20.

3. Werth, *France, 1940-1955*, 30-31.

4. Robert O. Paxton, *The Anatomy of Fascism* (New York: Knopf, 2004), 218-220. Whether Vichy was authoritarian or fascist is discussed by Paxton in his book on Vichy France: Robert O. Paxton, *Vichy France: Old Guard and New Order, 1940-1944* (New York: Columbia University Press, 2001), 251-257.

5. Mark J. Thériault, "Art as Propaganda in Vichy France, 1940-1944" (PhD dissertation, McGill University, 2007), 35

6. Moynahan, *The French Century*, 283.

7. Horne, Alistair. *Friend Or Foe: A History of France*. (United Kingdom: Orion, 2012), p. 1943.

8. Kundahl, *The Riviera at War*, p. 80.

9. Thériault, "Art as Propaganda in Vichy France."

10. From *Vérités et Rêveries sur l'éducation*, quoted in Francine Muel-Dreyfus, *Vichy and the Eternal Feminine: A Contribution to a Political Sociology of Gender*, trans. Kathleen A. Johnson (2001 Durham, NC: Duke Univ. Press, 2001), 225.

11. Gold, *Crossroads Marseille*, 226.

12. Thériault, "Art as Propaganda in Vichy France," 77-78.

13. Matisse railed against photographic mimicry, saying, "Exactitude is not truth."

14. Thériault, "Art as Propaganda in Vichy France," 21, 33. Note that Adolf Hitler was also depicted as a crusading mounted knight in armor. For *l'art maréchal*, see Cone, *Artists under Vichy*, 66.

15. Josse Bernheim had died in March 1941 in Lyon of natural causes.

16. Spotts, *The Shameful Peace*, 149.

17. See, e.g., *Omaha World-Herald* (Omaha, Nebraska, October 1, 1942), 9; and *NewsBank: America's Historical Newspapers*. https://infoweb.news bank.com/apps/news/document-view?p=EANX-K12&docref=image/ v2%3A1106B5BBD4B623A8%40EANX-K12-13725F4A9B63CCB9%40243 0634-1367858C10FA69BC%408-1367858C10FA69BC%40.

18. Matisse's correspondence with his son Pierre was to be interrupted by the war from October 1942 until July 1944.

19. Spotts, *The Shameful Peace*, 161.

20. Ibid., 161. The project with Courthion was never finished. Matisse thought little of his writing, and when Louis Aragon came into his life, Matisse had a far better chronicler.

21. Pierre Bonnard to Henri Matisse, Sept 8, 1940; Bonnard and Matisse, *Bonnard/Matisse*, 68.

22. Henri Matisse to Pierre Bonnard, Nov. 7, 1940.

23. The first letter was a postcard Matisse sent from Amsterdam that said, *"Vive le Peinture!!!"* (Long live Painting!!!); Bonnard and Matisse, *Bonnard/Matisse*, 33.

24. Pierre Bonnard to Henri Matisse at clinic, Jan. 14, 1941.

25. Kundahl, *The Riviera at War*, 27.

26. "It's the end of the beans!" Matisse, *The Missing Matisse*, 105.

27. Felstiner, *To Paint Her Life*, 134-135.

28. Soeur Jacques-Marie et al., "Henri Matisse," 78-89.

29. Felstiner, *To Paint Her Life*, 135.

30. Bonnard and Matisse, *Bonnard/Matisse*, 78.

31. *Le système D* derives from the verb *se débrouiller*—to manage, to get on. See, e.g., Sica, Mussolini's Army, 39.412. A *débrouillard* is a survivor.

32. Moynahan, *The French Century*, 285.

33. Michael Hodges, "Henri Matisse: Guns! Girls! Gestapo! The wild final years." DailyMail.com, March 29, 2014. https://www.dailymail.co.uk/home/event/article-2590862/Henri-Matisse-Guns-Girls-Gestapo-The-wild-final-years-Henri-Matisse.html; Aimé Maeght's small picture gallery in Cannes became the renowned Foundation Maeght in Saint-Paul-de-Vence.

34. Henri Matisse to Pierre Bonnard, Sept. 7, 1940.

35. Pierre Bonnard to Henri Matisse, Sept. 8, 1940.

36. Pierre Bonnard to Henri Matisse, Apr. 12, 1940; "This old carcass": Pierre Bonnard to Henri Matisse, n.d., winter 1942; Bonnard and Matisse, *Bonnard/Matisse*, 114.

37. Bonnard and Matisse, *Bonnard/Matisse*, 96.

38. Bonnard and Matisse, *Bonnard/Matisse*, 117. Letter from April 1, 1943.

39. Bonnard and Matisse, *Bonnard/Matisse*, 92.

40. Henri Matisse in Nice to Pierre Bonnard, Feb. 5, 1942. Bonnard and Matisse, *Bonnard/Matisse*, 103.

41. Pierre Bonnard to Henri Matisse, July 4, 1940; Bonnard and Matisse, *Bonnard/Matisse*, 66.

42. Matisse, *The Missing Matisse*, 96.

43. Matisse, *The Missing Matisse*, 97.

44. Pierre Bonnard to Henri Matisse, March 4, 1941.

45. Henri Matisse to Pierre Bonnard, Oct. 1940.

46. Pierre Bonnard to Henri Matisse, early February 1942; Bonnard and Matisse, *Bonnard/Matisse*, 101.

47. Henri Matisse to Pierre Bonnard, Feb. 23, 1942.

48. Quote from Julien Gracq, from Bonnard and Matisse, *Bonnard/Matisse*, 29.

49. Nicholas, *Rape of Europa*, 182-183.

50. Matisse and Flam, *Matisse on Art*, 91.

51. Pierre Bonnard to Henri Matisse, Feb. 1, 1935; Bonnard and Matisse, *Bonnard/Matisse*, 12.

52. Bonnard mentioned Lascaux in March 1941; Matisse spoke of Giotto on May 7, 1946. Bonnard and Matisse, *Bonnard/Matisse*, 130.

53. Russell, *Matisse: Father & Son*, 190.

CHAPTER ELEVEN: ESCAPE TO NEW YORK

1. Jackie Wullschlager, *Chagall: A Biography* (New York: Alfred A. Knopf, 2008), 395.

2. Russell, *Matisse: Father & Son*, 397.

3. Pierre Matisse to Henri Matisse, Dec. 8, 1926. The same Ritz Tower where his father stayed on the thirty-seventh floor in March 1930.

4. Russell, *Matisse: Father & Son*, 202.

5. Victor Semerjian, "Artists in Exile: The Great Flight of Culture," master's thesis, University of British Columbia, Sept. 1990, 15.

6. Victor Semerjian, "Artists in Exile: The Great Flight of Culture," master's thesis, University of British Columbia, Sept. 1990, 84 & n.187.

7. Stephen Birmingham, "Reckless: The Artistic Love Life of Peggy Guggenheim." *Vanity Fair*, 49 (Feb. 1986).

8. Transcript of an interview of Margaret Scolari Barr conducted between February 22 and May 13, 1974, by Paul Cummings for the Archives of American Art. See also: Christina Eliopoulos, "Safe Passage: Discover the extraordinary story of how one woman, Margaret Scolari Barr, helped MoMA save artist refugees during World War II." MoMa Magazine, Nov 17, 2020.

9. Victor Serge, *Memories of a Revolutionary, 1901-1941*, trans. Peter Sedgwick (Oxford University Press, 1963), 362.

10. Russell, *Matisse: Father & Son*, 226. Russell's book has this meeting in late summer 1941, at the end of Fry's mission in France. Sheila Isenberg's *A Hero of Our Own* describes this meeting as occurring in the winter of 1940-1941. Whenever it took place, the response was the same: Matisse was not leaving France.

11. Nicholas, *The Rape of Europa*, 149.

12. Gold, *Crossroads Marseille*, 296.

13. Isenberg, *A Hero of Our Own*, 191; Cynthia Jaffee McCabe. "Wanted by the Gestapo: Saved by America": Varian Fry and the Emergency Rescue Committee. In: Jarrell C. Jackman and Carla M. Borden, eds., *The Muses*

Flee Hitler: Cultural Transfer and Adaptation, 1930-1945, (Smithsonian Institution Press, 1983), 79-91.

14. Isenberg, *A Hero of Our Own*, 120. This could mean the studio in Issy-les-Moulineaux or perhaps it refers to Jean Matisse's structure in Montauban, north of Toulouse.

15. Isenberg, *A Hero of Our Own*, 134.

16. Jacqueline Bograd Weld. *Peggy: The Wayward Guggenheim* (United Kingdom: Bodley Head, 1986), 223.

17. Lionelli Venturi. *Marc Chagall* (Pierre Matisse Editions, Inc., Feb. 1945).

18. Ibid.

19. Wullschlager, *Chagall: A Biography*, 323.

20. Pierre Matisse to Jean Leymarie, March 11, 1977, in William Griswold, Jennifer Tonkovich, Alessandra Carnielli, and Margaret Loudon, *Pierre Matisse and His Artists* (New York: Pierpont Morgan Library, 2002).

21. Venturi, *Marc Chagall*.

22. Gold, *Marseille 1940*, 334.

23. Wullschlager, *Chagall: A Biography*, 395.

24. Russell, *Matisse: Father & Son*, 204.

25. John Russell, "Dean of Dealers Reflects on the Art World," *The New York Times* (July 5, 1981).

26. Gary Ferdman, "The Genius and the Gentiles: Chagall's American Odyssey," Jewish Currents, March 21, 2014.

27. Wullschlager, *Chagall: A Biography*, 402.

28. Venturi, *Marc Chagall*.

29. Jeffrey Meyers, "European Artists in American Exile," *The Article* (Apr. 17, 2023).

30. Venturi, *Marc Chagall*.

31. Sidney Alexander, *Marc Chagall: A Biography* (London: Cassell, 1978), 440.

32. The exhibition opened on Nov. 25 and ran until Dec. 27, 1941.

33. John Russell, GALLERY VIEW, *The New York Times* (June 5, 1977).

34. Griswold et al., *Pierre Matisse and His Artists*, 189.

35. Sabine Rewald and Magdalena Dabrowski, *The American Matisse: The Dealer, His Artists, His Collection: The Pierre and Maria-Gaetana Matisse Collection* (The Metropolitan Museum of Art and Yale University Press 2009), 16-17.

36. Russell, *Matisse Father and Son*, 201.

37. Maurice R. Davie, *Refugees in America: Report of the Committee for the Study of Recent Immigration from Europe* (Greenwood Press, 1974), 325.

38. Gold, *Crossroads Marseille*, 183.

39. Meyers, "European Artists in American Exile."

40. Edward Alden Jewell, "Noted Exiles' Art on Exhibition Here," *The New York Times* (March 7, 1942).

41. James Thrall Soby, *Artists in Exile Exhibition Catalog* (Pierre Matisse Gallery, March 1942).

42. Rosamund Frost, "First Fruits of Exile," *Art News* 15, no. 31 (March 7, 1942).

43. Ibid.

44. Grace Glueck, "Celebrating the Other Matisse: Dealer, Patron, and Son." *The New York Times* (Feb. 15, 2002).

45. "Pierre Matisse Gallery," *The Brooklyn Daily Eagle*, Feb. 14, 1943. The *New York Times* review said: "The artist who feels deeply the horror [of war] will be more apt to translate his reaction into familiar, everyday things . . . The result is not a battle picture, but a deepened and broadened interpretation of the surroundings and of his relation to them. See, Edward Alden Jewell, "Art in Time of War," *The New York Times*, March 14, 1943.

46. Russell, *Matisse: Father & Son*, 253.

47. Russell, *Matisse: Father & Son*, 252-254.

48. Lipchitz, quoted in McCabe, "Wanted by the Gestapo," 344; Victor Semerjian, "Artists in Exile: The Great Flight of Culture," master's thesis, University of British Columbia, Sept. 1990, 95.

49. Glueck, "Celebrating the Other Matisse."

CHAPTER TWELVE: THEMES AND VARIATIONS

1. *The Papers of George Catlett Marshall*, Larry I. Bland and Sharon Ritenour Stevens, eds. (Lexington, VA: The George C. Marshall Foundation, 1981). Electronic version based on *The Papers of George Catlett Marshall, Vol. 3, "The Right Man for the Job," December 7, 1941-May 31, 1943* (Baltimore and London: The Johns Hopkins University Press, 1991), 241-242.

2. M. Adereth. *Aragon, the Resistance Poems: (Le Crève-coeur, Les Yeux D'Elsa and La Diane Française)* (London: Grant & Cutler, 1985), 14.

3. "French Communists Continue Activities," *New York Times* (Feb. 21, 1941).

4. Monica Stirling, "Elsa Triolet," *The Atlantic* (September 1949).

5. Werth, *France, 1940-1955*, 44, 197. "Anger with elegance" comes from Monica Stirling, "Elsa Triolet."

6. Gilot, *Matisse and Picasso*, 254-255.

7. Stirling, "Elsa Triolet."

8. Gilot, *Matisse and Picasso*, 254-255. The little hats, *les petits bibis*, she wore perched "dangerously forward."

9. Stirling, "Elsa Triolet."

10. Monica Stirling, "A Touch of Magnificence," *Vogue* (1945).

11. For apartment, see Gilot, *Matisse and Picasso*, 254.

12. Adereth, *Aragon: The Resistance Poems*, 24.

13. Rodney T. Swan, "Cultural Resistance in Henri Matisse's Poèmes de Charles d'Orléans." *Visual Resources* 36, no. 1 (2018).

14. Richard, "Matisse in Morocco."

15. David Carrier. "The Beauty of Henri Matisse," *Journal of Aesthetic Education* 38, No. 2 (Summer 2004).

16. Bonnard and Matisse, *Bonnard/Matisse*, 95.

17. Hilary Spurling, "Matisse's Pajamas," *The New York Review*, Aug. 11, 2005.

18. Adereth, *Aragon: The Resistance Poems*, 23-24.

19. The model was Annelies Nelck; the painting is at Musée Matisse in Nice.

20. Aparna Nayak-Guercio, "The Project of Liberation and the Projection of National Identity: Calvo, Aragon, Jouhandeau, 1944-45" (PhD dissertation, University of Pittsburgh, 2006), 62.

21. Adereth, *Aragon: The Resistance Poems*, 39.

22. Adereth, *Aragon: The Resistance Poems*, 53. An example of a militant poem from Aragon is *Les Roses de noël*, which contains the lines, *"Entendez Francs-Tireurs de France/Renaisse de votre colère/Comme une voile dans le vent."* "Listen, partisans of France/Refill your anger/like a sail in the wind" (my translation). *La Diane française*, 16.

23. Gilot, *Matisse and Picasso*, 240-241.

24. Ibid.

25. Rabinow, "The Legacy of la Rue Férou," 109.

26. Author interview with Jennifer Farrell, Jordan Schnitzer Curator, The Metropolitan Museum of Art, New York, NY. April 17, 2024.

27. Barr, *Matisse: His Art and His Public*, 269; Sarah Wilson and Henri Matisse, *Matisse* (New York: Rizzoli, 1992), 22-24; John Klein, *Matisse and Decoration* (New Haven, CT: Yale Univ. Press 2018), 96-97.

28. Phrase from Werth, *France, 1940-1955*: "all-out collabos and traitors—the French Gestapo men, who . . . for mercenary reasons or a fanatical belief in Hitler . . . staked everything on the German horse."

29. Werth, *France, 1940-1955*, 44.

30. Ibid., 44.

31. Spurling, *The Conquest of Color*, 406.

32. Author interview with Jennifer Farrell, Jordan Schnitzer Curator, The Metropolitan Museum of Art, New York, NY, March 6, 2024.

33. Spotts, *The Shameful Peace*, 164.

34. Matisse and Flam, *Matisse on Art*, 92, citing 1942 radio interview #1.

35. "Henri Matisse or the French Painter," in *Henri Matisse: Retrospective Exhibition of Paintings, Drawings & Sculpture* (Philadelphia Museum of Art, 1948), 28.

36. Louis Aragon, *Henri Matisse: A Novel*, Vol. I, United Kingdom: Harcourt Brace Jovanovich, 1972 49.

37. Spurling, "Matisse's Pajamas," *The New York Review*, Aug. 11, 2005, referring to Aragon's essay, "A Character Called Pain."

38. Louis Aragon, *Henri Matisse: A Novel*, Vol. I, United Kingdom: Harcourt Brace Jovanovich, 1972 169-170.

39. Louis Aragon, *Henri Matisse: A Novel*, Vol. I, (United Kingdom: Harcourt Brace Jovanovich, 1972), 173.

40. Natalya Azarenko, "Love story in paintings. Henri Matisse and Lydia Délectorskaya," July 9, 2020, arthive.com. Friend was the writer Konstantin Paustovsky.

41. Russell, *Matisse: Father & Son*, 382.

42. Barbara Freed film.

43. Soeur Jacques-Marie et al., "Henri Matisse," 78-89.

44. Ibid., 78-89.

45. Barbara Freed, director. *A Model for Matisse: The Story of Henri Matisse, Sister Jacques-Marie and the Vence Chapel.* (First Run Features, 2003).

46. Soeur Jacques-Marie, "Henri Matisse," 78-89.

47. Barbara Freed, a professor of French studies at Carnegie Mellon University in Pittsburgh, who directed a 2003 documentary on their relationship, *A Model for Matisse: The Story of Henri Matisse, Sister Jacques-Marie and the Vence Chapel.*

48. Soeur Jacques-Marie, Henri Matisse, and Barbara F. Freed, *Henri Matisse: The Vence Chapel*, new edition, trans. Barbara Freed (Paris: Bernard Chauveau Éditeur, 2014), 93.

49. Soeur Jacques-Marie et al., "Henri Matisse," 78-89. Matisse's mellow voice is from Gilot, *Matisse and Picasso*, 85.

50. Sister Jacques-Marie et al., *The Vence Chapel*, 18.

51. Freed, *A Model for Matisse: The Story of Henri Matisse, Sister Jacques-Marie and the Vence Chapel.*

52. Soeur Jacques-Marie et al., "Henri Matisse," 78-89.

53. Freed, *A Model for Matisse.*

54. Soeur Jacques-Marie et al., "Henri Matisse," 78-89.

55. Spurling, *The Conquest of Color*, 411; "Bolshevik": Marie-France Boyer, Hélène Adant, and Henri Matisse, *Matisse at Villa Le Rêve* (Thames & Hudson, 2004), 9.

56. Soeur Jacques-Marie, *The Vence Chapel*, 26.

57. Ibid., 26.

58. Ibid., 31.

59. Freed, *A Model for Matisse: The Story of Henri Matisse, Sister Jacques-Marie and the Vence Chapel.* "Inferiority": Soeur Jacques-Marie et al., "Henri Matisse," 78-89.

60. Gilot, *Matisse and Picasso*, 184.

61 Boyer, *Matisse at Villa Le Rêve*, 76.

62. *Monique* (Dec. 4, 1942); *The Idol* (Dec. 1942); *Monique in Green Dress and Oranges* (Jan. 1943); and *Tabac Royal* (March 1943).

63. J. Flam, "Matisse's Dessins Thèmes et variations: A Book and a Method," exh. cat., Staatsgalerie, Stuttgart op. cit., p. 122.

64. Matisse in "Notes of a Painter on His Drawing," 1939, in Matisse and Flam, *Matisse on Art*, 130-131.

65. Henri Matisse, Jean Leymarie, Herbert Read, and William S. Lieberman. *Henri Matisse*, Berkeley, CA: University of California Press, 1966, 26.

66. Swan, "Symbolism in Jazz," 63.

67. Louis Aragon, *Henri Matisse: A Novel*, Vol. I, (United Kingdom: Harcourt Brace Jovanovich, 1972), 17.

CHAPTER THIRTEEN: A MEASURE OF SOVEREIGNTY

1. Charles d'Orléans, *One Hundred Selected Ballades and Rondeaux*, trans. A. S. Kline (2019). https://www.poetryintranslation.com/PITBR/French/OrleansPoems.php

2. Laurence Bertrand Dorléac, *L'Art de la Défaite: (1940-1944)* (N.p.: Seuil), 2010.

3. Spurling, *The Conquest of Color*, 412, citing report of Marguerite on her father's health.

4. Swan, "Cultural Resistance," 25.

5. Kathryn Brown, "Influence as Appropriation of the Creative Gesture: Henri Matisse's Poèmes de Charles d'Orléans." In: Thomas Baldwin, James Fowler, and Ana de Medeiros, eds., *Questions of Influence in Modern French Literature* (New York: Palgrave MacMillan, 2013), 92.

6. In Act II of Shakespeare's *Henry V*, on the eve of the English departure for France, the king is betrayed by three friends: Lord Scroop, the Earl of Cambridge, and Sir Thomas Grey. Henry has the three executed for treason.

7. Gilot, *Matisse and Picasso*, 239-240.

8. Pierre Reverdy, Pablo Picasso, and François Chapon. *Le Chant des Morts* (Paris: Gallimard, 2016).

9. Susan Halstead, "History Written by the Victors, Poetry by the Losers? Charles d'Orléans, the Prisoner-Poet of Agincourt," British Library blog, Oct. 25, 2015. https://blogs.bl.uk/european/2015/10/history-written-by-the-victors-poetry-by-the-losers.html

10. Matisse in bed in this manner comes from Marguette Bouvier's recollections of her visit to Matisse in Vence. See also Matisse and Flam, *Matisse on Art*, 96-97.

11. Henri Matisse to André Rouveyre, Oct. 25, 1942.

12. Swan, "Cultural Resistance," 29.

13. Gilot, *Matisse and Picasso*, 240-41.

14. Henri Matisse to André Rouveyre, March 11, 1943.

15. Spurling, *The Conquest of Color*, 421.

16. Felstiner, *To Paint Her Life*, 136.

17. Miranda Pollard. "A Question of Silence? Odette Rosenstock, Moussa Abadi, and the Réseau Marcel." *French Politics, Culture and Society* 30, no. 2 (2012). Himmler quota from Paxton, *Vichy France*, 181.

18. Jean-Louis Panicacci and Jean Combes, *Les Alpes-Maritimes dans la Guerre: 1939-1945* (Paris: De Borée, 2013), 186.

19. Sica, *Mussolini's Army*, 77.

20. Matisse, *The Missing Matisse*, 155-156.

21. Sica, *Mussolini's Army*, 104-105.

22. Ibid., 101.

23. Rodney T. Swan. "Cultural Resistance in Henri Matisse's 'Poèmes de Charles d'Orléans.'" *Visual Resources* 36 (March 2020), pp. 21–42.

24. Aparna Nayak-Guercio, "The Project of Liberation and the Projection of National Identity: Calvo, Aragon, Jouhandeau, 1944-45" (PhD dissertation, University of Pittsburgh, 2006), 53.

25. "Examined by the control authorities."

26. June 6, 1944.

27. Jennifer Stafford Brown, "'Au feu de ce qui fut brule ce qui sera'": Louis Aragon and the Subversion of the Medieval," *Romantic Review* (2010).

28. Gilot, *Matisse and Picasso*, 240-241.

29. Ibid., 146.

30. Charlie Rose interview. A conversation with artist and author Françoise Gilot about her life and career. Feb. 13, 1998.

31. Swan, "Cultural Resistance," 34.

32. Cowart, Jack. *Henri Matisse: Paper Cut-outs*. United States, St. Louis Art Museum, 1977, 101-105. Matisse would use this same symbol in his powerful *Nightmare of the White Elephant* later in the war.

33. As Swan notes, Matisse's illustrated book on Charles d'Orléans is 108 pages, the fleur-de-lys appears on forty-eight pages; there are more flowers than poems: on the front cover, the opening four pages, the last two pages, and paired with each of the thirty-five poems by way of the verso.

34. Nayak-Guercio, "The Project of Liberation."

35. Swan, "Cultural Resistance," 32.

36. Gilot, *Matisse and Picasso*, 90.
37. Brown, "Influence as Appropriation."
38. Henri Matisse to André Rouveyre, Oct 25, 1942.
39. Swan, "Cultural Resistance," 31.
40. Barr, *Matisse*, 273. Barr suggests that of all his *livres d'artists*, the book on the Duke of Orléans gave Matisse the greatest joy.

CHAPTER FOURTEEN: THE WAR WITHIN

1. Kundahl, *The Riviera at War*, 26
2. Malraux at Moulin memorial. Also: "It was not he who created the regiments, but it was he that created the army."
3. Thomas Wieder. "Disparitions: Colette Pons-Dreyfus," *Le Monde* (July 6, 2007).
4. Paxton, *Vichy France*, 292-293.
5. Dominique Aury, "Departure," *Defeat and Beyond: An Anthology of French Wartime Writing 1940-45* (New York: Pantheon Books, 1970), 234.
6. Werth, *France, 1940-1955*, 159.
7. "Italian Soldiers Attacked in Nice," *The New York Times* (May 12, 1943).
8. Jean-Louis Panicacci, ed., *La Résistance Azuréene* (Nice: Editions Serre, 1994), 248-249.
9. "The Underground Press of France, Belgium, Norway, Denmark and the Netherlands." *Quarterly Journal of Current Acquisitions* 2, no. 3/4 (1945), 3-29. http://www.jstor.org/stable/29780384
10. *Action*, Organe Social du M.L.N. et des Corps-Francs de la Libération, October 1943.
11. Kundahl, *The Riviera at War*.
12. Jean was stationed at Moissac.
13. Matisse, *The Missing Matisse*, 76.
14. Ibid., 193
15. Ibid., 11.
16. Ibid., 99.
17. Russell, *Matisse: Father & Son*.
18. Matisse, *The Missing Matisse*, 105.
19. Ibid., 130-131.
20. Lisa Bartelt, "Art, War & Resistance: A Review of the Missing Matisse by Pierre H. Matisse," Jan. 27, 2017.
21. Matisse, *The Missing Matisse*, 140-141.
22. Matisse, *The Missing Matisse*, 142-143.
23. Kundahl, *The Riviera at War*, 54.
24. Gilot, *Matisse and Picasso*, 241.

25. Thomas Fontaine, "Joseph Darnand," Sciences Politique, Mass Violence and Resistance—Research Network, Nov. 18, 2007.

26. Paxton, *Vichy France*, 297.

27. "Foreign News: New Bully," *TIME*.

28. *L'Eclairieur de Nice*, March 1, 1943.

29. The Germans' gammadion, the *Hakenkreuz* (hooked cross), and the French *croix gammée* derive from the medieval Latin, *crux gammata*.

30. Stephen Cullen, *World War II Vichy French Security Troops* (Osprey, 2018), 37-38.

31. For example, Victor Basch and prewar conservative leader Georges Mandel.

32. Victor Basch, age 81.

33. "Foreign News: New Bully," *TIME*.

34. Malraux speech at Moulin memorial.

35. Kundahl, *The Riviera at War*, 73.

36. Horne, *La Belle France*, 365.

37. Kundahl, *The Riviera at War*, 49-50, citing the work of authority, Jean-Louis Paniacci.

38. Paxton, *Vichy France*, 298-299.

39. Kundahl, *The Riviera at War*, 55.

40. Colin W. Nettlebeck, ed., *War and Identity: The French and the Second World War. An Anthology of Texts*. (London: Methuen, 1987), 55.

41. See Gold, *Crossroads Marseille*, photo insert.

CHAPTER FIFTEEN: FALLING TO EARTH

1. Aragon, *La Diane Française*, 26.

2. DiCrescenzo, Casimiro. *Tériade and Matisse: A Friendship*. N.p.: Yoshii Gallery, 1997.

3. Gilot, *Matisse and Picasso*, 134-135.

4. "Deeply impressed": Spurling, *The Conquest of Color*, 419; "Dazzling": see DiCrescenzo, *Tériade and Matisse*, 58; Matisse himself reported a "great breakthrough in color." See Rabinow, "The Legacy of la Rue Férou," 94.

5. Kundahl, *The Riviera at War*, 63.

6. "Corpse": Louis Aragon, *Henri Matisse: A Novel*, Vol. II, United Kingdom: Harcourt Brace Jovanovich, 1972, 35.

7. Some scholars have likened Matisse's figure to Robert Capa's famous photograph of the falling partisan from 1936, during the Spanish Civil War. See, e.g., Alastair Sooke, *Henri Matisse: A Second Life* (London: Penguin Books, 2014), 25. Regarding the acrobat comment, *Icarisme* is the French word for "acrobatic feats."

8. Louis Aragon, *Henri Matisse: A Novel*, Vol. II, (United Kingdom: Harcourt Brace Jovanovich, 1972), 33-35.

9. Schneider et al., *Matisse*, 661.

10. Adam Harrison Levy, "Henri Matisse: The Lost Interview," Jan. 21, 2015.

11. Spurling, *The Conquest of Color*, 419, citing Henri Matisse to Marguerite Matisse, Jan. 10, 1943.

12. Marguerite Matisse to Henri Matisse, May 20, 1943, AMP; Spurling, *The Conquest of Color*, 416.

13. Louis Aragon, *Henri Matisse: A Novel*, Vol. II, (United Kingdom: Harcourt Brace Jovanovich, 1972), 33.

14. Goats grazing from Sister Jaques-Marie, *The Vence Chapel*, 157.

15. Boyer, *Matisse at Villa Le Rêve*, 9.

16. Pinkie finger: *A Model for Matisse* film; "Nothing grew": Soeur Jacques-Marie, Henri Matisse and Arthur Goldhammer, "Henri Matisse," *Grand Street*, Autumn, 1994, No. 50, Models (Autumn, 1994), 85.

17. Local butcher: see Spurling, *The Conquest of Color*, 417.

18. Russell, *Matisse: Father & Son*, 246; Henri Matisse to Pierre Matisse, March 10, 1946.

19. Henri Matisse to Marguerite Matisse, July 11, 1943; Spurling, *The Conquest of Color*, 419.

20. Gilot, *Matisse and Picasso*.

21. *"Belle, bonne, nompareille, plaisant...Comme celle qui me peut conforter/Car je vous tiens pour ma seule maitresse."*

22. Marguette Bouvier, "Henri-Matisse at Home, 1944." Printed in Matisse and Flam, *Matisse on Art*, 96-97.

23. Boyer, *Matisse at Villa Le Rêve*.

24. Gilot, *Matisse and Picasso*, 136. On 142 she says these objects "danced a recurrent, elusive saraband in his pictures."

25. Gilot, *Matisse and Picasso*, 262.

26. Boyer, *Matisse at Villa Le Rêve*, 83.

27. Matisse and Flam, *Matisse on Art*, 96-97, citing Marguette Bouvier's "Henri-Matisse at Home, 1944," 96-98.

28. Boyer, *Matisse at Villa Le Rêve*, 14.

29. Matisse and Flam, *Matisse on Art*, 96-97, citing Marguette Bouvier's "Henri-Matisse at Home, 1944," 96-98.

30. Boyer, *Matisse at Villa Le Rêve*, 26.

31. Gilot, *Matisse and Picasso*, 23.

32. Matisse and Flam, *Matisse on Art*, 96-97, citing Marguette Bouvier's account.

33. Gilot, *Matisse and Picasso*, 138.

34. Ibid., 137.

35. Sooke, *Henri Matisse: A Second Life*, 38.
36. Samatha Friedman, "Matisse: The Same Thing, Different Means," MoMA, MoMA PS1 Blog, Nov. 11, 2014.
37. Sooke, *Henri Matisse: A Second Life*, 29-30.
38. Ibid., 21.
39. Rabinow, "The Legacy of la Rue Férou," 100, citing interviews in Oct. and Nov. 1943 at Saint-Jean-Cap-Ferrat with Tériade and his assistant Agathe Lamotte.
40. The maquettes at the Musée Matisse in Nice bear pencil marks, handwriting on some of the pieces, pins, and pinholes.
41. Rabinow, "The Legacy of la Rue Férou," 95.
42. Matisse also illustrated a book of poems by Stéphane Mallarmé and an American edition of James Joyce's *Ulysses*, among others.
43. Rabinow, "The Legacy of la Rue Férou," 89.
44. Gilot, *Matisse and Picasso*, 60.
45. Boyer, *Matisse at Villa Le Rêve*, 119.
46. Klein and Matisse, *Matisse and Decoration*, 188.
47. DiCrescenzo, *Tériade and Matisse*, 58.
48. Freed, *A Model for Matisse: The Story of Henri Matisse, Sister Jacques-Marie and the Vence Chapel.*
49. Soeur Jacques-Marie et al., "Henri Matisse," 78-89.
50. Gilot, *Matisse and Picasso*, 300.
51. *"Vous allez simplifier la peinture."* Museum of Modern Art 1931 catalog.
52. Schneider et al., *Matisse*, 662. As Schneider points out, these lines were not included in the final text that was published with *Jazz* in 1947.
53. Gilot, *Matisse and Picasso*, 146.
54. Lemon quote is from Gilot, *Matisse and Picasso*, 146.
55. Louis Aragon, *Henri Matisse: A Novel*, Vol. II, (United Kingdom: Harcourt Brace Jovanovich, 1972), 35.
56. Aragon, *Henri Matisse; A Novel [by] Aragon*, Vol. 2, p. 35; Sooke, *Henri Matisse: A Second Life*, 25. Also Barr, Matisse: *His Art and His Public*. Gowing says specifically "anti-aircraft shells" (Lawrence Gowing, *Matisse*. New York: Oxford University Press, 1979).
57. Edward Alden Jewell, "Art in Time of War," *The New York Times*, March 14, 1943.

CHAPTER SIXTEEN: THE HUNTING GROUND

1. Paxton, *Vichy France*, 182-183.
2. Sica, 165-166.
3. Paxton, *Vichy France*, 182-183.

4. Felstiner, *To Paint Her Life*, 161.

5. Martin Gilbert. *The Righteous: The Unsung Heroes of the Holocaust* (New York: Henry Holt & Sons, 2003), 359.

6. Felstiner, *To Paint Her Life*, 165.

7. I am indebted to scholars of Charlotte Salomon, including David Foenkinos, whose novel *Charlotte* was published in 2014; Griselda Pollack; Toni Bentley; and most of all, Mary Felstiner, author of *To Paint Her Life*.

8. Felstiner, *To Paint Her Life*, 180-181. General Eisenhower's broadcast resulted in the cancellation of a plan to evacuate Jews from Nice to Allied-controlled areas of North Africa.

9. Toni Bentley, "The Obsessive Art and Great Confession of Charlotte Salomon," *The New Yorker* (July 15, 2017).

10. Kundahl, *The Riviera at War*, 65.

11. Michel Laffitte. "Brunner, Alois, Mass Violence & Résistance" [online], published November 18, 2007, sciencespo.fr, 1961-9898; Felstiner, *To Paint Her Life*, 183.

12. Felstiner, *To Paint Her Life*, 91.

13. Felstiner, *To Paint Her Life*, 161.

14. Felstiner, *To Paint Her Life*, 116.

15. Shoah Resource Center, The International School for Holocaust Studies, entry on Alois Brunner.

16. Felstiner, *To Paint Her Life*, 166.

17. Mémorial de la Shoah/Drancy Musée, "The history of the 'Cité de la Muette' no author, no date.

18. Mary Felstiner, "Commandant of Drancy: Alois Brunner and the Jews of France." *Holocaust and Genocide Studies* 2, No. 1 (1987), 21-47.

19. Union of Jews for Resistance and Mutual Aid, Nice.

20. Spurling, *The Conquest of Color*.

21. Ibid., 11.

22. Spurling, *The Conquest of Color*, 211-213; see also Gilot, *Matisse and Picasso*, 21.

23. Spurling, *The Conquest of Color*, 419.

24. The ground floor of the villa was taken over by a German detachment. See Spurling, *The Conquest of Color*, 419.

25. Rodney T. Swan, "Resistance and Resurgence: The Cultural and Political Dynamic of the Livre d' Artiste and the German Occupation of France" (PhD dissertation, University of New South Wales, 2016), 162.

26. Gisèle Sapiro. *The French Writers' War, 1940-1953* (Duke University Press, 2014), 578n59, citing Jean Turlais, "Introduction à l'histoire de la littérature 'fasciste.'" *Les Cahiers français* (May 6, 1943).

27. Swan, "Resistance and Resurgence," 162.

28. Cowart, Jack. *Henri Matisse: Paper Cut-outs.* (United States, St. Louis Art Museum, 1977), 45.

29. Spurling, *The Conquest of Color*, 188.

30. Gilot, *Matisse and Picasso*, 48.

31. Spurling, *The Conquest of Color*, 188, quoting letter from G. Duthuit.

32. In 1928, Paul Schultz-Naumburg, an architect and Nazi activist, set forth this argument in his pseudo-scientific book *Kunst und Rasse (Art and Race).* See article at: https://www.vam.ac.uk/articles/entartete-kunst-the-nazis -inventory-of-degenerate-ar

33. Matisse, Henri, and Jack D. Flam. *Matisse on Art.* New York: E.P. Dutton, 1978, 110-111.

34. "Art for Extraordinary Circumstances: Henri Matisse's 'Jazz' and More" (May 15, 2020), Jennifer Farrell, Curator, Department of Drawings and Prints; and The Digital Editors, Digital Department.

35. Author's interview with Dr. Rebecca Rabinow, April 2, 2024.

36. Schneider, *Matisse*, 661.

37. On a misty spring day, curator Jennifer Farrell graciously spent time with me examining no. 79/100 of Matisse's book.

38. DiCrescenzo, *Tériade and Matisse.*

39. Author interview with Jennifer Farrell, Jordan Schnitzer Curator, The Metropolitan Museum of Art. New York, NY. April 17, 2024.

40. Swan, "Symbolism in Jazz," 33.

41. Rabinow, "The Legacy of la Rue Férou," 100-101.

42. Felstiner, *To Paint Her Life*, 185.

43. Renée Poznanski, *Les Juifs En France Pendant La Seconde Guerre Mondiale.* Nouv. ed., mise à jour et corr ed. (Paris: Hachette, 1997), 568-571.

44. Serge Klarsfeld. *Vichy-Auschwitz: la rôle de Vichy dans la solution finale de la question juive en France, 1942.* Paris: Fayard, 1983, 302-303.

45. Felstiner, *To Paint Her Life*, 184.

46. Klarsfeld, *Vichy-Auschwitz*, 310; Kundahl, *The Riviera at War*, 95-100.

47. Robert Levitt, "City of Nice remembers the thousands forcibly deported," *Jewish News*, Jan. 31, 2020.

CHAPTER SEVENTEEN: THE STUFF OF WARRIORS

1. Description of Marguerite Matisse's clothes from Roger Faligot and Rémi Kauffer, *Service B* (Paris: Fayard, 1985), 227.

2. Marguerite Matisse to Henri Matisse, Nov. 23, 1943; Spurling, *The Conquest of Color*, 420.

3. Weiss, Steve. "The Resistance as Part of Anglo-American Planning for the Liberation of Northwestern Europe." *La Résistance Et Les Français*, edited

by Jacqueline Sainclivier and Christian Bougeard, presses universitaires de Rennes, 1995, doi.org/10.4000/books.pur.16351, 53-66 citing SHAEF joint paper of Dec. 29, 1943.

4. Roderick Miller, "Jacques Cartier Prison," Frank Falla archive, not dated.

5. *Series B*, 227-228; Thomas Le Grand and George-Michel Thomas. *1939-1945 Finistère* (Brest-Paris: Éditions de la Cité, 1987), 301-310.

6. The description of the cells at Jacques-Cartier Prison is from the "detailed account" of a male prisoner named Henry Mainguy. See Roderick Miller, "Jacques Cartier Prison," Frank Falla archive, not dated. frankfallaarchive.org.

7. Entry on Thérèse Pierre, Accueil Mémoire de Guerre, site by Jean Paul Louvet.

8. Kundahl, *The Riviera at War*, 107.

9. Matisse, *The Missing Matisse*, 157.

10. Fraser, *Ornament and Silence*, 85-98.

11. Matisse, *The Missing Matisse*, 157.

12. Spurling, Hilary. *The Unknown Matisse: A Life of Henri Matisse, the Early Years, 1869-1908*. 3rd ed. (New York: Alfred A. Knopf, 2008), 148.

13. Gilot, *Matisse and Picasso*, 319.

14. Olivier Wievieorka. *The French Resistance* (Cambridge, MA: The Belknap Press of Harvard University Press, 2016), 407.

15. Camoin et al., *Correspondance Entre Charles Camoin et Henri Matisse*, 200.

16. French government report on Allied bombings from the Ministry of the Interior, Paris.

17. Henri Matisse to Charles Camoin, Camoin et al., *Correspondance Entre Charles Camoin et Henri Matisse*.

18. Hayden Herrara. *Matisse: A Portrait* (New York: Harcourt Brace & Company, 1993), 188-189.

19. Rabinow, "The Legacy of la Rue Férou," 100, citing Lamotte's notes from conversation with Matisse in Oct./Nov. 1943.

20. Elizabeth Vihlen McGregor, *Jazz and Postwar French Identity: Improvising the Nation* (New York: Lexington Books, 2016), 1-10.

21. Gold, *Crossroads Marseille*, 311.

22. For Henri Matisse's friendship with Django Reinhardt, see Lisa Bartelt, "Art, War & Resistance: A Review of the Missing Matisse by Pierre H. Matisse," Jan. 27, 2017. https://lisabartelt.com/2017/01/art-war-resistance-review-of-the-missing-matisse-by-pierre-h-matisse/.

23. Kundahl, *The Riviera at War*, 61; "Casino at Nice Is Razed," *The New York Times* (May 22, 1944).

24. Erik Satie remarked that jazz "shouted its sorrows." See Matisse and Flam, *Matisse on Art*, 111.

CHAPTER EIGHTEEN: WOUND MY HEART

1. Camoin et al., *Correspondance entre Charles Camoin et Henri Matisse*, 202-203.
2. Pierre H. Matisse, *The Missing Matisse*, 193-194.
3. Matisse, *The Missing Matisse*, 196.
4. Matisse, *The Missing Matisse*, 193-194.
5. Ibid.
6. Matisse, *The Missing Matisse*, 209-211.
7. Victor Davis Hanson. *The Second World Wars: How the First Global Conflict Was Fought and Won* (New York: Basic Books, 2017).
8. Mary K. Barbier, *D-Day Deception: Operation Fortitude and the Normandy Invasion* (Bloomsbury Publishing, 2007), 190.
9. SHAEF: Supreme Headquarters Allied Expeditionary Force; Werth, *France, 1940-1955*, 167-168.
10. Aparna Nayak-Guercio, "The Project of Liberation." "La bataille de la France est engagée, il faut la gagner. (. . .) Tous les Français veulent se battre." Avante-Guard: Nos Alliés ont enfin débarqué! Les Français . . . ils doivent y prendre part. Avec raison, le Général de Gaulle a proclamé que le devoir simple et sacré de tous les fils de France est de combattre par tous les moyens pour faire repasser le Rhin.
11. *"Jeunes Français aux armes!"* in L'Avant-Garde. Zone Sud (June 8, 1944).
12. "Appel du Conseil National de la Résistance pour le 14 juillet 1944" in L'Aurore 13 (July 1944). Que chaque Français fasse ce jour-là un acte de patriotisme, un acte de guerre contre l'envahisseur.
13. "Ils sont la force et nous sommes le nombre." Aragon, *Les Yeux d'Elsa*, 74.
14. Stephen E. Ambrose. "Eisenhower, the Intelligence Community, and the D-Day Invasion." *The Wisconsin Magazine of History* 64, no. 4 (1981): 261-277. http://www.jstor.org/stable/4635547
15. Nayak-Guercio, "The Project of Liberation," 55-56, citing *Louis Aragon et Elsa Triolet* by M. Adereth.
16. See Jennifer Stafford Brown, *Aragon Medieval Poems*; Matisse frontispiece Swan, "Symbolism in Jazz," 63.
17. All this from Matisse, *The Missing Matisse*, 202-203.
18. Matisse, *The Missing Matisse*, 202-203.
19. Ibid., 220.
20. This episode is from Matisse, *The Missing Matisse*, 242-243. Rugles was officially liberated by the Royal Dragoon Guards on August 23, 1944.

CHAPTER NINETEEN: THE WOLF

1. Camoin et al., *Correspondance Entre Charles Camoin et Henri Matisse*, 205.

2.   Ibid., 202. Henri Matisse to Charles Camoin, May-June 1944.

3.   Ibid., 201, 204.

4.   Russell, *Matisse: Father & Son*, 238-239.

5.   Ibid., 238-239.

6.   Spurling, *The Conquest of Color*, 422.

7.   Russell, *Matisse: Father & Son*, 238-239.

8.   Camoin et al., *Correspondance Entre Charles Camoin et Henri Matisse*, 201.

9.   Henri Matisse and Riva Castleman, *Jazz*, George Braziller, Inc., 1992, "Introduction to Jazz", xii-xiii (introduction by Castleman).

10. Author interview with Jennifer Farrell, Jordan Schnitzer Curator, The Metropolitan Museum of Art, New York, NY. April 17, 2024.

11. In her dissertation, "The Legacy of la Rue Férou," Rebecca Rabinow cites an unpublished letter from Matisse to Tériade dated July 4, 1944, in which he alludes to *Little Red Riding Hood*. Rabinow, "The Legacy of la Rue Férou," iii.

12. Le Grand and Thomas, *1939-1945 Finistère*, 301-310.

13. Spurling, *The Conquest of Color*, 424, citing unpublished typescript by Claude Duthuit, *Résistantes*.

14. Service B was a series of networks tracking German movements and passing that intelligence to the FTP.

15. Le Grand and Thomas, *1939-1945 Finistère*, 301-310.

16. Ibid., 301-310.

17. The memorial at the Gare de Langeais lists the names of the American and Allied soldiers who lost their lives in the attack.

18. Le Grand and Thomas, *1939-1945 Finistère*, 301-310.

19. Horne, *Seven Ages of Paris*, 370.

20. The American Seventh Army, led by General Alexander Patch, landed with three experienced infantry divisions, the Third, Thirty-Sixth, and Forty-Fifth. French Army B, soon renamed the First Free French Army, under the command of General Jean de Lattre de Tassigny, landed shortly after the American divisions. The First Free French, First Armored (France), and Third Algerian Infantry Divisions were all experienced units that had extensive combat experience in the Italian campaign.

21. "Allied Forces Help French to Rid Capital of Nazis," *The New York Times*, Aug. 26, 1944, as reprinted here: archive.nytimes.com: "In the latter stages of the war, General Charles de Gaulle gave the Resistance factions a unifying name, French Forces of the Interior, or FFI, or more casually, *Fifis*."

CHAPTER TWENTY: *LA LIBERATION!*

1.   Horne, *Seven Ages of Paris*, 370-373. See also: Mark T. Calhoun, "The Liberation of Paris," National World War II Museum (August 25, 2023).

2. Horne, *Seven Ages of Paris*, 370-373.

3. Author interview with Colette Chauvelot and Gérard Francès, June 25, 2024.

4. Horne, *Seven Ages of Paris*, 370-373.

5. As Kundahl describes in *The Riviera at War*.

6. Sica, *Mussolini's Army*, 101.

7. "Nazi Guns at Nice Face Wrong Way," *The Philadelphia Inquirer* (Sept. 9, 1944).

8. Jean-Louis Panicacci, *Les lieux de mémoire – De la deuxième guerre mondiale dans les Alpes-Maritimes* (Éditions Serre, 1997), 11-13, 18, 22, 27, 44, 83, 86, 104-105.

9. The hour-by-hour details of the Nice liberation are from *Lemagazine*, No. 22, Mai-Juin 2024, "80e anniversaire de la Libération de Nice, 1944-2024" (encart special).

10. Spurling, *The Conquest of Color*, 423, citing Annelies Nelck, *L'Olivier Du Rêve: Matisse à Vence: Témoignage* (Nice: Achevé d'imprimer sur les presses d'Imprimix, 1999), 110.

11. Spurling, *The Conquest of Color*, 423, citing Nelck, *L'Olivier du Rêve*, 110.

12. The rectangular plates are 16 5/8 × 25 5/8 in. (42.2 × 65.1 cm).

13. Spotts, *Hitler and the Power of Aesthetics*, 347.

14. Arnold Whittick, *Symbols, Signs and Their Meaning and Uses in Design* (London: Leonard Hill, 1971), 18-19, 300-301 for the symbolism of red.

15. Author interview with Jennifer Farrell, Jordan Schnitzer Curator, The Metropolitan Museum of Art. New York, NY. April 17, 2024.

16. Russell, *Matisse: Father & Son*, 300-301.

17. Ibid.

18. Rabinow, "The Legacy of la Rue Férou," 121.

19. Claude Morgan. "Matisse montre toujours de nouveaux chemins," *Le lettres françaises*, VIII, no. 190 (Jan. 8, 1948).

20. Gilot, *Matisse and Picasso*, 59. For the symbolism of red, see, e.g., Whittick, *Symbols, Signs and Their Meaning*, 18-19, 301.

21. Vivian Jacobs and Wilhelmina Jacobs, "The Color Blue: Its Use as Metaphor and Symbol." *American Speech* 33, no. 1 (1958): 29-46. https://doi .org/10.2307/453461

22. Gilot, *Matisse and Picasso*, 98.

23. Ibid., 99.

24. Sooke, *Henri Matisse: A Second Life*, 89.

25. Rabinow, "The Legacy of la Rue Férou," 93.

26. Museum of Modern Art catalog 1931, p. 17. The paintings are from 1909-1910 and were at the Museum of Modern Western Art in Moscow.

27. Fraser, *Ornament and Silence*, 85-98.

28. Richard, Paul. "'Matisse in Morocco': Dreaming in Color." *The Washington Post*, March 18, 1990.

29. Charlie Rose interview. A conversation with artist and author Françoise Gilot about her life and career. Feb. 13, 1998.

30. Henri Matisse to Charles Camoin, Sept. 6, 1944; Russell, *Matisse: Father & Son*, 238.

31. She was released in October after serving two consecutive three-month sentences.

32. Rabinow, "The Legacy of la Rue Férou," 108.

33. Morgan, "Matisse montre toujours de nouveaux chemins."

34. Rabinow, "The Legacy of la Rue Férou," 109.

CHAPTER TWENTY-ONE: THE MIRACLE OF MARGUERITE

1. Les Roses de noël, *La Diane française*, 71. See Adereth, *Aragon, the Resistance Poems*, 19.

2. KdS Rennes was located at Foyer des Étudiantes, Avenue Jules Ferry.

3. Russell, *Matisse: Father and Son*, 240; Henri Matisse to Pierre Matisse, Feb. 12, 1945.

4. Karen Wilkin, "Through Her Father's Eyes," *The Wall Street Journal* (Nov. 5, 2013).

5. Spurling, *The Conquest of Color*, 178.

6. Wilkin, "Through Her Father's Eyes."

7. Fraser, *Ornament and Silence*, 85-98.

8. Hanne Finsen (ed.), *Matisse Rouveyre correspondance*, Paris: Flammarion 2001, letter no. 456, 301.

9. Russell, *Matisse: Father & Son*, 239; Henri Matisse to Pierre Matisse, Feb. 12, 1945.

10. Russell, *Matisse: Father & Son*, 239.

11. Spurling, *The Conquest of Color*, 425.

12. Le Grand and Thomas, *1939-1945 Finistère*, 301-310.

13. Roger Faligot and Rémi Kauffer, *Service B* (Paris: Fayard, 1985) 227-246.

14. Spurling, *The Conquest of Color*, 424.

15. Ibid., 424.

16. Russell, *Matisse: Father & Son*, 240.

17. "Stupefied": Russell, *Matisse: Father & Son*, 239. Rest of quote from Schjeldahl, "The Matisse We Never Knew."

18. Russell, *Matisse: Father & Son*, 239.

19. Henri Matisse to Monique Bourgeois, Feb. 12, 1945; Soeur Jacques-Marie et al., *The Vence Chapel*, 140.

20. Henri Matisse to Pierre Matisse, Feb. 12, 1945; Russell, *Matisse: Father & Son*, 239.

21. Katherine Boyle, "In Baltimore, an unparalleled look at Matisse and his daughter." *The Washington Post*, Jan. 3, 2014.

22. Henri Matisse to Pierre Matisse, Feb. 12, 1945; Russell, *Matisse: Father & Son*, 239.

CHAPTER TWENTY-TWO: ONLY FOR THE LIGHT

1. Soeur Jacques-Marie, Henri Matisse and Arthur Goldhammer, "Henri Matisse," *Grand Street*, Autumn, 1994, No. 50, Models (Autumn, 1994), 87-88.

2. Ibid., 86-87.

3. Sister Jacques-Marie, *Henri Matisse: The Vence Chapel*, 51-52.

4. Freed, *A Model for Matisse: The Story of Henri Matisse, Sister Jacques-Marie and the Vence Chapel.*

5. Soeur Jacques-Marie, Henri Matisse and Arthur Goldhammer, "Henri Matisse," *Grand Street*, Autumn, 1994, No. 50, Models (Autumn, 1994), 89.

6. Henri Matisse to Pierre Matisse, Feb. 12, 1945; Russell, *Matisse: Father & Son*, 239.

7. Ibid., 240.

8. See Christopher C. Gorham, "The Handshake that Ended the War." We're History (April 25, 1918). https://werehistory.org/the-handshake-that-ended-the-war/

9. Tériade to Henri Matisse, March 20, 1945, in Claude Duthuit, Françoise Garnaud, and Jean Guichard-Meili *Henri Matisse: Catalogue raisonné des ouvrages illustrés*. Paris: Imprimerie Union, 1988, 446.

10. Russell, *Matisse: Father & Son*, 241.

11. Russell, *Matisse: Father & Son*, 242.

12. Marcelle Poirier, "Brighter Days in Paris," *London Daily Post*, Nov. 1, 1945.

13. "Review of Verve," *Art Digest* XX, no. 13 (April 1, 1946).

14. Russell, *Matisse: Father & Son*, 242-243.

15. Edward Allen Jewell, "Accent on Modernism," *The New York Times* (March 24, 1946).

16. Author interview with Jennifer Farrell, Jordan Schnitzer Curator, The Metropolitan Museum of Art, New York, NY. April 17, 2024.

17. Morgan, "Matisse montre toujours de nouveaux chemins."

18. Ibid.

19. Sooke, *Henri Matisse: A Second Life.*

20. "Tragic ambience": Rabinow, "The Legacy of la Rue Férou," 109.

CHAPTER TWENTY-THREE: THE LANGUAGE OF DREAMS

1. Russell, *Matisse: Father & Son*, 246; Henri Matisse to Pierre Matisse, March 19, 1946.
2. Gilot, *Matisse and Picasso*, 137.
3. Ibid., 89.
4. Ibid., 316.
5. Ibid., 90.
6. Jack D. Flam, *Matisse and Picasso: the story of their rivalry and friendship* (Cambridge, MA: Icon Edition/Westview Press, 2003), xi.
7. Elizabeth Cowling, et al. eds. *Matisse Picasso*. The Museum of Modern Art, 2003, p. 24.
8. Matisse et al., *Matisse Picasso*, 24.
9. Russell, *Matisse: Father & Son*, 246; Henri Matisse to Pierre Matisse, March 19, 1946.
10. "seesaw of esteem": Schjeldahl, "The Matisse We Never Knew."
11. Gilot and Lake, *Life with Picasso*, 240.
12. Elizabeth Cowling, et al. eds. *Matisse Picasso*. The Museum of Modern Art, 2003, 334.
13. Gilot, *Matisse and Picasso*, 90-95.
14. Elizabeth Cowling, et al. eds. *Matisse Picasso*. The Museum of Modern Art, 2003, 334.
15. Weber was a young artist in Matisse's class. Transcript of interviews of Max Weber conducted by C. S. Gruber for the Oral History Research Office of Columbia University, 1958, 80.
16. Harris, *Contemporary Portraits*, 142.
17. Henri Matisse to Pierre Matisse, Jan. 1945; Russell, *Matisse: Father & Son*, 240.
18. Harris, *Contemporary Portraits*, 137.
19. Gilot, *Matisse and Picasso*, 90.
20. Sister Jacques-Marie, *Henri Matisse: The Vence Chapel*, 56.
21. Henri Matisse to André Rouveyre, Apr. 27, 1947.
22. Freed, *A Model for Matisse: The Story of Henri Matisse, Sister Jacques-Marie and the Vence Chapel*.
23. Ibid.
24. Soeur Jacques-Marie et al., *The Vence Chapel*, 64.
25. D. P. Barritt, "Modern Church Design: Matisse's Dominican Chapel at Vence," *The Irish Monthly* 80, no. 949 (1952), 276-278. http://www.jstor.org/stable/43649555
26. Bernier, "Matisse Designs a New Church."
27. Ibid.
28. Dudley, "Notes on Painting."
29. Father Couturier, "The Church of Joy," *Vogue* (Dec. 1951).

30. Fourcade, 123, and note also Spurling, *The Conquest of Color*, 205.
31. Rebecca Rabinow and Dorthe Aagesen, eds. *Matisse: In Search of True Painting* (Yale Univ. Press 2012), 142
32. Gilot, *Matisse and Picasso*, 277.
33. Louis Aragon, *Henri Matisse: A Novel*, Vol. I, (United Kingdom: Harcourt Brace Jovanovich, 1972), 208. This was 1942.
34. Schjedjahl, "The Matisse We Never Knew."
35. Matisse and Flam, *Matisse on Art*, 207.
36. Transcript of interviews of Max Weber conducted by C. S. Gruber for the Oral History Research Office of Columbia University in 1958, 84.
37. Soeur Jacques-Marie, *The Vence Chapel*, 91.
38. Ibid., 91, 123.
39. Matisse, *The Missing Matisse*, 116.
40. Soeur Jacques-Marie, *The Vence Chapel*, 72, see also 83-84.
41. Ibid., 151.
42. Gilot, *Matisse and Picasso*, 178.
43. Schjeldahl, "The Matisse We Never Knew."
44. Henri Matisse to Pierre Matisse, March 19, 1946; Russell, *Matisse: Father & Son*, 246.
45. Soeur Jacques-Marie, *The Vence Chapel*, 87, 109.
46. Museum of Modern Art exhibition press release 1951.
47. Ibid.
48. Gilot, *Matisse and Picasso*, 194.
49. Actually, he proposed a fruit-and-vegetable market, to which Matisse "was proud of snapping back that his greens were greener and his oranges more orange than any actual fruit."
50. One reported she felt "very at rest" in the intimate sanctuary. Barritt, "Modern Church Design," 276-278.
51. Schjeldahl, "The Matisse We Never Knew," citing Spurling, *The Conquest of Color*.
52. Tériade in DiCrescenzo, *Tériade and Matisse*.
53. Richard, "'Matisse in Morocco.'"
54. Gilot, *Matisse and Picasso*, 5.

EPILOGUE

1. Russell, *Matisse: Father & Son*, 380-382.
2. See, e.g., John Russell. "An Artist Who Shook the World," *New York Times* (Nov. 25, 1984); Lydia Delectorskaya obituary, "Model and Muse to Matisse," from April 3, 1998, reprinted in the *London Daily Telegraph* and in newspapers around the world.